T0331063

Data Analytics for Smart Infrastructure

This book presents, for the first time, data analytics for smart infrastructures. The authors draw on over a decade's experience working with industry and demonstrating the capabilities of data analytics for infrastructure and asset management.

The volume gives data-driven solutions to cover critical capabilities for infrastructure and asset management across three domains: (1) situation awareness, (2) predictive analytics, and (3) decision support. The reader will gain from various data analytic techniques including anomaly detection, performance evaluation, failure prediction, trend analysis, asset prioritisation, smart sensing, and real-time/online systems. These data analytic techniques are vital to solving problems in infrastructure and asset management. The reader will benefit from case studies drawn from critical infrastructures such as water management, structural health monitoring, and rail networks.

This groundbreaking work will be essential reading for those studying and practicing analytics in the context of smart infrastructure.

Yang Wang is a professor at UTS Data Science Institute, leading advanced data analytics for smart infrastructure. Yang keeps actively engaged with industry partners and delivers innovative data-driven solutions for critical infrastructures including supply water and transport network, structural health monitoring, etc. Yang has received various research and innovation awards including Eureka Prize, iAwards, and AWA water awards.

Associate professor Zhidong Li at UTS is an award-winning expert in data science and machine learning, with a notable tenure at Data61, CSIRO, and a history of significant contributions to translate machine learning into industrial fields, including infrastructure, finance, environment, and agriculture.

Ting Guo is a senior research fellow in the Data Science Institute at UTS. He has 10 years of experience in collaborative research with industry partners in infrastructure failure prediction and proactive maintenance. His research interests include deep learning, graph learning, and data mining.

Bin Liang, a senior lecturer at UTS, is an accomplished data scientist with extensive industry and research experience. With publications in top venues and successful industry project deliverables, his expertise in data analytics, artificial intelligence (AI), and computer vision has driven significant academic, social, and economic advancements.

Hongda Tian is a research and innovation-focused senior lecturer at the UTS Data Science Institute. By leveraging the power of AI, he has been focusing on research translation through working with government and industry partners and providing data-driven solutions to real-world problems.

Distinguished professor Fang Chen is the Executive Director at the UTS Data Science Institute. She is an award-winning, internationally recognised leader in AI and data science, having won the Australian Museum Eureka Prize 2018 for Excellence in Data Science, NSW Premier's Prize of Science and Engineering, and the Australia and New Zealand "Women in AI" Award in Infrastructure in 2021. Her extensive expertise is centred around developing data-driven innovations that address complex challenges across large-scale networks in different industry sectors.

Data Analytics for Smart Infrastructure
Asset Management and Network Performance

Yang Wang, Zhidong Li, Bin Liang, Hongda Tian, Ting Guo, and Fang Chen

CRC Press
Taylor & Francis Group
Boca Raton London New York

CRC Press is an imprint of the
Taylor & Francis Group, an **informa** business

Designed cover image: Sydney CBD is the central business district of Sydney, Australia; Shutterstock

First edition published 2025
by CRC Press
2385 NW Executive Center Drive, Suite 320, Boca Raton FL 33431

and by CRC Press
4 Park Square, Milton Park, Abingdon, Oxon, OX14 4RN

CRC Press is an imprint of Taylor & Francis Group, LLC

ISBN: 978-1-032-75416-1 (hbk)
ISBN: 978-1-032-75415-4 (pbk)
ISBN: 978-1-003-47389-3 (ebk)

DOI: 10.1201/9781003473893

Typeset in Nimbus Roman font
by KnowledgeWorks Global Ltd.

Publisher's note: This book has been prepared from camera-ready copy provided by the authors.

Contents

Preface

In an era where the seamless integration of technology into our daily lives becomes ever more apparent, the concept of smart infrastructure stands at the forefront of innovation and progress. This book, for the first time, presents a comprehensive exploration of data analytics for smart infrastructures. Leveraging over a decade of industry experience, we aim to demonstrate the transformative potential of data analytics in the realm of infrastructure and asset management.

The advent of smart infrastructure presents a unique set of challenges and opportunities. With the increasing complexity of infrastructure systems and the vast amounts of data generated daily, there is an urgent need for advanced analytical methods to enhance efficiency, reliability, and sustainability. This book is dedicated to addressing this need by introducing data-driven solutions that are critical for infrastructure and asset management across three key domains: situation awareness, predictive analytics, and decision support.

To provide a holistic understanding, we delve into various data analytics techniques, including anomaly detection, performance evaluation, status monitoring, failure prediction, long-term prediction, demand prediction, asset prioritisation, real-time/online systems, and smart sensing. Each technique is explained in the context of its application to infrastructure management, showcasing its role in improving operational efficiency and decision-making processes.

The importance of these techniques cannot be overstated, as they offer robust solutions to some of the most pressing issues in infrastructure management, such as handling heterogeneous data, navigating complex network structures, managing dynamic systems, and mitigating the uncertainty inherent in analytical processes. By addressing these challenges, the techniques presented in this book pave the way for more resilient, adaptable, and intelligent infrastructure systems.

To illustrate the practical applications of these concepts, we include detailed case studies from various critical infrastructure sectors, including water and wastewater management, structural health monitoring, and transport and rail networks. These case studies not only demonstrate the effectiveness of data analytics in real-world scenarios but also highlight the potential for these techniques to revolutionise infrastructure management practices.

We believe this book will serve as an essential resource for students, researchers, and professionals engaged in the study and practice of data analytics within the context of smart infrastructure. As we stand on the brink of a new era in infrastructure management, we hope this work inspires further innovation and collaboration, driving forward the development of smarter, more efficient, and more sustainable infrastructure systems.

Author

Yang Wang is a professor at UTS (University of Technology Sydney, Australia) Data Science Institute, leading advanced data analytics for smart infrastructure. Yang keeps actively engaged with industry partners and delivers innovative data-driven solutions for critical infrastructures including supply water and transport network, structural health monitoring, etc. Yang has received various research and innovation awards including Eureka Prize, iAwards, and AWA water awards.

Associate professor Zhidong Li at UTS is an award-winning expert in data science and machine learning, with a notable tenure at Data61, CSIRO, and a history of significant contributions to translate machine learning into industrial fields, including infrastructure, finance, environment, and agriculture.

Ting Guo is a senior research fellow in the Data Science Institute at UTS. He has 10 years of experience in collaborative research with industry partners in infrastructure failure prediction and proactive maintenance. His research interest includes deep learning, graph learning, and data mining.

Bin Liang, a senior lecturer at UTS, is an accomplished data scientist with extensive industry and research experience. With publications in top venues and successful industry project deliverables, his expertise in data analytics, artificial intelligence (AI), and computer vision has driven significant academic, social, and economic advancements.

Hongda Tian is a research and innovation focused senior lecturer at the UTS Data Science Institute. By leveraging the power of AI, he has been focusing on research translation through working with government and industry partners and providing data-driven solutions to real-world problems. .

Distinguished professor Fang Chen, UTS Data Science Institute's Executive Director, is globally recognized in AI and data science, earning accolades like the Eureka Prize.

1 AI Empowering Infrastructure: The Road to Smartness

To do a good job, one must first sharpen one's tools.

— Confucius

1.1 INTRODUCTION

Modern infrastructure is a vital cornerstone of a well-functioning society, significantly transforming our lives by enhancing convenience, efficiency, effectiveness, and cost reduction. However, challenges within infrastructure encompass various issues. These include aging infrastructure demanding extensive maintenance, repairs, and upgrades, leading to safety hazards and service disruptions, particularly concerning the deterioration of bridges, roads, and utilities. Transportation congestion not only impedes productivity but also contributes to environmental pollution. Crucial to both urban and rural areas, effective water resource management involves overseeing supply, treatment, and distribution while ensuring water quality and availability. The development of smart grids, essential for efficient energy production, distribution, and consumption, presents the complex task of balancing supply and demand within power grids. Additionally, in recent times, the focus on cybersecurity and infrastructure protection has become increasingly significant.

In the face of the vast scale of modern civilization's infrastructure, it's unrealistic to rely solely on manual efforts for the smooth operation of these extensive systems. Even in ancient times, people utilized various tools for infrastructure building and maintenance. However, due to the enormity of infrastructure, construction and maintenance costs tend to be high. Modern society heavily depends on intricate networks of infrastructure encompassing transportation, energy, water supply, communication, and more. Yet, the escalating complexity, aging components, and urban expansion present significant challenges to their seamless operation. Addressing these challenges within budget constraints requires optimized planning and operations. Achieving this optimization proves to be a daunting task as it demands a comprehensive understanding of the extensive infrastructure network, future predictions, and making the best decisions. This book delves into how the integration of artificial intelligence (AI) technologies has emerged as a potent tool to optimize, predict, and manage various aspects of infrastructure. It discusses how AI can assist humans in dealing with these challenging tasks.

DOI: 10.1201/9781003473893-1

AI has surged in popularity, particularly in this era marked by the proliferation of large data and extensive models. Recent innovations like ChatGPT have gained significant traction, aiding individuals in composing lengthy texts and facilitating language understanding and creation. Moreover, the advancement of generative AI has enabled its application in image and video production. These developments have spurred the belief that machine learning-based AI can formulate algorithms akin to the human brain, potentially capable of human-like thinking and behaviour. Consequently, there's optimism that AI might surpass human capabilities, foresee hidden information and future events, and autonomously make optimal decisions.

However, it's crucial to recognize that the efficacy of AI is inherently linked to the data it represents. This capability can be dissected across three key aspects. Firstly, we need sufficient data to cover a wide range of situations. It's essential to understand that it's not necessary for the data to represent every single scenario comprehensively. Think of it like creating a topographic map; we focus on identifying critical points. A well-designed model can extrapolate and understand the nuances between these significant points. Secondly, as previously mentioned, the model must fit the data representation and connect these crucial data points. This requires a meticulous analysis of data alongside incorporating relevant physical knowledge to structure an appropriate model. Thirdly, AI systems must adapt to changes as no infrastructure remains static. The dynamic nature and evolving patterns must be ingrained within the model to enable predictive capabilities. This also involves continuous validation processes to ensure accuracy and relevance.

1.2 STATISTICS AND MACHINE LEARNING: TWO SIDES OF THE SAME COIN

Machine learning and statistics are not polar opposites. Mathematics is fundamental to statistics, making it a powerful tool for bridging the gap between data and real-world problems. Similarly, machine learning acts as another layer, connecting fundamental theory to practical applications. In this way, machine learning also bridges the gap between applications and data. Moreover, machine learning often serves as a link between statistics and applications, while statistical techniques remain crucial for data processing. Machine learning techniques in this process strive for increased agility, efficiency, replicability, capacity, and applicability. These properties of machine learning can fill different needs, and they are usually not isolated but overlapped. That is, some machine-learning techniques will fulfil more than one need with multiple properties displayed.

1.2.1 AGILITY

Agility becomes essential when a user lacking comprehensive background knowledge encounters a data-driven problem. In such situations, opting for a machine learning tool to interpret the data and obtain desired results is a more agile approach. Conversely, traditional statistical models typically demand a profound understanding of the problem, underlying theories, and the establishment of relationships to reconstruct the targeted (dependent) variable using observable (independent) variables based on theory. Employing these statistical models necessitates users to undergo a lengthy process to design and create them, particularly when addressing novel problems for which no solutions exist.

1.2.2 REPLICABILITY

Furthermore, statistical models must be designed to ensure computational convenience. Hence, they either require careful design as approximations for simplified computation or users must identify a specified and appropriate inference method to solve for the parameters. This necessitates users to design a specified model and involves manual work and programming for each specified problem, although some existing tools, albeit limited, can offer assistance.

In contrast, achieving replicability is more straightforward when using machine learning models for such data-driven problems. With machine learning models, a regular user only needs a basic grasp of data quality, particularly for tabular data. They can then utilize readily available model packages, such as Python packages in Scikit-learn [1], to swiftly establish a relationship between input variables and the target. Even a junior data scientist or machine learning researcher can promptly deploy an application and test it without model redesign to adapt to the problem and data.

The replicability achieved by the machine learning model is primarily due to its uniform input and generalized problem definition. For instance, in most structured data prediction problems, there exists a matrix X, where each sample is represented in a row and each variable (referred to as a feature) in a column. The problem is typically defined as finding a projection f that can map $X \rightarrow \vec{y}$, where $\vec{y}$ represents the target, and each element corresponds to the target for the data given in the same row in X. Such a definition of X', within infrastructure, might encompass all assets and their attributes. $\vec{y}$ could represent maintenance prices. Machine learning aims to fit f into the optimized cost function to ensure the projected prices closely align with the real prices. Consequently, machine learning can be used to address problems such as estimating maintenance prices for newly constructed assets. A simple Python code of fewer than 20 lines can entirely fulfil this basic function, with the model-building process to achieve the goal. For different problems, the only part to be reprogrammed is to use different data files and specify the columns as features and targets.

1.2.3 APPLICABILITY

The applicability of machine learning lies in adapting and designing models to meet specific requirements in real-world applications. For instance, to address privacy concerns, model designers may not have access to the raw data. Algorithms like federated learning [2] have been developed for this purpose, enabling the learning of models across distributed terminals without sharing the underlying data. Instead, the model updates are aggregated into a central server.

In addition, in many real-world projects, the data extends beyond structured table data and includes various formats such as images, documents, sound files, or network data. These diverse data types are common in applications. Often, these diverse data types are transformed into structured formats to suit statistical models. However, the methods of data processing can significantly influence the final outcome. This influence is not isolated but generally intertwines with the model employed after processing.

Machine learning design views both data processing and modelling as an integrated problem. This integration does not demand extensive additional efforts to design a new model for every instance. Techniques like embedding and representation learning are tailored for this purpose and can be swiftly implemented alongside any model. This flexibility allows machine learning to accommodate most requirements in applications despite their complexity and uncertainty.

1.2.4 EFFICIENCY

The machine learning models can achieve runtime efficiency. Data-driven problems usually exhibit complexity, and both the complexity and data size significantly influence runtime speed. Exploiting efficient hardware and utilizing the parallel processing capabilities of modern hardware can further enhance runtime efficiency. In addition, employing algorithms such as XGBoost (a faster version of Random Forest) and optimizing software integration can all contribute to performance gains in software. Many existing machine learning tools offer a more efficient structure and implementation, highlighting the key aspects of efficiency in machine learning. They also emphasize the importance of balancing efficiency with other critical considerations, such as interpretability and validity.

1.2.5 CAPABILITY

The term "capacity" refers to the machine learning model's ability to handle more complex relationships via data fed in. There are two dimensions of capacity.

First, data capacity and the types of data the model can handle, which may include high-dimensional data, large-scale data, unstructured data, dynamic data, etc. These types of data are typically different from normal structured data. In the case of high-dimensional data, for example, traditional modelling involves considering how to model the impact for each dimension. In contrast, machine learning models can incorporate all dimensions and compress them within the model. For instance, techniques like Lasso, which adds dimension regularization to the model, bridge the gap between statistics and machine learning. Lasso imposes the constraint that a minimum number of features should be used for learning. Other methods, such as deep learning, can take the entire image as input (by dimensions in the image resolution scale), integrating dimensions with convolution to generate higher-level features through layers. These higher-level features can help reduce dimensionality. Machine learning models are also adept at learning from unstructured data, such as images and graph networks. Additionally, for dynamic data like streaming and online data, machine learning models do not need to be retrained every time. Techniques like incremental learning and online learning facilitate model updating, especially for large-scale data.

The other dimension is machine learning's capacity to fit many types of learning scenarios. The fundamental scenario categories are supervised learning and unsupervised learning. Supervised learning is commonly used when labelled ground truth data is available, enabling the model to fit parameters and features to approximate labels closely. Unsupervised learning is more challenging as it lacks labelled data, and its goal is different, mainly focusing on clustering observations or compressing data from high dimensions to critical dimensions. Machine learning also addresses scenarios with additional learning difficulties, such as noisy labels, small or sparse datasets, imbalanced categories, and unclear data dependencies. Learning can be applied to scenarios with requirements beyond data, such as privacy, security, and fairness. Solutions in these cases usually involve model development in the pre-process, in-process, and post-process stages, providing the flexibility to apply machine learning to various applications.

1.3 HOW MACHINE LEARNING MAKES INFRASTRUCTURE SOLUTIONS SMARTER

In this book, we would like to introduce modern machine-learning techniques that can be applied to infrastructure areas. We hope that we can provide smarter ways to understand, plan, and manage the infrastructure assets, both tangible and intangible. We will focus on three sections: Situation Awareness, Predictive Analytics, and Decision Support.

1.3.1 SITUATION AWARENESS

Many infrastructure structures are difficult to inspect. In this case, how can we know the health status of the structure at any time? There are also many infrastructures that are in the model of operating, such as traffic, communication, and commuting, which are very large systems. We may be able to use simulation technology to test their robustness, but the simulation system cannot completely and truly include all factors. Therefore, when an unwanted situation occurs or is about to occur, how can we be sure that we can know these situations? When the system's operating efficiency is low, how can we find the key causes? Therefore, we introduce data-driven situation awareness here. Unlike simulation, data-driven situation awareness can use actual observations as the basis for inference. Based on the possible observed crisis data, it can help infer the health of the system and conduct further analysis. We demonstrate data-driven situation awareness in Chapters 2, 3, and 4.

Chapter 2 focuses on asset anomaly identification, the purpose of which is to be aware of whether there is any fault/failure associated with infrastructure. Since data associated with normal states of infrastructure are only available generally, an unsupervised approach is more suitable. Damage identification in structural health monitoring is used to illustrate the scenario. Some techniques addressing the challenges of damage identification in structural health monitoring will be presented, including dimensionality reduction, damage detection, damage localization, and damage estimation. Some case studies on damage identification in structural health monitoring will also be provided.

In Chapter 3, we focus on the evaluation of railway network performance, specifically addressing the issue of delays and their propagation within large-scale networks. They present a detailed case study and aim to contribute to the existing knowledge of network performance evaluation by providing valuable insights into delay phenomena and their implications for railway operations and management. We begin by introducing the problem formulation and background information, including the different types of delays and their categorization based on causes. We then propose a conditional Bayesian model for predicting delay propagation, which allows for the estimation and analysis of future delay consequences in various scenarios. The model takes into account factors such as single train delays, subsequent train delays, crossing-line propagation, and connected trains. By utilizing this model, the authors demonstrate how the future impacts of delays can be estimated and analyzed under different conditions, providing valuable information for railway network planning and management. Overall, this chapter offers a comprehensive study on railway network performance evaluation, with a specific focus on delay propagation. The information and insights provided can be valuable for stakeholders involved in railway operations and management, helping them enhance the efficiency and reliability of railway networks.

In Chapter 4, we focus on signal aspect transition detection for railway networks which presents a comprehensive exploration of the development of an AI-driven object detection methodology specifically tailored for one NSW railway utility, a pivotal rail service provider in the Greater Sydney area. The research underscores the critical significance of accurately identifying signal aspect states and transitions in railway operations to enhance safety, efficiency, and overall customer experience. By leveraging video footage captured from front-facing cameras on Waratah train sets, the study aims to provide a detailed understanding of historical performance metrics and facilitate rapid incident recovery, thereby contributing to the continuous improvement of operational processes. Through the amalgamation of advanced machine learning techniques, such as a unified neural network-driven process for signal detection and an innovative image segmentation method for track detection, the research endeavours to revolutionize traditional train signal detection practices. This pioneering approach not only aims to optimize the safety and dependability of railway operations but also seeks to drive strategic planning enhancements for large-scale rail systems. By harnessing cutting-edge technologies and methodologies, the study aspires to transform the landscape of railway operations, fostering increased reliability, efficiency, and sustainability. The collaborative efforts with train operators exemplify a commitment to innovation and industry collaboration, with a shared goal of advancing the field of transportation through research-driven solutions that benefit both individual commuters and society at large.

1.3.2 PREDICTIVE ANALYSIS

Situation awareness is only for the current moment, focusing on event detection or performance, which mainly relies on static information. However, dynamic change should be included if we need to make plans for the future, and then we consider predictive analysis. The purpose of predictive analysis is to forecast what will happen in the future. The traditional methods use an analytic method to find out the influencing factors. Such structural models or parametric models are based on expertise and knowledge. Such, a model is correct only when all factors and how the factors influence the outcome have been known. Therefore, such a method does not require a large amount of data. However, the reality is that most of the factors and influences are latent. So, we need machine learning to create a mapping of data that does not require these latent relationships to be known. Our book presents three chapters about predictive analysis, showing how we use machine learning to predict water pipe failures for the short-term future and long-term future. We also use an example of transport demand for prediction.

Chapter 5 gives an example of predicting water pipe failures by machine learning. Machine learning techniques aren't just a myth when it comes to making predictions. These models take in data and forecast what might occur within a known range of outcomes. To illustrate, let's delve into the issue of predicting water pipe failures. Water pipes, often buried underground for many years without direct monitoring, are costly to inspect or replace. The dilemma lies in avoiding the excessive response of fixing pipes after a burst, which incurs higher costs. Utility companies typically plan and allocate budgets for inspecting, repairing, or replacing pipes before they fail. This proactive strategy relies on planning to prevent two potential wastes. First, unnecessary spending on inspecting pipes that are in good condition. Second, a budget spent on inspecting good pipes results in no failures found, failing to reduce bursts. If we convert this problem into an optimization challenge, where inspecting n pipes and each failure costs a loss of b, we aim to maximize the benefits (saved cost) by evaluating $\sum_{i=1 \cdots n} bm_i$, where m_i denotes pipe i in the set of n pipes. Here, m_i equals 1 if the pipe is expected to fail soon, otherwise 0. Machine learning aims to discover a model f that projects $x_i \rightarrow s_i$ for all pipes, predicting the likelihood of failure (s_i). Two strategies are discussed for machine learning in pipe failure prediction: replacement and maintenance. Replacement focuses on predicting when a pipe should be retired based on its lifespan. Maintenance, on the other hand, involves frequent inspections, using machine learning to estimate failure frequency, and determining how often inspections should occur. It's important to note that a higher score doesn't guarantee imminent failure over a smaller score. Predictions provide supportive suggestions rather than definitive information for decision-making. Users can adjust the score definition according to their needs.

Chapter 6 gives an example to predict water pipe failures in the long-term future by machine learning. When it comes to predicting which pipes might burst, using data on pipe features, inspections, and past bursts can prevent costly damages. However, decisions made by water utilities must consider budget constraints. Planning for the budget involves thinking about the long-term future because implementing changes takes some time. Machine learning steps in to help with this issue. It offers suggestions for budget planning that look far ahead, often called long-term prediction. In our discussion about long-term prediction, we address the challenges and methods involved. Long-term prediction faces challenges, especially when trends change over extended periods. We explore clues that aid prediction, such as change points, adapting data from similar but older assets, and predicting mean trends with uncertainty bands. These clues provide a framework for machine learning algorithms. Within machine learning, various algorithms help in different ways. Some focus on digitizing knowledge about the future, predicting step-by-step into the future for a long time, grouping assets based on similarities, or using sequence-to-sequence learning, projecting historical data from one asset to another. Additionally, we touch on Conformal Prediction for uncertainty predictions. In the chapter, we also provide details about existing models.

In Chapter 7 on Service Demand Prediction in urban rail networks, we delve into the development of Intelligent Transport Systems (ITS) within smart cities, with a specific focus on railway networks and the integration of Internet of Things (IoT) devices for real-time monitoring of passenger numbers. The challenges of coarse data granularity, dynamic transfers leading to unpredictable variations in passenger numbers, and the need for real-time prediction capabilities are highlighted. To address these challenges, the study introduces a dual-phase, self-adjusting model designed for precise and expeditious prediction of commuter traffic. The model incorporates innovative techniques such as data decomposition methods and a self-attention mechanism to capture long-term patterns in time series data, enabling accurate minute-level granularity predictions. By transforming discrete entry records into continuous patterns and adapting predictions in response to immediate emergencies and short-term fluctuations, the model offers a comprehensive solution for enhancing operational efficiency and decision-making in urban rail networks. The successful implementation of this model in the railway network of the Greater Sydney Area in Australia demonstrates its capacity to provide accurate forecasts essential for scheduling and real-time strategic guidance to operators during urgent situations. The feedback received from front-line railway staff further informs potential enhancements to the framework, emphasizing the practical significance and ongoing research potential of this innovative approach to service demand prediction in urban rail networks.

1.3.3 DECISIONS SUPPORT

Decision-making is a multifaceted process that involves the consideration of various factors and the ability to anticipate future events. One crucial aspect of decision-making is the need for information. This information can be based on Situation Awareness (SA), which is centred on the present moment, emphasizing event detection and performance assessment. Situation awareness primarily relies on static information, offering insights into the current state of affairs. On the other hand, the decision-making process also requires dynamic considerations, making predictive analysis imperative. Predictive analysis is geared towards forecasting future events so that decisions can be planned proactively before things happen. Chapters 8, 9, and 10) illustrate how machine learning is employed in the decision-making process.

Chapter 8 delves into the critical importance of strategic asset prioritization in infrastructure management, especially amidst growing populations and aging networks. It discusses the shift towards data-driven models for identifying and managing high-risk assets, emphasizing aspects like feature engineering, model evaluation, and the significance of real-world case studies, particularly within the water industry. Through advanced risk management strategies and the integration of machine learning techniques, the chapter highlights the potential for enhancing infrastructure resilience and financial sustainability. It underscores the transformative role of data-driven approaches in optimizing asset maintenance and prioritization, offering a robust framework for effective water utility management amidst contemporary challenges.

Regarding data-driven solutions for asset and infrastructure maintenance, one challenge arises from online applications, where data arrive continuously in the form of a stream and a decision on whether they are anomalous needs to be made for each incoming sample. In many real-world applications, the underlying distributions of data vary over time. This implies that normal behaviour may evolve with time, and a current notion of normal behaviour may not be sufficiently representative in the future, which poses a great challenge for infrastructure monitoring when dealing with non-stationary data streams. Chapter 9 will discuss how to accommodate normal behaviour evolution in the non-stationary data stream. Taking structural health monitoring as an example, the problem is formulated from the concept drift adaptation perspective. Case studies on three bridge structures are presented as well.

Chapter 10 outlines the implementation and effectiveness of deploying acoustic sensors in targeted areas to detect leaks and breaks in water mains, a crucial endeavour for water utilities aiming to minimize water loss and enhance infrastructure resilience. Through the integration of predictive analytics and intelligent sensing technologies, the research focuses on preemptive leak detection by prioritizing high-risk zones and strategically situating sensors. Leveraging data collected from these sensors, machine learning models are developed to enable predictive maintenance, aiming to mitigate water loss and improve overall system efficiency. The chapter underscores the significance of a data-driven approach in automating leak detection processes and emphasizes the validation of this approach.

1.4 PURPOSE OF THIS BOOK

The book serves two purposes, offering valuable insights into both the infrastructure society and the AI society. Our objectives revolve around enhancing the understanding of AI capabilities for infrastructure users and guiding AI developers toward a clear aim. These dual purposes can be categorized as follows:

First, showcasing AI techniques in Infrastructure Scenarios: for infrastructure developers, we would like to show examples of how AI techniques can be used to solve real problems. Therefore, we have selected typical issues, including performance analysis, detecting unusual situations, predictions, decision optimization, ongoing system monitoring, and data acquisition. All these problems are data-driven, showcasing how machine learning can play a role in supporting manually designed statistical work in infrastructure. This involves fast responses to situations or identifying patterns that are complex for humans to analyze. It is also our pleasure to see infrastructure users absorb the experiences presented in these chapters and adapt the elementary solutions to their own problems. They can then develop solutions tailored to their specific purposes based on these examples. Additionally, we aim to present data-driven infrastructure problems from the perspective of data scientists and AI researchers. We explore the commonalities and distinctions of this data compared to other datasets typically handled by AI.

Secondly, we would like to discuss how machine learning development is influenced by the needs of smart infrastructure. The book chapters are grounded in real developments within the realm of smart infrastructure. All the work is the result of collaboration among experienced data scientists, machine learning researchers, and domain experts. The discussions in real projects typically extend over a considerable duration for each individual step, and the overall development process often spans several years. These discussions are rooted in actual problems that domain experts may have faced, as well as newly discovered challenges encountered during the problem-solving process. Our discussions have also illuminated various areas and brought to light challenges that machine learning had not previously considered. Machine learning researchers, with experience in developing algorithms, expand their knowledge by applying these algorithms to real-world applications. This affords them the opportunity to test and reconsider their design purposes. This process prompts us to reflect on the most crucial needs in infrastructure when developing AI to maximize its impact.

In this book, we also discuss how we deal with two challenges, one for infrastructure and the other for machine learning. When applying machine learning research to infrastructure problems, it is crucial and challenging to bridge the professional knowledge of machine learning and infrastructure. The goal is to discover and identify suitable problems in infrastructure that can be feasibly solved by machine learning. As a result, our discussions are conducted on a case-by-case basis, showcasing identified infrastructure problems, elementary and necessary machine-learning knowledge required for solving these problems. We illustrate the progressive steps for each implementation and emphasize how to ensure the work is both useful and impactful. Some chapters also delve into philosophical discussions on why machine learning is chosen and why the identified infrastructure problem is suitable. The knowledge and techniques presented in these discussions are versatile and can be applied to other areas.

This challenge also extends to machine learning. The methods discussed in this book differ from prevalent AI techniques that often focus on images and text due to the nature of data. Many AI techniques, like the ChatGPT, are based on multimedia data where humans can clearly see patterns, making it easier to confirm that the data can be used to solve a problem. For instance, recognizing a human face is successful because the face is visible and distinguishable. However, in this book, we discuss infrastructure data where patterns are not always visible. We emphasize that our focus is not solely on designing models; instead, we also explore why the model can make predictions with the given data.

1.4.1 AUDIENCE OF THE BOOK

This book targets a diverse readership spanning professionals and individuals involved in various facets of the infrastructure and machine learning industries. Our primary audience comprises those actively engaged in the practical application and management of infrastructure systems. This encompasses professionals from sectors like transportation, water and sewage, energy, and structural health monitoring. However, the book also welcomes a broader audience of professionals and enthusiasts working in the fields of machine learning and data science. It provides a platform to explore cutting-edge research, innovative applications, and theoretical advancements at the intersection of AI and infrastructure domains. By bridging these realms, the book aims to foster cross-pollination of ideas and promote interdisciplinary collaboration towards developing intelligent infrastructure solutions.

Some of the figures in this book are originally generated in colours. Refer to the electronic version for the best visual effects of those figures.

2 Asset Anomaly Identification – Damage Detection in Structural Health Monitoring

2.1 BACKGROUND

With regards to asset/infrastructure maintenance, one extremely important aspect is to grasp the working or operating status of them in a timely manner, so as to carry out corresponding maintenance work when necessary. In order to be aware of whether there is any fault/failure associated with infrastructure, the traditional approach is to conduct regular inspections of related facilities. However, this method has limitations in terms of both space and time. On the one hand, it may be difficult or even impossible to inspect certain key parts of infrastructure in actual operations. On the other hand, in order to ensure the timeliness of inspection and maintenance while reducing maintenance costs, how to devise an appropriate inspection cycle is also a challenge. In recent years, with the rapid advancement of sensing technology and data science, data-driven situation awareness for asset/infrastructure has received extensive attention from both academia and industry. Its essence is to perform analysis by means of machine learning on sensor data collected from asset/infrastructure. The status of the related facilities could be derived based on advanced analytics. Compared with traditional time-based maintenance approach, this type of intelligent fault/failure detection makes it possible to perform condition-based maintenance.

Structural health monitoring (SHM) [11] utilises sensor systems to offer actionable insights into the present and future conditions of civil infrastructures, which are vital for supporting the flow of people and goods within cities. By leveraging advanced sensing technologies and data analytics, SHM systems enable a transition from time-based (such as visual inspections at predetermined intervals) to condition-based maintenance[56]. Consequently, SHM holds the promise of further reducing both economic losses and potential human casualties.

A typical model-driven approach in SHM adopts a numerical model of the structure, usually based on finite element analysis, which relates differences between measured data and the data generated by the model to the damage identification [11]. However, a numerical model may not always be available in practice and does not always correctly capture the exact behaviour of the real structure. On the other hand, a data-driven approach establishes a model by learning from measured data and then makes a comparison between the model and measured responses to detect damage.

DOI: 10.1201/9781003473893-2

This approach uses techniques in pattern recognition, or more broadly, in machine learning [179]. Patterns in data that deviate from the anticipated normal behaviour are referred to as anomalies or outliers[1]. The process of pinpointing these divergent patterns is commonly known as anomaly detection [31], which has seen widespread application across various domains including intrusion detection for cyber-security and fault detection in safety-critical systems.

Damage identification represents a pivotal challenge in SHM. Rytter categorizes it into four distinct levels of complexity [153]:

- Level 1 (Detection): to detect if damage is present in the structure.
- Level 2 (Localization): to locate the position of the damage.
- Level 3 (Assessment): to estimate the extent of the damage.
- Level 4 (Prediction): to give information about the safety of the structure, e.g. a remaining life estimation.

Out of these four levels, level 4 necessitates comprehension of the physical attributes of structural damage progression. Machine learning techniques can address levels ranging from 1 to 3, with level 1 manageable through unsupervised learning, while levels 2 and 3 typically require a supervised learning methodology (Worden & Manson, 2007). Given that data pertaining to the healthy states of structures are typically more accessible, an unsupervised approach proves to be more feasible.

In SHM, data often exhibit high redundancy and correlation. Multiple sensors positioned at various locations gather similar vibration data over time, such as on a long-span bridge where numerous sensors detect signals generated by traffic loading. Each vehicle event produces multiple signals recorded by different sensors. These measured variables not only correlate with each other at specific times but also exhibit autocorrelation over time. Traditional two-way analysis using matrices, common in SHM, may not fully capture these intricate relationships and correlations. Typically, such analyses involve matricizing multiway arrays followed by matrix-based techniques like principal component analysis (PCA) or singular value decomposition (SVD). However, unfolding multiway data and analyzing them using two-way methods can lead to information loss and misinterpretation, especially in the presence of noise [5]. Tensor analysis, on the other hand, enables simultaneous analysis of data across multiple modes [89].

Following this introduction, some techniques addressing the challenges for damage identification in SHM will be presented in 2.2. Specifically, dimensionality reduction is usually performed due to data redundancy. Then how damage detection, localization, and estimation can be achieved using machine learning is described. Some case studies on damage identification in SHM will be provided in 2.3.

---

[1] In this chapter, anomaly and outlier are used interchangeably

2.2 TECHNIQUES

2.2.1 DIMENSIONALITY REDUCTION

The data in SHM are are frequently high-dimensional, exhibiting significant redundancy and correlation. This complexity can impede the detection process and render underlying patterns more intricate to discern. Furthermore, processing high-dimensional data can be resource-intensive, necessitating increased data transmission and imposing higher computational demands on the sensor network. Let the data matrix be denoted as $X \in \mathbb{R}^{n \times d}$, where n is the number of data instances and d is the data dimension. Since d is large, the aim here is to transform X to $Y \in \mathbb{R}^{n \times k}$ where $k \ll d$.

Principal component analysis (PCA) is a popular technique for dimensionality reduction in SHM [137]. It's a process of transforming a vector space from a higher dimension to a lower one. PCA entails computing the eigenvectors of a data covariance matrix, with the mean of each feature subtracted beforehand. This method is straightforward and commonly employed for reducing dimensionality. Sohn et al.[162] employed PCA with the statistical process control for damage detection. In addition, Zang and Imregun [188] used PCA to compress frequency response function (FRF) data for damage detection. However, PCA has some drawbacks including 1) when the data dimension is exceedingly high, performing PCA becomes computationally expensive; 2) its performance is sensitive to the number of selected components. PCA entails eigen decomposition of the data covariance matrix with a complexity of $O(d^3)$, where d represents the data dimension. This computation becomes costly when d is exceedingly large, a typical scenario in SHM sensing data. Although we can mitigate the computation cost by computing only the first few eigenvectors, it remains impractical for extremely high-dimensional data.

PCA transforms original features from data onto a new set of axes known as the principal components of the transformation. Each principal component corresponds to an eigenvector of the covariance matrix of the original dataset. Generally, the first few principal components capture the majority of the variance in the data, allowing the subsequent principal components to be omitted with minimal loss of information. Hence, PCA facilitates the reduction of data dimensionality.

The transformation operates as follows: assuming each column of X has a zero mean, the covariance matrix of X is denoted as $C = (1/(n-1))X^T X$. A matrix V whose columns are d eigenvectors of the covariance matrix C forms a set of d principal components. It is computed from the decomposition $C = VDV^T$ where D is the diagonal matrix whose ith diagonal element represents the eigenvalue λ_i. Conventionally, the eigenvectors in V have unit lengths and are arranged based on their eigenvalues in descending order.

Let k represent the number of the first eigenvectors that capture the majority of the data variance ($k < d$), and $P(d \times k)$ represent a matrix formed by the first k eigenvectors as the columns. A projection of a data matrix X onto a subspace spanned by eigenvectors in P

$$Y = XP \tag{2.1}$$

represents the dimensionality reduction of X.

PCA's complexity is $O(d^3)$ because of the eigen decomposition of the data co-variance matrix. Despite potential reductions in computation by focusing on the first few eigenvectors, this approach remains impractical for extremely high-dimensional data. As an alternative, random projection (RP) offers a less expensive method for dimensionality reduction in such cases [6]. As per the Johnson–Lindenstrauss lemma, if data is randomly projected onto a subspace defined by $O(\log n)$ columns, the pairwise Euclidean distances between data points are maintained. Consequently, the dimension of the projected space relies solely on the number of data points, irrespective of the original data dimension. The RP thus reduces the data dimension from d to $k = O(\log n)$. In practice, k can be relatively small while still preserving the pairwise distances within the projected space. RP emerges as an effective and efficient method for dimensionality reduction in high-dimensional data [19].

Zang et al. [187] employed independent component analysis (ICA) for dimensionality reduction in time domain signals, subsequently utilising neural networks for damage detection. ICA serves as a method to decompose signals into uncorrelated independent components. However, similar to PCA, the efficacy of this approach hinges significantly on the number of selected components.

Moreover, Keogh et al. [85] introduced a technique known as piecewise aggregate approximation (PAA) for reducing the dimensionality of large time series data. This method is characterized by its speed, simplicity, and ability to accommodate flexible distance measures, facilitating rapid similarity search in extensive time series datasets. The original signal, represented by each row x_i of X, is segmented into k equal-sized parts. Each element in the reduced data is then computed as the mean value of the corresponding segment in the original data. Specifically, each element j of each row y_i of Y is computed as

$$y_{ij} = \frac{k}{d} \sum_{d(j-1)/k+1}^{dj/k} x_{ij} \tag{2.2}$$

2.2.2 DAMAGE DETECTION

Worden et al.[180] employed Mahalanobis distance to detect anomalies in data, indicative of potential damage events. Anomalies in this context refer to data points whose Mahalanobis distances from training events exceed a specified threshold. However, it's important to note that this approach assumes data adherence to a normal distribution, which may not always be the case in practical scenarios.

Neural networks [20] are popular techniques for damage detection in SHM. Zang and Imregun [188], Lee et al. [99] and Zang et al. [187] employed neural networks for detecting structural damage in a supervised context, necessitating data from both healthy and damaged states. Chan et al. [30] utilised auto-associative neural networks for damage detection in several cable-supported bridges in Hong Kong including the Tsing Ma Bridge, Kap Shui Mun Bridge and Ting Kau Bridge. The networks served as a novelty filter for detecting damage occurrence in an unsupervised manner. An auto-associative network, a type of multilayer feedforward neural network with a bottleneck layer, was employed. This network architecture aims to replicate input patterns at the output layer while filtering out redundant information and noise through the bottleneck layer. Subsequently, a novelty index is defined as the disparity between the target output and the network's estimated output. In the event of abnormal structural conditions in the bridge, a notable increase in the novelty index is anticipated. However, overfitting remains a significant drawback of neural networks.

The support vector machine (SVM) is a supervised learning method rooted in the Vapnik–Chervonenkis theory [41]. With robust theoretical foundations, SVM exhibits a notable regularization property, enabling effective generalization to new data and mitigating overfitting, a common challenge encountered in neural networks. Additionally, SVM possesses the capability to integrate various types of discriminant functions, including linear, non-linear, and radial basis functions, within a unified framework.

In practical scenarios, it's often the case that there are no labeled damage data available for supervised learning. Unsupervised methods, therefore, train models without relying on class information, thus framing the classification task as an anomaly detection problem. Within this framework, data objects that exhibit significant deviations from the learned normal behaviour are identified as anomalies or indicative of damage. Worden et al. utilised Mahalanobis distance to find anomalies in the data, which are likely to be damage [180]. Chan et al. [30] employed auto-associative neural networks for damage detection of the three cable-supported bridges in Hong Kong. One-class SVM (OCSVM) [157, 166] is a robust technique for this purpose. Unsupervised methods in SHM normally train the model using only healthy data. Events which significantly deviate from the normal behaviour of the trained model are considered as damage.

Consider a set of training data denoted as $\mathscr{X} = \{\mathbf{x}_i\}_{i=1}^m$, where $\mathbf{x}_i$ represents a feature vector representing a training sample and m signifies the number of training samples. OCSVM first maps these training data points into a high-dimensional feature space using a function $\boldsymbol{\phi}$ defined by the kernel $k(\mathbf{x}_i, \mathbf{x}_j) = \boldsymbol{\phi}(\mathbf{x}_i)^T \boldsymbol{\phi}(\mathbf{x}_j)$. Subsequently, it aims to identify a hyperplane that maximizes the margin between the data points and the origin [157]. For this purpose, a quadratic optimization problem is formulated as follows:

$$\min_{\mathbf{w},\xi,\rho} \frac{1}{2}\|\mathbf{w}\|^2 + \frac{1}{vm}\sum_{i=1}^m \xi_i - \rho \qquad (2.3)$$

$$s.t. \quad \mathbf{w}^T \boldsymbol{\phi}(\mathbf{x}_i) \geq \rho - \xi_i, \quad \xi_i \geq 0,$$

where ξ_i is a slack variable, $v \in (0, 1]$ controls the amount of penalization incurred by these slack variables, ρ is the bias term, and $\mathbf{w}^T \boldsymbol{\phi}(\mathbf{x}_i) - \rho$ is the separating hyperplane or decision boundary in the feature space. After introducing Lagrange multipliers

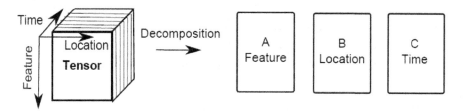

Figure 2.1   Tensor data in SHM [87]

$\alpha = \{\alpha_1,\ldots,\alpha_m\}$, the dual problem can be derived as follows [158]:

$$\min_{\alpha,\rho} \frac{1}{2} \sum_{i=1}^{m} \sum_{j=1}^{m} \alpha_i \alpha_j k(\mathbf{x}_i, \mathbf{x}_j) + \rho\left(1 - \sum_{i=1}^{m} \alpha_i\right) \tag{2.4}$$

$$s.t. \ 0 \le \alpha_i \le 1, \ \sum_{i=1}^{m} \alpha_i = \frac{1}{\nu m}.$$

After obtaining the optimal solution of Equation (2.4), the decision value for a new sample $\mathbf{x}$ is determined using the following decision function:

$$g(\mathbf{x}) = \sum_i \alpha_i k(\mathbf{x}_i, \mathbf{x}) - \rho, \tag{2.5}$$

with its magnitude $|g(\mathbf{x})|$ reflecting the distance from $\mathbf{x}$ to the decision boundary and its sign $sign(g(\mathbf{x}))$ indicating the class label. Moreover, the training data can be classified into three sets: samples with α_i lying in the range $(0,1)$ are termed margin support vectors and comprise the set $\mathscr{S}$; samples having $\alpha_i = 1$ are termed error support vectors and constitute the set $\mathscr{E}$; the remaining data with $\alpha_i = 0$ are referred to as reserve vectors and are denoted by the set $\mathscr{R}$.

2.2.3   DAMAGE LOCALIZATION AND ESTIMATION

Due to the limitation of unsupervised learning techniques as noted in [179], the methods presented in 2.2.2 are only able to detect damage. There is not much work available in discussing damage localization and estimation in unsupervised setting.

Actually in SHM, it's common to utilise multiple sensors placed at various locations to capture vibration signals continuously. These data can be regarded as a three-dimensional tensor (feature × location × time) as illustrated in Figure 2.1. Features refer to the information derived from raw signals in the time domain (such as frequency domain features). Location denotes the sensors, while time represents the data snapshots captured at different timestamps. Each cell within the tensor contains a feature value extracted from a specific sensor at a particular moment. Every slice along the time axis, as depicted in Figure 2.1, constitutes a frontal slice illustrating all feature signals across all sensor locations at that particular time. For simplicity, we represent a tensor as a three-dimensional array here, which is often applicable in

SHM. Nonetheless, it's also feasible to extend all theories to an n-dimensional array. Tensor analysis has proven successful across various domains of application, spanning chemistry, neuroscience, social network analysis, and computer vision [5, 90]. Prada [148] employed three-way analysis of SHM data to detect damage and select features. However, the focus of their tensor analysis was solely on detecting damage, without addressing the localization and estimation of its extent.

There are two primary methods for tensor decomposition: CANDECOMP/-PARAFAC (CP) decomposition and Tucker decomposition [89]. Following decomposition of a three-way tensor, three component matrices can be derived, each representing information in a specific mode. In the context of SHM data, as depicted in Figure 2.1, these modes correspond to features (represented by matrix A), locations (matrix B), and time (matrix C), respectively. The CP method allows for the independent interpretation of artifacts within each mode using its associated component matrix. Conversely, in the Tucker method, any component can interact with another component in different modes, as quantified by the core tensor [4]. This interaction complexity makes the interpretation of a Tucker model more challenging than CP. Hence, for the purpose of damage identification, we exclusively utilise the CP method.

CP decomposition breaks down a tensor into a combination of a finite number of rank-one tensors. In the case of a three-way tensor $\mathscr{X} \in \mathbb{R}^{I \times J \times K}$, it is expressed as

$$\mathscr{X} = \sum_{r=1}^{R} \lambda_r A_{:r} \circ B_{:r} \circ C_{:r} + \varepsilon, \tag{2.6}$$

where R is the latent factor, $A_{:r}$, $B_{:r}$, and $C_{:r}$ are r-th columns of component matrices $A \in \mathbb{R}^{I \times R}$, $B \in \mathbb{R}^{J \times R}$, and $C \in \mathbb{R}^{K \times R}$, respectively, and λ is the weight vector so that the columns of A, B, C are normalized to length one. The symbol '∘' represents a vector outer product. ε is a three-way tensor containing the residuals. It can also be written in terms of the k-th frontal slice of $\mathscr{X}$:

$$X_k = AD_kB^T + E_k, \tag{2.7}$$

where the diagonal matrix $D_k = diag(\lambda C_{k:})$ ($C_{k:}$ is the k-th row of matrix C).

The typical approach to solving CP decomposition involves alternating least squares (ALS) technique. This method iteratively addresses each component matrix using a least square approach, while keeping all other components fixed. This iterative process continues until convergence is achieved [89]. CP yields unique results as long as we permute the rank-one components accordingly [90].

Given a three-way tensor $\mathscr{X}$ ($feature \times location \times time$), representing data in a healthy condition of a structure, the objective is to determine whether a new event X_n (a frontal slice of size feature $\times$ location) is an anomaly compared to all other healthy events in the training dataset. Therefore, we utilise the subspace corresponding to the time mode after decomposition to detect damage. $\mathscr{X}$ undergoes CP decomposition, resulting in three component matrices: A, B, and C. Each row of C represents an event in the time mode. Using OCSVM, we construct a model using healthy training events, which are represented by rows of the component matrix C.

With the arrival of a new event (a new frontal slice in the time mode), an extra row will be appended to the component matrix C. As in Equation (2.7), when a new frontal slice X_n comes, we have:

$$X_n \approx AD_nB^T, \tag{2.8}$$

where $D_n = diag(\lambda C_{n:})$ which is a diagonal matrix based on the new row $C_{n:}$ of component matrix C caused by the new slice X_n. The new row $C_{n:}$ can be obtained via D_n [148]:

$$D_n = \arg\min \|X_n - AD_nB^T\|, \tag{2.9}$$

which can be solved using a least square method. Once $C_{n:}$ is obtained, this new row will undergo validation against the benchmark model established during training, assessing the structural condition. In the context of OCSVM, a negative decision value suggests that the new event is likely indicative of structural damage.

To pinpoint the location of damage, the components of the decomposed matrix in the location mode are analysed to extract meaningful artifacts from various states of the structure. Through analysis and comparison of these components, anomalies indicative of damaged locations can be identified.

To assess the extent of damage, we examine the decision values provided by the OCSVM model. The premise is that a structure experiencing more significant damage (such as a longer crack) will exhibit greater deviation from normal behaviour. Distinct ranges of decision values may indicate varying severity levels of damage. These analyses will be detailed in 2.3.

2.3 CASE STUDIES

2.3.1 A LABORATORY-BASED BUILDING STRUCTURE

2.3.1.1 Dataset

A dataset called bookshelf was obtained from Los Alamos National Laboratory (LANL)[2]. The data come from a three-story building structure constructed with unistrut columns and aluminium floor plates. The dimensions of the structure and floor layout are illustrated in Figure 2.2. Excitation was induced using a shaker, affixed at corner D to enable both translational and torsional motions. Twenty-four piezoelectric single-axis accelerometers were positioned on all joints of the structure. As depicted in Figure 2.2, two accelerometers were affixed to each joint, totaling eight accelerometers per floor.

A total of 270 vibration events were generated, each comprising 8192 data points sampled at a rate of 1600 Hz. Within this dataset, 150 events represented the healthy state of the structure, encompassing various shaker input levels and bandwidths to simulate diverse environmental and operational conditions. Among the remaining

---

[2]http://institute.lanl.gov/ei/software-and-data/

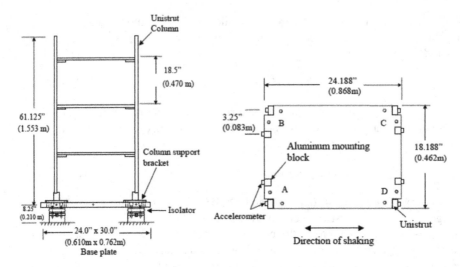

Figure 2.2 Three-story building and floor layout (image is obtained from the data description)

120 events, there were 30 instances of damage occurring at location 1A (corner A at level 1), 60 events with damage at location 3C, and 30 events with damage occurring at both locations (1A and 3C). Damage was induced by either loosening and hand-tightening bolts or by removing bolts and brackets at the joints, allowing free movement of the plate relative to the column.

For each vibration event, the data captured by each accelerometer underwent normalization by subtracting the mean and dividing by the standard deviation. This procedure standardized all events to have a mean of zero and a standard deviation of one. Subsequently, the data were transformed into the frequency domain using Fourier transform. The difference between the readings of two sensors affixed to one joint (with a total of 12 joints across three stories) in the frequency domain was utilised as a feature vector. Consequently, a total of 3240 events were obtained from all locations, each comprising a feature vector of 8192 elements.

2.3.1.2 Dimensionality Reduction and Damage Detection

Figure 2.3 shows the computational time and detection accuracy of unsupervised SVM (OCSVM) in the original feature space and in the reduced dimensional spaces computed using three methods presented in 2.2.1, namely PCA, RP, and PAA. As noted, OCSVM combined with RP and PAA had similar running time and was the fastest. PCA was the slowest method among the three.

Accuracy, measured on a scale from 0 to 1, represents the ratio of correctly predicted test events to the total number of test events. Both RP and PCA demonstrated high accuracies with a small value of k. Conversely, PAA necessitated a larger value of k to sustain a comparable accuracy level to that of the original feature space.

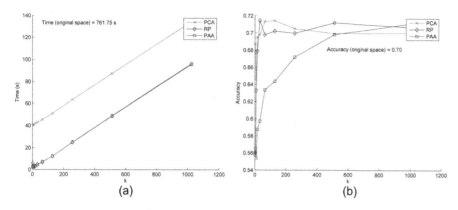

Figure 2.3 (a) Computational time and (b) detection accuracy of unsupervised SVM on building data. RP: random projection; SVM: support vector machine; PCA: principal component analysis; PAA: piecewise aggregate approximation [86]

In the case of the building data with $k = 32$, the RP method attained an accuracy of 0.71, compared to 0.70 without dimensionality reduction, and exhibited a speed improvement of 175 times. These results indicate that RP strikes a balance between computational efficiency and detection accuracy. It substantially reduces computational time while preserving detection accuracy. Although PCA yielded a similar level of accuracy, its execution time was longer. Conversely, PAA presented a comparable runtime to RP but with reduced detection accuracy.

2.3.1.3 Damage Localization and Estimation

Tensor-based techniques presented in 2.2.3 were further employed for damage localization and estimation. We only selected frequencies up to 150 Hz as features, resulting in the data being structured as a tensor of dimensions (768 features × 12 locations × 270 events). For the building dataset, 100 healthy events were randomly selected as training data, while the remainder were used for testing purposes.

To enhance result reliability, multiple testing was employed. Instead of computing decision values for each event individually (single testing), we calculated the median value for a block of 10 sequential events in chronological order. The reported accuracy reflects the accuracy of this block. This approach is based on the assumption that while individual events may contain noise, the health status of sequential events within a short period should be highly similar. All presented results were averaged over ten experimental trials.

We use $F_1 = 2 \frac{precision*recall}{precision+recall}$ to evaluate the damage detection accuracy. The F_1 scores for all new test instances using both single testing and multiple testing are shown in Figure 2.4. In order to decide the number of rank-one tensors R in the CP method, core consistency diagnostic technique (CORCONDIA) described in [25] was applied, in which a Tucker core is used for assessing the appropriateness of a CP model. CORCONDIA selected $R = 1$ for the building data. Since $R = 2$ also

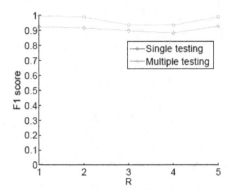

Figure 2.4   Damage detection accuracy using different values of R for the building dataset [87]

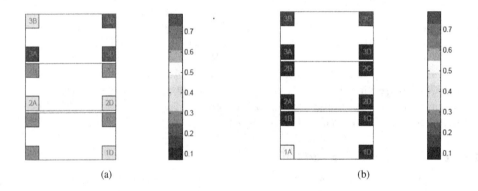

Figure 2.5   Damage localization for building dataset ((a) Location mode – First component, (b) Location mode – Second component) [87]

gave similar results for the building data, we selected $R = 2$ to be used for damage localization and estimation. Then we have F_1 score of 0.99 (using multiple testing) for the building dataset. The results also show that multiple testing can significantly improve the detection results.

Two components of the location mode ($R = 2$) with colour-coded values representing all sensor locations in the building data are shown in Figure 2.5. The first component depicts the building in a healthy state, devoid of damage, while the second component corresponds to a damaged state. Notably, during the damaged state, regions with high colour values accurately correspond to the locations with known damage (1A and 3C). This illustrates the potential of tensor analysis in effectively localizing damage within structures.

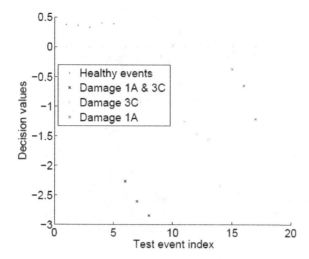

Figure 2.6 Damage characterization using decision values obtained by CP and OCSVM for the building dataset [87]

The decision values provided by the OCSVM model were utilised to assess the extent of damage. Figure 2.6 illustrates the decision values of each test event within the building dataset, as determined by the OCSVM. Dotted lines delineate the boundary between healthy and damaged events. Distinct ranges of decision values correspond to various severity levels of damage, as outlined in the dataset.

In Figure 2.6, the initial 50 events (equivalent to 5 blocks) represent decision values derived from healthy data. Subsequently, the next 30 events pertain to damaged data, wherein damage occurred simultaneously at locations 1A and 3C. Among these, the first and the next 15 events had different levels of severity. Following this, the subsequent 60 events correspond to damage solely at location 3C, spanning four severity levels. Lastly, the remaining 30 events depict decision values for damaged events occurring exclusively at location 1A, with two severity levels. Notably, for instances of identical damage types, the decision values are lower when damage occurs at both locations compared to occurrences at only one location.

2.3.2 THE SYDNEY HARBOUR BRIDGE

2.3.2.1 Real Bridge Data

The Sydney Harbour Bridge [169] stands as an iconic structure in Australia, inaugurated in 1932. Lane 7 of the bridge's underside, illustrated in Figure 2.7 (a), features 800 jack arches, exclusively dedicated to buses and taxis. Constructed from steel-reinforced concrete, these arches are susceptible to cracks developing along their joints over time, primarily due to the aging of the bridge and the significant loads imposed by buses traversing the deck. It is very critical to detect any

(a)   (b)

Figure 2.7   The Sydney Harbour Bridge and a sensor node attached to it. (a) lane 7 of the bridge: the first lane from the left, (b) a sensor node with three accelerometers attached to a joint [169]

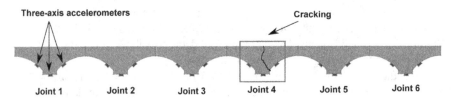

Figure 2.8   Schematic illustration of the evaluated joint with cracking [86]

deterioration in the status of the arches as soon as it occurs in order to schedule necessary inspection and repair.

Vibration data stemming from passing vehicles were captured using three-axis accelerometers positioned beneath the deck of lane 7. Each joint was equipped with a sensor node connected to three accelerometers, placed at the left, middle, and right positions on the joint, as depicted in Figure 2.7(b). For this particular case study, attention was focused solely on six instrumented joints, designated as joints 1 through 6, as delineated in Figure 2.8. The data collection spanned from early August to late October in 2012. Notably, a known crack was identified at joint 4, while the remaining joints were deemed to be in good condition.

A machine learning flow chart, which has been used as a damage detection solution for the Sydney Harbour Bridge is shown in Figure 2.9. This approach can be generic and may be applied to other types of civil structures.

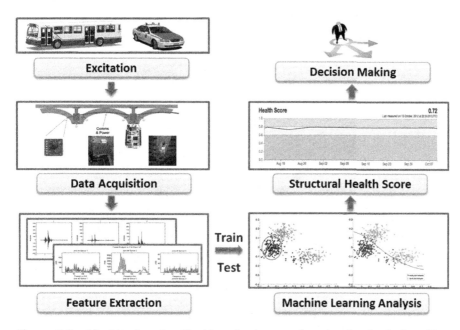

Figure 2.9   Machine learning flowchart for damage detection for the Sydney Harbour Bridge [86]

Initially, excitation events are captured using accelerometers or alternative sensor types, then transmitted and stored via a data acquisition system. Subsequently, a training set is chosen, followed by the extraction of features from the raw acceleration data in the time domain. Following this, the dimensionality of the features is reduced using techniques for dimensionality reduction. Finally, a model is trained using OCSVM.

Upon the arrival of a new event, the process involves feature extraction and dimensionality reduction steps, akin to those in the training phase. Subsequently, the event with reduced features is inputted into the trained model, which then generates a structural health score. This score, depicted as an SVM decision value in 2.2.2, indicates the condition of the structure. A negative value suggests an abnormal structural condition, and the absolute value of this negativity signifies the severity level of the damage. The greater the negativity, the more severe the damage is. Given that the data originate from a known location (such as a joint on the Sydney Harbour Bridge), this approach facilitates the provision of information regarding changes in the structural state, including the location and severity of the damage.

In this context, an event is defined as the duration when a motor vehicle traverses across an instrumented joint. Typically, an event is initiated once the acceleration value surpasses a pre-established threshold. Upon triggering, the node records data for a duration of 1.5 seconds at a sampling rate of 400 Hz. Each event encompasses 100 samples before the event trigger and 500 samples during and after the event occurrence. Similar to the feature extraction process for the building data, the data

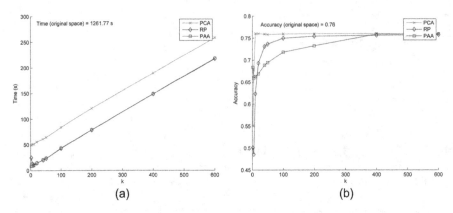

Figure 2.10 (a) Computational time and (b) detection accuracy of unsupervised SVM on Sydney Harbour Bridge data. RP: random projection; SVM: support vector machine; PCA: principal component analysis; PAA: piecewise aggregate approximation [86]

from each accelerometer for every vibration event undergo normalization to achieve a mean of zero and a standard deviation of one. Subsequently, they are transformed into the frequency domain using Fourier transform.

In Figure 2.10, the computational time and detection accuracy of unsupervised SVM (OCSVM) are illustrated for both the original feature space and reduced dimensional spaces generated using three methods discussed in 2.2.1: PCA, RP, and PAA. SVM combined with RP and PAA demonstrated comparable running times, being the fastest among the methods considered. Conversely, PCA exhibited the slowest performance among the three methods. In the case of the bridge data with $k = 100$, RP achieved comparable accuracy with a speed improvement of 29 times.

2.3.2.2 Specimen Data

A steel-reinforced concrete beam, as depicted in Figure 2.11, was fabricated with a geometry resembling that of structures found on the Sydney Harbour Bridge. Data were gathered from two sets of sensor nodes situated at the base of the joint: one set positioned at the tip and the other mounted 750 mm away from the tip. Each node features three accelerometers, similar to those affixed to the joints of the bridge. Excitation was induced using an impact hammer. Upon triggering by the hammer, the node records data for a duration of 3 seconds at a sampling rate of 500 Hz, resulting in 1500 samples for each event.

Following the benchmark testing under healthy conditions, a crack was systematically introduced into the specimen with four varying levels of crack dimensions: (75×50) mm, (150×50) mm, (225×50) mm, and (270×50) mm. Subsequently, identical tests were performed for each severity level of damage. Approximately 200 events were collected under healthy conditions, as well as for each level of damage severity.

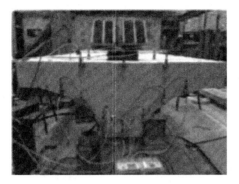

Figure 2.11   A steel reinforced concrete cantilever beam with a similar geometry to those on the Sydney Harbour Bridge

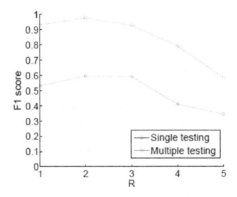

Figure 2.12   Damage detection accuracy using different values of R for the specimen dataset [87]

Following a process akin to feature extraction performed for other structures, the data from each accelerometer for every vibration event were normalized to achieve a zero mean and a standard deviation of one. Subsequently, they underwent conversion to the frequency domain using Fourier transform.

For each sensor node, the disparities between the features of accelerometers 1 and 2, 1 and 3, and 2 and 3 in the frequency domain were employed as features. Only frequencies up to 150 Hz were considered. Consequently, a tensor of dimensions $(450 \times 6 \times 960)$ was obtained. From this dataset, 150 healthy events were randomly selected as training data for the specimen.

The F_1 scores for all new test instances in specimen dataset using both single testing and multiple testing are shown in Figure 2.12. CORCONDIA selected $R = 2$ for the specimen data. Then we have F_1 score of 0.98 (using multiple testing) for the specimen dataset.

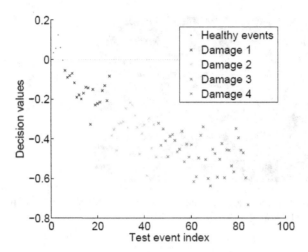

Figure 2.13   Damage characterization using decision values obtained by CP and OCSVM for the specimen dataset [87]

The decision values provided by the OCSVM model were utilised to assess the extent of damage. Figure 2.13 illustrates the decision values of each test event within the specimen data, as determined by OCSVM. Dotted lines delineate the boundary between healthy and damaged events. Distinct ranges of decision values correspond to various severity levels of damage, as outlined in the dataset.

Figure 2.13 demonstrates the successful differentiation between healthy and damaged events based on decision values. Furthermore, events exhibiting more severe damage tended to have lower decision values. Hence, this suggests that the decision values obtained through CP and OCSVM could serve as structural health scores for characterizing damage severity in an unsupervised manner.

2.4   SUMMARY

Smart detection aims to detect and raise alerts for failures/defects in urban infrastructure facilities in a well-timed manner. Practically there are two long-standing issues for smart detection, namely low detection rate and high false alarm rate. These practical issues can be attributed to the following research problems: 1) how to cover the diverse types of detection; 2) how to adapt to the dynamic evolution of detection; 3) how to overcome data sparsity and imbalance; and 4) how to fuse multi-modality sensor data. Under the deep learning framework, the problems could be addressed through large-scale normality learning, enhancing anomaly supervisory knowledge, deep weakly supervised learning, and devising innovative fusion network architectures. With these promising directions, more robust smart detection is expected for timely maintenance of infrastructure.

3 Network Performance Evaluation – Delay Propagation on Large Scale Railway Systems

3.1 BACKGROUND

In contemporary urban development, most infrastructure systems consist of various elements and components that are interconnected and form complex network structures [69, 159]. These infrastructure networks include water distribution networks, power grids, transportation systems, and telecommunication networks [190, 102, 145]. The emergence of network structures in these domains can be attributed to several factors. Firstly, the need for efficient and reliable service delivery necessitates the interconnection and coordination of multiple nodes and components. Secondly, the network structure allows for better resource allocation and utilization, enabling optimized performance and improved system resilience. Additionally, the network topology facilitates the flow of resources, information, and services, enhancing connectivity and accessibility.

However, evaluating the performance of these networked infrastructure systems presents significant challenges. The complexities arise from various factors, including the large-scale nature of the networks, the inherent uncertainties associated with their operation, and the dynamic interactions among the network components. For instance, these systems often operate in highly dynamic and uncertain environments affected by factors such as changing demand patterns, environmental conditions, and human behaviours [7]. Moreover, the inter-dependencies and interactions among different components within the network introduce further complexities, as disruptions or failures in one component can propagate and impact the overall network performance. These challenges make the assessment and prediction of network performance a non-trivial task that requires sophisticated analysis techniques and models [22]. In this context, understanding and evaluating the performance of networked infrastructure systems have become critical for efficient operation, planning, and decision-making. The ability to assess and predict the performance of these systems not only ensures their optimal functioning but also supports effective resource allocation, risk management, and infrastructure investment strategies.

Based on the challenges mentioned above, we take on one representation case study of the network performance evaluation to illustrate our proposed methods: the influence and prediction of delays and their propagation on large-scale railway

DOI: 10.1201/9781003473893-3

networks. Delay and its propagation significantly impact the operational performance of railway systems, making it a crucial concern for railway managers. A train delay in a railway network can trigger a chain reaction of subsequent delays, causing disruptions across the entire network [68]. Despite introducing measures such as adding buffer times and signal control in timetable design, train delays remain inevitable due to various stochastic factors. These factors include escalating passenger demand, equipment and asset malfunctions, passenger and driver behaviour, or external factors like extreme weather. In the intricate web of a railway network system, delays are not confined to a single train, station, or line. Instead, they propagate throughout the network, giving rise to secondary delays and a cascade of traffic issues, such as operational disorder within the railway network. These problems ultimately lead to diminished service quality, decreased punctuality, and reduced reliability. Consequently, it is imperative to undertake a comprehensive analysis of the causes of delay, as well as develop strategies for managing and predicting delays to uphold the reliability of the railway network system [67].

In the realm of practical train operations, the prediction of delays heavily relies on the experience and intuition of local train controllers instead of relying on computational methods that encompass the entire network [101, 129, 149, 176]. Given the intricate structure of a railway network and the interdependencies among train operations across numerous origins and destinations, estimating delays and making subsequent decisions typically depends on the traffic conditions within a specific local geographic area or line. However, in the real world, the consideration of secondary delays should not be limited solely to trains operating on the same service line. Factors such as conflicts between crossing or merging lines, train driver changes, and train connections can all contribute to secondary delays. With the escalating demand and the presence of extensive and densely interconnected networks in large cities, a railway network performance evaluation tool is badly needed to assist railway managers and controllers in empowering their replies to real-time emergencies and offering optimal or approximate optimal solutions.

In this chapter, we aim to predict delay propagation in a large-scale railway network located in the Greater Sydney Area. To achieve this, we propose a data-driven conditional Bayesian delay propagation model. However, the development of a prediction model on a complex network faces two fundamental challenges. Firstly, it is difficult to learn the station-level delay patterns due to the vast amount of operational data from a large railway system. Secondly, there is a lack of models that can effectively consider both the intricate structure of the railway network and the interdependencies among multiple trips for propagation and prediction tasks. In order to address these challenges, we introduce a conditional Bayesian model in this study. The Bayesian-based approach serves as a representation-learning method to capture complex structures and organize knowledge about the situation into a coherent framework [43]. Furthermore, it enables the integration of extensive historical data to identify relationships between various events and update different variables based on real-time feed data.

In our conditional Bayesian model, we assume that delay propagation follows the Markov property, which indicates the future delay condition is solely determined by the current state, and the previous delays have no impact on future delays, despite having access to the complete train operational records. The introduction of this Markov assumption facilitates the discovery of delay dependencies and reduces the computational complexity of our model. To address the challenges posed by the complex network structure, we divide the context of delay and its propagation into four scenarios: (1) Self-propagation: This scenario focuses on the impact of delays on its current trip, which caused the primary delays; (2) Backward propagation: We consider the influence of delays on the following trips along the same service line; (3) Cross-line propagation: It focuses on the impact of delays on trips from cross-service lines that interact with intersection stations of the current trip; and (4) Train-connection propagation: We analyze the impact of delays on trips that have a train connection with the current trip (i.e., a train connection occurs when a train starts a new trip after reaching the destination of a previous trip, the delay of the preceding trip will always cause a secondary delay for the following trip at the origin.). By considering these four scenarios, we encompass all the dependencies among different trips based on the railway network and operation timetable. This approach effectively reduces the complexity of delay propagation. Consequently, our proposed model benefits from scalable computing time and simplified complexity while still adhering to the Markov property. Compared to traditional delay-propagation models, the implementation of our model has demonstrated its effectiveness and efficiency in numerous experiments.

The task of modelling and analyzing delay propagation has been explored using various empirical statistical methods. Carey and Kwiecinski [26] developed a stochastic simulation method that measured delay propagation by considering stochasticity between trains. Chen and Harker [32] improved upon this approach by explicitly considering the uncertainty in actual train departure times. Florio and Mussone [59] proposed a solution for a moderately complex railway scheme, but their model did not consider runtime delay and dwell delay. Jovanovic [82] analyzed buffer times between trains in a periodic schedule, while [68] used regression analysis to predict departure delays from arrival delays. However, these methods may not effectively handle complex scenarios and networks. Goverde [67] introduced an advanced model that calculates the propagation of primary delays throughout an entire network within a timetable period. They also devised a graph-based method for storing and computing propagated delay information. However, this method was based on a linear system and did not account for the distribution of runtime delay and dwell time delay. Although various attempts have been made to address delay propagation modelling, challenges remain when dealing with complex scenarios and networks. Future research should focus on developing models that capture the dependence between different types of delay scenarios and consider the runtime delay and dwell time delay.

With the emergence of machine learning methods, researchers have started to approach delay prediction as a time series prediction task, mainly focusing on predicting delays at the node level (train stations) while disregarding delay propagation within the network as a whole. Previous studies, such as those by Oneto et al. [141], Jiang et al. [80], and Oneto et al. [140], have primarily focused on predicting station-level delays on a single line without considering the interaction of delays in complex railway networks, such as cross-line delay propagation or the impact of connected trips. Consequently, the capability and applicability of these approaches to entire railway networks have not been sufficiently demonstrated. Similarly, Heglund et al. [76] proposed a deep graph-based model for delay prediction on railway network structures. However, their method requires a long computing time, as reported in their study, which makes it impractical for real-world applications. In addition, Wu et al. [183] explored the use of Long Short-Term Memory (LSTM) for predicting primary delays. Nonetheless, as mentioned earlier, these existing works are still in the early stages and have not undergone extensive testing on large datasets or real-world network evaluations. Therefore, there is a need for further research and development to address the limitations of existing delay prediction methods, including the incorporation of delay propagation mechanisms in complex railway networks, scalability to large datasets, and comprehensive evaluation in real-world scenarios.

3.2   METHODOLOGY

To optimize capacity utilization and train schedule design in large-scale railway systems relies on predicting the reliability and punctuality of train operations, which are influenced by train delays and their propagation. Delay propagation commonly occurs during the arrival and departure of trains at stations, as the crossing or merging of lines and platform tracks often act as bottlenecks in heavily utilized railway networks. In this section, we introduce the problem formulation of delay propagation and provide relevant background information. Subsequently, we will introduce a conditional Bayesian model for predicting delay propagation. This model aims to estimate the future impact of a delay in various scenarios, including a single train, subsequent trains, crossing-line propagation, and connected trains. By utilizing this model, the future consequences of a delay can be estimated and analyzed under different conditions.

3.2.1   PROBLEM FORMULATION AND BACKGROUND

Notations

Here we summarize the notations used in this chapter in Table 3.1.

Train Delay

The term "delay" in the context of railway networks refers to the difference between the actual time and the scheduled time. It can be further categorized into different types based on various standards, as introduced in Figure 3.1. One fundamental categorization of delay is into **primary delay** and **secondary delay**, based on their dependency relationship. Primary delay is defined as the earliest self-caused delay, while secondary delay encompasses all delays caused by the primary delay. We consider both primary delay and secondary delay in this chapter. We categorize them

Table 3.1
Notations Used in this Chapter

Notations	Description
$t_i^{a/d,x}$	t^x represents the train x. a/d represents arrive/departure of the train. i represents Station i.
R_{ij}	Runtime delay for a train from Station i to j.
D_i	Dwell delay for a train at Station i.
$\Delta t_i^{a/d}$	Arrive/Departure delay time at Station i.
$P(A \mid B)$	The likelihood of event A occurring given that B is true.

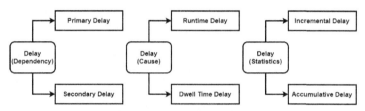

Figure 3.1   Delay Types under different standards [104]

based on their causes, estimate the distribution of incremental delay at the station level using historical data, and analyze the accumulative delay and its impact on the entire railway network. Furthermore, delay can be classified as either **incremental delay** or **accumulative delay**, depending on whether the stacking effect of delays for the same trains is taken into account.

Additionally, delay can be divided into two types based on its causes: **runtime delay** and **dwell time delay**. Runtime delay refers to the variation in time concerning the scheduled runtime, while dwell time delay refers to the variation in time concerning the scheduled dwell time at stations. The incremental runtime from Station i to Station j is defined as:

$$R_{ij} = t_j^a - t_i^d \tag{3.1}$$

Where t_j^a is the arrival time at Station j and t_i^d is the departure time at Station i. Then the incremental runtime delay from Station i to Station j is calculated by $\mathscr{A}(t_j^a) - \mathscr{S}(t_i^d)$, where $A(\cdot)$ is the actual time function and $S(\cdot)$ is the scheduled time function. Similarly, the incremental dwell time at Station j is:

$$D_j = t_j^d - t_j^a \tag{3.2}$$

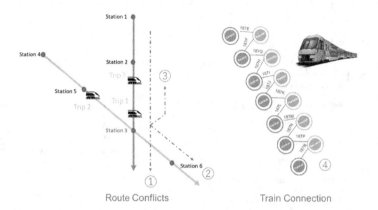

Figure 3.2 Four scenarios of delay propagation on a large railway network:(1) Self-propagation; (2) Cross-line propagation; (3) Backward propagation; and (4) Train connection propagation [104]

Therefore, the incremental dwell time delay can be calculated by $\mathscr{A}(t_j^d - t_j^a) - \mathscr{S}(t_j^d - t_j^a)$.

Delay Propagation

As mentioned in the introduction, delays in railway systems can propagate and affect subsequent trains, as well as trains on crossing lines, which is known as delay propagation. To comprehensively capture all possibilities of delay propagation, four typical scenarios have been defined, as depicted in Figure 3.2. These scenarios are:

- **Self-propagation**: If a train T experiences a delay at a given station (excluding the destination), the delay may propagate and affect T itself at subsequent stops along its route.
- **Cross-line propagation**: If a train T encounters a delay at a given station (excluding the destination), the delay may propagate and impact trips from other lines that arrive at the same station during the time period when T is unscheduled to be stationed there.
- **Backward propagation**: If a train T occurs a delay at a given station, the delay may propagate and influence the subsequent trains that are scheduled to arrive at the same station during the time period when T is stationed there.
- **Train connection propagation**: Due to the nature of train operations involving round trips or connected trips, a train connection effect occurs when a train arrives late at its destination, it can cause a delayed departure for its next trip.

To help better understand the different kinds of delay propagation, we introduce four specific examples to illustrate different instances of delay propagation and help

Table 3.2
Sample of Self-Propagation

Station	Station 1	Station 2
Planned Arrival Time	2019/7/24 16:25:48	2019/7/24 16:28:36
Planned Departure Time	2019/7/24 16:26:48	2019/7/24 16:29:36
Actual Arrival Time	2019/7/24 16:28:06	2019/7/24 16:30:25
Actual Departure Time	2019/7/24 16:28:50	2019/7/24 16:31:33
Delay Time (S)	138	109
Planned Dwell Time (S)	60	60
Actual Dwell Time (S)	44	68

Table 3.3
Sample of Cross-Line Propagation

Station	Station 1 – Train T_1	Station 1 – Train T_2
Planned Arrival Time	2019/7/24 10:03:48	2019/7/24 10:07:48
Actual Arrival Time	2019/7/24 10:08:24	2019/7/24 10:11:11
Delay Time (S)	276	203

Table 3.4
Sample of Train Connection Propagation

Station	$Trip_i$ Destination	$Trip_{i+1}$ Origin Station
Planned Arrival Time	2019/7/24 08:08:42	2019/7/24 08:13:00
Actual Arrival Time	2019/7/24 08:10:38	2019/7/24 08:16:45
Delay Time (S)	116	225

in gaining a better understanding of the various forms of delay propagation in railway systems. Here we choose some sample data from railway operational data in the Greater Sydney area, which are shown in Tables 3.2 to 3.4:

- **Sample of Self-propagation**: We use Train T that travels from Station 1 to Station 2 (next station, not the destination) as an example, as shown in Table 3.2. Firstly, we can find that Train T arrived at Station 1 with 138 seconds delay (not a busy station). Meanwhile, its dwell time on Station 1 reduces from 60 seconds to 44 seconds with the aim to make up for the delay. Secondly, Train T arrives at Station 2 with 109 seconds delay because of its delay at Station 1. Moreover, its dwell time on Station 2 increases by 8 seconds because it needs more time for boarding the accumulating passengers (busy station).

- **Sample of Cross-line Propagation**: Table 3.3 shows a sample of cross-line propagation between Train T_1 and T_2 at Station 1. Train T_1 and Train T_2 are on two different trips, but they need to arrive at Station 1 in a similar period. When Train T_1 arrives at Station 1, it gets 276 seconds arrival delay than its planned time. Meanwhile, the planned arrival time of Train 2 overlaps with the period that Train 1 stays at Station 1. Therefore, Train T_2 needs to wait before Train T_1 leaves Station 1, which causes a 203-second delay.
- **Sample of Backward Propagation** For backward propagation, is similar to cross-line propagation. The difference is that the backward propagation happens between different trains in the same series trip, as shown in Figure 3.2. Besides, these are similar to Table 3.3.
- **Sample of Train connection propagation** Table 3.4 shows a sample of Train connect propagation. Train connection propagation happens when Train T arrives late at its last trip destination, and it will influence its next trip. We can find Train T arrives at its destination of Trip$_i$ with a 116-second delay. Therefore, Train T needs more time to prepare for its next Trip$_{i+1}$. Hence it has a delay when it starts Trip$_{i+1}$.

3.2.2 PRELIMINARY

Delay propagation has significant implications for the daily operations of railway networks, and accurate prediction of delay propagation can greatly assist train planners and controllers in making informed decisions. In this study, we propose a conditional Bayesian model with the incorporation of the Markov property to predict and estimate delay propagation. This model takes into account the complex scenarios encountered in real-world railway systems by considering both run-time delay and dwell delay.

To facilitate a better understanding of the model, we provide a concise overview of the relevant background knowledge. This background knowledge encompasses the fundamental concepts and factors related to delay propagation in railway networks. Building upon this understanding, we present the detailed design of our conditional Bayesian model, which captures the dependencies and dynamics of delay propagation. By incorporating both run-time delay and dwell delay, our model offers a comprehensive and accurate representation of delay propagation in railway systems.

Bayesian Inference

The proposed model adopts a Bayesian inference framework, which has been extensively studied in empirical machine learning literature. Bayesian inference leverages Bayes' Theorem, expressed as $P(A \mid B) = \frac{P(B|A)P(A)}{P(B)}$, to model random variables. In this equation, the denominator, $P(B)$, represents the evidence or normalizing constant. To simplify the notation, the equation is often written as $P(A \mid B) \propto P(B \mid A)P(A)$, where $P(A \mid B)$ is the posterior distribution, proportional to the likelihood $P(B \mid A)$ multiplied by the prior $P(A)$.

In the Bayesian inference framework, the prior distribution is typically defined first, and then the posterior distribution is computed using Bayes' Theorem. However, in cases where conjugate priors are not applicable, it becomes necessary to compute intractable integrals that cannot be evaluated analytically to obtain the posterior distribution.

In the context of the proposed delay propagation model, Bayesian inference is employed to capture the relationships and dependencies among variables involved in delay propagation. By specifying appropriate priors and likelihood functions, the model aims to estimate the posterior distribution of delay propagation given observed data. This Bayesian framework enables the integration of historical data and real-time information, allowing for more accurate and reliable predictions of delay propagation in railway networks.

Markov Property

The Markov property, in the context of train delay propagation, refers to the independence of the future delays from the past delays, given the current delay status. Mathematically, if we define a one-parameter process X as a Markov process with respect to a filtration $\mathscr{F}_t$, then for any time points s and t, where $s > t$, the delay X_s is independent of the information in $\mathscr{F}_t$ given the current delay X_t. This can be expressed as $X_s \perp\!\!\!\perp \mathscr{F}_t \mid X_t$.

In the case of train delay propagation, the Markov property holds because the delays at a station are influenced solely by the delay status at the immediate preceding station. For example, if a train at Station 1 experiences a primary delay and transmits the delay to Station 2, which in turn propagates it to Station 3, the delay at Station 3 is solely influenced by the delay at Station 2. In other words, the delay at Station 3 is conditionally independent of the delays at Station 1, Station 4, and any other stations, given the delay at Station 2. This relationship can be mathematically expressed as follows: $P(\tau_{i+1}^{delay} \mid \tau_i^{delay}, \tau_{i-1}^{delay}, \cdots, \tau_1^{delay}) = P(\tau_{i+1}^{delay} \mid \tau_i^{delay})$.

By assuming the Markov property, the proposed delay propagation model takes into account the immediate preceding delay at each station when predicting the delay at the next station. This simplifies the modelling process and reduces the complexity of considering the entire history of delays. The Markov property allows for efficient estimation and prediction of delay propagation in railway networks.

3.2.3   CONDITIONAL BAYESIAN DELAY PROPAGATION

Delay Self-propagation

Scenario (1) in Figure 3.2 demonstrates the phenomenon of delay self-propagation within a single trip. The figure illustrates that delays occurring at one station can propagate to subsequent stations, resulting in accumulated delays (referred to as secondary delays) at those stations. It is evident that the extent of delay accumulation at the next station is solely influenced by the delays experienced at preceding stations, exhibiting the characteristic of the Markov property. To elucidate the modelling of delay propagation from one station to another within a single trip, and its seamless extension to the entire trip, we utilize a specific delay example occurring consecutively at two stations. This example serves to elucidate the application of Bayesian theory in capturing the dynamics of delay propagation and its potential for broader implementation within the context of a single trip.

Let $R_{i(i+1)}$ denote the normal incremental runtime from Station i to Station $i+1$ (consecutive stations), and D_{i+1} represent the normal incremental dwell time at Station $i+1$. We assume that both $R_{i(i+1)}$ and D_{i+1} follow normal distributions without losing much accuracy as the empirical study shows. It is important to note that our experiments indicate that delays, encompassing both runtime delay and dwell time delay, tend to follow gamma distributions with a long right tail. However, for the development of the delay propagation model in subsequent steps, we employ normal distributions to capture the delay patterns. This choice is motivated by the fact that the normal distribution is symmetric, and our focus lies on the positive values (representing delay times) on the right side of the X-axis. Negative values, on the other hand, indicate that the train's actual arrival time is earlier than its scheduled time. It is customary for train drivers to wait until the planned time for passenger convenience, thereby not affecting the subsequent timetable. In this paper, we fit various normal distributions to historical data obtained from different stations, allowing us to learn the parameters $\mu^R_{i(i+1)}$, $\sigma^R_{i(i+1)}$, μ^D_{i+1}, and σ^D_{i+1}. These parameters can be estimated from the historical data, expressing the relationship as $R_{i(i+1)} \sim N(\mu^R_{i(i+1)}, \sigma^R_{i(i+1)})$ and $D_{i+1} \sim N(\mu^D_{i+1}, \sigma^D_{i+1})$.

If a primary or secondary delay occurs at Station i (departure delay of Station i: Δt^d_i), it has an impact on both the driver's behaviour (e.g., speeding up to compensate for the delay in the subsequent trip) and the passenger flow pattern (e.g., increased number of passengers on the platforms) at Station $i+1$, resulting in an arrival delay (Δt^a_{i+1}). Therefore, based on the Markov property, the runtime between Station i and $i+1$ as well as the dwell time at Station $i+1$ can be expressed as follows:

$$R'_{i(i+1)} = R_{i(i+1)} + (\Delta R_{i(i+1)} \mid \Delta t^d_i) \tag{3.3}$$

$$D'_{i+1} = D_{i+1} + (\Delta D_{i+1} \mid \Delta t^a_{i+1}) \tag{3.4}$$

where $\Delta t^a_{i+1} = \Delta t^d_i + (\Delta R_{i(i+1)} \mid \Delta t^d_i)$. $(\Delta R_{i(i+1)} \mid \Delta t^d_i)$ and $(\Delta D_{i+1} \mid \Delta t^a_{i+1})$ are the incremental delays caused by Δt^d_i for the runtime and dwell time, respectively.

Incremental runtime delay: In the presence of a delay at Station i (Δt^d_i), the train driver may increase the power to accelerate the train in order to make up for the delay in the subsequent trip. This acceleration directly impacts the actual runtime to the next station (Station $i+1$). The incremental runtime delay varies for different values of Δt^d_i. If Δt^d_i is small, the driver can easily compensate for the delay, resulting in no additional delay at Station $i+1$. However, if Δt^d_i is significantly large, even with the train running at full speed, it becomes impossible for the driver to recover the delay at Station $i+1$. To analyze actual operational records, we categorize Δt^d_i into several bins: (1) ΔT^1_i: $0 < \Delta t^d_i \leq 3$ minutes; (2) ΔT^2_i: 3 minutes $< \Delta t^d_i \leq 5$ minutes; (3) ΔT^3_i: 5 minutes $< \Delta t^d_i \leq 10$ minutes; and (4) ΔT^4_i: $\Delta t^d_i > 10$ minutes. For each bin, we learn distinct normal distributions to model them individually. Specifically,

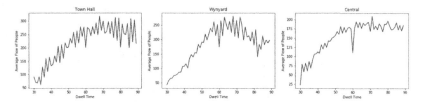

Figure 3.3 The linear relationship between dwell time and average passenger flow has been observed across three stations. Our experimental findings suggest that similar patterns can be observed in the majority of other stations as well

the conditional distribution of the incremental runtime $(\Delta R_{i(i+1)} \mid \Delta t_i^d, \Delta t_i^d \in \Delta T_i^k)$ is represented as $(\Delta R_{i(i+1)} \mid \Delta T_i^k) \sim N(\mu_{i(i+1)}^{\Delta T_i^k}, \sigma_{i(i+1)}^{\Delta T_i^k})$.

Hence, the incremental runtime delay, given $\Delta t_i^d \in \Delta T_i^k$, can be also expressed using the superposability of Gaussian distribution.

Incremental dwell time delay: In the event of an arrival delay at Station i (arrival delay of Station i: Δt_i^a), the number of awaiting passengers at the station increases, thereby affecting the actual dwell time when the delayed train arrives at Station i. Through an analysis of historical train running data from the railway network, we have discovered a strong linear relationship between the actual dwell time and the accumulated awaiting passengers to some extent. Figure 3.3 illustrates this relationship, demonstrating its linearity within the range of 30 to 60 seconds (30 seconds being the scheduled dwell time for most stations in the Greater Sydney area's railway network). This finding has inspired us to develop and train a piece-wise function that fits this relationship. In this function, we employ α_i and β_i as parameters in the linear function for dwell times under 60 seconds, while a constant c_2 represents the situation when the dwell time exceeds 60 seconds:

$$\Delta D_i \mid \Delta t_i^a = \begin{cases} \alpha_i(\Delta t_i^a) + \beta_i, & \Delta t_i^a < 60s \\ c_2, & \Delta t_i^a \geq 60s \end{cases} \tag{3.5}$$

Consequently, the incremental dwell delay D'_{i+1} at Station $i+1$, given Δt_1^d, can be calculated accordingly based on Equation 3.5:

Accumulative departure delay: During the process of delay propagation within a single trip, our focus lies on the accumulated delay at each station rather than the incremental runtime or dwell time. Furthermore, the value of Δt_i^d as a secondary delay follows a normal distribution, propagated from preceding stations, rather than being fixed. Specifically, Δt_i^d can be modelled as $\Delta t_i^d \sim N(\mu_i, \sigma_i)$. Consequently, it is essential to consider the delay components $(\Delta R_{i(i+1)} \mid \Delta t_i^d)$ and $(\Delta D_{i+1} \mid \Delta t_{i+1}^a)$. Under the framework of Bayesian theory, the probability of these components $(P(\Delta R_{i(i+1)} \mid \Delta t_i^d))$ can be calculated by using the conditional addition rule. And the probability of the arrival delay and dwell delay at Station $i+1$ can be calculated respectively. The detailed derivation process can be found in [104].

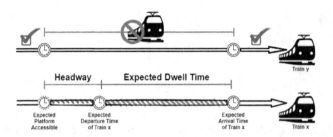

Figure 3.4   The delay propagation between trains occurs when Train x and Train y are scheduled to stop consecutively at Station $i + 1$. If the expected arrival time of Train y at Station $i + 1$ is earlier than the expected platform accessibility time, it implies that Train y needs to wait and experience a delay [104]

Finally, with the given departure delay of Station i: $\Delta t_i^d \sim N(\mu_i, \sigma_i)$, the departure delay of Station $i + 1$ (Δt_{i+1}^d) is the addition of Δt_i^a, $\Delta R_{i(i+1)|\Delta t_i^a}$ and ΔD_{i+1}. The calculation of delay propagation between two consecutive stations in a single trip can be achieved through the utilization of the equations mentioned above. However, these equations represent segmented functions that pose challenges in terms of computation. To address this, we employ the Belief Propagation (BP) method in our model, which facilitates the transfer of delays across consecutive stations. By fitting the segmented functions to normal distributions, a minor amount of information loss occurs. Nonetheless, this approach ensures that the delay distributions continue to follow normal distributions, resulting in a significant improvement in computational efficiency.

Cross-line, Backward, and Train Connection Delay Propagation

The remaining delay scenarios exhibit a consistent structure of delay propagation, wherein delays can transmit from one trip to the next by considering the scheduled interval and the unscheduled arrival time of a preceding train, which referred to cross-line propagation, backward propagation, or train-connected trip propagation. The specific distinction lies in how the scheduled interval is determined, either by the headway between consecutive trips on the same line or cross-line trips, or by the turn-round time resulting from round-trip journeys. Despite these variations, cross-line, backward, and train connection scenarios share the same mode of delay propagation due to their underlying structure. It is important to note that conflicts may arise at Station $i + 1$ between Train x and Train y (representing a cross-line, backward, or connected trip) if either Train x or Train y experiences an unscheduled arrival time at Station $i + 1$, resulting in delay propagation between trains, as depicted in Figure 3.4. In order to estimate the delay propagation from Train x to Train y at Station $i + 1$, we make the following assumption as a precondition:

- **Train x**:
  - Scheduled arrival time at Station $i + 1$: $t_{i+1}^{a,x}$

- Scheduled departure time at Station $i+1$: $t_{i+1}^{d,x}$
- Accumulative arrival delay at Station $i+1$ with a departure delay $\Delta t_i^{d,x}$ at Station i:

$$\Delta t_{i+1}^{a,x} = \Delta t_i^{d,x} + (\Delta R_{i(i+1)^x} \mid \Delta t_i^{d,x})$$

- Accumulative departure delay at Station $i+1$ with a departure delay $\Delta t_i^{d,x}$ at Station i:

$$\Delta t_{i+1}^{d,x} = \Delta t_i^{d,x} + (\Delta R_{i(i+1)^x} \mid \Delta t_i^{d,x}) + (\Delta D_{i+1}^x \mid \Delta t_{i+1}^{a,x})$$

- Estimated arrival time at Station $i+1$: $t_{i+1}^{a,x} + \Delta t_{i+1}^{a,x}$
- Estimated departure time at Station $i+1$: $t_{i+1}^{d,x} + \Delta t_{i+1}^{d,x}$
- **Train y**:
  - Scheduled arrival time at Station $i+1$: $t_{i+1}^{a,y}$
  - Accumulative arrival delay from Station j to Station $i+1$ with a departure delay $\Delta t_j^{d,y}$ at Station j:

$$\Delta t_{i+1}^{a,y} = \Delta t_j^{d,y} + (\Delta R_{j(i+1)}^y \mid \Delta t_j^{d,y})$$

  - Estimated arrival time at Station $i+1$: $t_{i+1}^{a,y} + \Delta t_{i+1}^{a,y}$

If Train y is affected by Train x as illustrated in Figure 3.4, the expected arrival time of Train y at Station $i+1$ will fall within the time period between the expected arrival time of Train x and the expected platform accessibility time. To ensure that Train y can smoothly pass through the platform without being affected by Train x, we define S as the minimum interval time (headway) between Train x and Train y at Station $i+1$. This implies that the following conditions must hold: $Z_1 = t_{i+1}^{a,y} + \Delta t_{i+1}^{a,y} - t_{i+1}^{a,x} - \Delta t_{i+1}^{a,x} > 0$ and $Z_2 = t_{i+1}^{a,y} + \Delta t_{i+1}^{a,y} - t_{i+1}^{d,x} - \Delta t_{i+1}^{d,x} - S < 0$. Based on these conditions, the probability of delay propagation from Train x to Train y can be defined as follows:

$$P(\delta t_{i+1}^{a,y} > 0 \mid \Delta t_{i+1}^{a,y}, \Delta t_i^{d,x}) = P(Z_1 > 0, Z_2 < 0) \tag{3.6}$$

where $\delta t_{i+1}^{a,y}$ is the delay propagation from Train x to y. As Δt_{i+1}^a and Δt_{i+1}^d follow normal distribution in our propagation model, it is hard to directly calculate the probability in Equation 3.6. We still use a normal distribution to estimate it. Given the schedule interval between two trains are $t_s^{x,y}$, and we have $\Delta t_{i+1}^{a,y} \sim N(\mu_{a,y}, \sigma_{a,y})$ and $\Delta t_{i+1}^{d,x} \sim N(\mu_{d,x}, \sigma_{d,x})$, then the secondary delay of y propagated from x can be estimated as $\Delta t_{i+1}^{x \to y}$, which is the distribution superposition of $t_s^{x,y}$, $\Delta t_{i+1}^{a,y}$ and $\Delta t_{i+1}^{d,x}$.

It is important to note that we only consider the positive part of $\Delta t_{i+1}^{x \to y}$. By incorporating the estimated delay propagation (secondary delay of Train y) from Train x to Train y into the departure delay estimation equation, we can obtain the estimated accumulated departure delay at Station $i+1$ of Train y, as shown in the equation below:

$$\Delta t_{i+1}^{d,y} = \Delta t_{i+1}^{a,y} + (\Delta D_{i+1}^y \mid \Delta t_{i+1}^{a,y}) + \Delta t_{i+1}^{x \to y} \tag{3.7}$$

Figure 3.5 The railway tracks and stations in the Greater Sydney Area

In our propagation model, the fitted delay distributions encompass a range of values $(-\infty, +\infty)$, implying that all trains passing through the same station have a certain probability of experiencing delay interaction. However, this does not reflect real-life conditions. Therefore, in this paper, we only consider the 95% confidence interval of each delay distribution and its corresponding propagation to other trains. This approach significantly reduces computational complexity while maintaining accuracy.

For each trip affected by delay propagation, we categorize them into one of the four previously analyzed delay propagation scenarios. It is important to note that the set of classified delayed trips is mutually exclusive. This means that each trip influenced by delay propagation will only be categorized into one scenario to analyze its impact on future events. In the prediction phase, we uniformly analyze all the delayed propagation scenarios to provide comprehensive insights.

3.3 CASE STUDY

Our proposed delay propagation prediction model has been deployed on a real-world large-scale railway system in the Great Sydney Area, yielding promising outcomes. The application has led to a significant reduction in delay-caused losses and an increase in operational performance. The railway network in the Greater Sydney Area contains over 1600 km of track and encompasses 175 stations with 700+ platforms, operating on nine service lines as shown in 3.5. With annual patronage of around 350 million passengers, the railway network is extensive and densely populated.

In the Experiments section, our proposed model is adopted to predict train delays using real-world railway operational data. Our model takes into account both spatial and temporal information simultaneously, enhancing its predictive capabilities. To

Table 3.5
Details of Experimental Setup

Experimental setup	Details
Operation System	64-bit Linux Server
CPU Frequency	2.20 GHz
CPU Cores	26
RAM	88.0 GB
Implementation Environment	Python 3.7

comprehensively evaluate the model's performance, we divide the experiments into spatial and temporal dimensions. In the temporal dimension, we focus on predicting the accumulated delays of trains over time. This analysis helps us understand how delays propagate and accumulate throughout the network. In the spatial dimension, we predict the trips that are influenced by previous delayed trips, aiming to uncover the mechanisms through which delay propagates in the network. The experiment results demonstrate the strong performance of our model across different dimensions. We achieve accurate predictions of accumulated train delays over time and effectively capture the propagation of delays in the network. Additionally, we provide a detailed case study comparing our prediction results with real-world data, further illustrating the capabilities and benefits of our model.

3.3.1 EXPERIMENTAL SETTING

To verify the performance of our model, we utilized real-world railway operational records and data. This dataset consists of the train service schedule and historical real running data, specifically the Train Log System-On Track Record (TLS-OTR) data. The dataset provides comprehensive information for each train trip, including the planned and actual train timetable, unique trip identifiers (representing trips that occur only once per day), and other relevant details. By comparing the planned schedule with the actual running data, we can determine whether a train experienced a delay. This data set serves as a valuable resource for evaluating the accuracy and effectiveness of our delay propagation model. Through the analysis of the actual train running records, we can assess how well our model predicts delays and captures the delay propagation. Here we show the experimental environment in Table 3.5.

Experimental Dataset

In our experiments, we utilized a 10-month dataset (May 1 to December 30, 2019) comprising historical operational data of the railway system to train our model to derive the delay propagation distributions for various delay types. It is important to note that only delay records was considered during the training process, and other data variables were excluded.

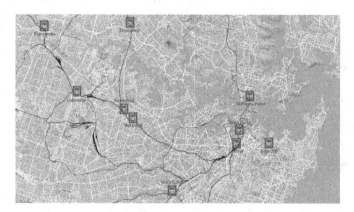

Figure 3.6 Location of the selected ten stations

Table 3.6

Statistics of Railway Operational Data for Selected Ten Stations

Data Description	Statistic
Total Number of Operational Records for Selected Station	36394
Total Number of Records for Selected Station Delay	24566
The Percent of Delay Trip	67.50%
Min of Delay Record Time	1.0 s
Max of Delay Record Time	5460.0 s
Mean of Delay Record Time	112.5
Standard Deviation of Delay Record Time	184.48

For the testing phase, we selected a specific date range (July 1 to July 31, 2019), which corresponds to the last month of the Australian financial year. This time range was chosen due to its significance as the busiest time of the year for residents, resulting in a higher frequency of train usage. Consequently, the demand for train services escalates, leading to an increased number of scheduled trips and a greater volume of passengers on platforms. This intensified usage scenario provides a more intricate and frequent occurrence of train delays compared to other periods.

To evaluate our model comprehensively, we carefully handpicked ten stations from the railway network that are prone to experiencing delays. These stations are strategically from different core commercial areas in Sydney to ensure a comprehensive evaluation of our model's performance. The selection of stations aimed to cover a wide range of scenarios and capture the diversity of delay patterns. The geographical distribution of these selected stations is depicted in Figure 3.6. Detailed statistics of the data collected from these ten stations are presented in Table 3.6. Our evaluation encompasses temporal prediction, examining how delays propagate over time, as well as spatial prediction, investigating how delays propagate across

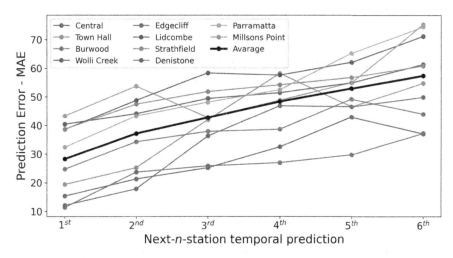

Figure 3.7 Temporal prediction performance for the next-6-station conditions from delayed trips of selected ten stations

different trips. These two dimensions provide a comprehensive assessment of our model's predictive capabilities.

Benchmark Methods

We compare our delay propagation model with the following representative delay prediction baselines: (1) **Linear Regression**: This approach involves modelling the relationship between variables by fitting a linear equation to the observed data. Linear regression is widely used in various fields for predictive analysis [160]. (2) **Random Forest**: This ensemble technique leverages multiple decision trees to perform regression tasks. It has proven effective in handling complex datasets and capturing nonlinear relationships [119]. (3) **N-Markov Model**: The N-Markov Model is a zero-shot Markov model specifically designed for predicting train delay time. It incorporates the principles of Markov processes to estimate the future delay based on historical data [64].

3.3.2 DELAY PROPAGATION PREDICTION FROM THE TEMPORAL DIMENSIONS

For the delay propagation prediction from the temporal dimensions, we adopt the accumulated delay time of delayed trips from selected ten stations to predict the future running conditions of the subsequent six stops for these delayed trips. To evaluate the prediction performance of our model, we compare the predicted results with the actual operating data. The evaluation metric used for this comparison is the mean absolute error (MAE), measured in seconds, which the performance is shown in Figure 3.7. For each line in the Figure, we present the MAE of the comparison between predicted and actual delay time at the next station for trips experiencing a

Table 3.7

Performance Compared with Other Baselines: Next-6-Station Temporal Prediction by Capturing the Average Delay Value on Ten Stations

Model \ MAE	1st	2nd	3rd	4th	5th	6th
Linear Regression	68.23	85.69	99.30	111.52	125.35	140.31
Random Forest	43.98	58.96	72.35	83.62	90.60	106.5
N-Markov Model	48.96	62.75	77.33	90.78	103.8	120.58
Our Model	**28.27**	**37.21**	**42.80**	**48.40**	**52.94**	**57.44**

Table 3.8

Performance Compared with Other Baselines in Multi-Evaluation Metrics, the Result is the Average Values of the Next-6-Station Temporal Prediction

Model	Total		
	MAE	RMSE	R2
Linear Regression	108.4	148.2	0.52
Random Forest	77.23	93.78	0.72
N-Markov Model	85.62	102.72	0.68
Our Model	**42.87**	**62.13**	**0.87**

major delay at the chosen station. Taking the blue line (Central Station) in the figure as an example, each node represents the MAE of the predicted delay time at the next station for trips with delays. The black bold line in the figure represents the average MAE of delay propagation across the selected ten stations. From the figure, it is evident that the majority of predicted delays have errors of less than 1 minute, even after propagating through six stations.

In terms of the comparison with other baselines shown in Tables 3.7 and 3.8, our model outperforms the other methods. The reason for this superior performance lies in the fact that our model takes into account the delay propagation influence and the complex network structure of the railway system. In contrast, the other methods do not adequately consider delay propagation and struggle with error propagation in step-by-step predictions. This is due to the dynamic changes in delay patterns under the control of complex railway controllers. Moreover, the other methods are affected by noise data (outliers), which hampers their final performance. Conversely, our model, based on a conditional Bayesian model with the introduction of the Markov property, is capable of handling noise data by learning historical delay distributions and focusing solely on the most recent train conditions. It is noteworthy that railway controllers often manually reschedule trains to respond to delays, where our model's performance maintains fairly accurate, making it highly suitable for applications in real-world large-scale railway networks.

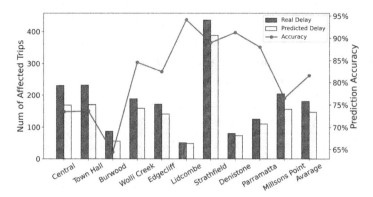

Figure 3.8 Performance of spatial prediction on ten stations: the real delay refers to the number of train delays more than 5 minutes at selected stations in July, and predicted delay refers to the predicted number of future delay trips which are affected by the previous delayed trip [104]

3.3.3 DELAY PROPAGATION PREDICTION FROM THE SPATIAL DIMENSIONS

For the delay propagation prediction from the spatial dimensions, we feed the delayed trips from the selected ten stations into our model to predict subsequent trips passing through the same station that will experience delays due to the previous delayed trips. The importance of spatial prediction lies in the model's ability to forecast the impact of delays on cross-line trips and backward trips, thus capturing how delays propagate throughout and influence the entire railway network. In this context, we define a delayed trip as one whose actual arrival time at the terminal station exceeds the planned arrival time by 5 minutes. To evaluate the spatial prediction performance of our model, we compare the predicted trips with the actual operational data. Instead of measuring the accuracy of individual delay predictions, which we have already assessed in the temporal prediction task, our focus is on predicting the number of trips affected by delays and the extent to which delays spread across the railway network. Therefore, we employ the prediction success ratio as the evaluation metric. The results are presented in Figure 3.8. Taking the first group of bars in the figure to illustrate, we selected delay timestamps at Central Station and obtained a prediction that the following 169 trips passing through the Station would be affected by delays. In reality, there were 230 delayed trips at Central Station. This indicates that our model successfully predicted 73.47% of the actually delayed trips for that month. Overall, the delay accuracy rate for the selected ten stations is 81.53%.

In comparison to other methods, as shown in Table 3.9, our model still outperforms them from the view of spatial dimension. The performance is consistent with the findings of the temporal prediction experiments, where the other baselines exhibited poor accuracy due to their failure to consider the structure of the railway network. Furthermore, these methods suffered from error propagation in

Table 3.9

Performance of Spatial Prediction Comparing to Other Methods, Both the Predicted and Real Delay are the Average Value of ten Stations

Affected Model	Predicted Delay	Real Delay	Accuracy
Linear Regression	119.3	180.3	66.16%
Random Forest	132.8	180.3	73.66%
N-Markov Model	128.6	180.3	71.32%
Our Model	**147**	**180.3**	**81.53%**

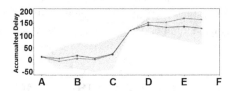

Figure 3.9   Delay Self-propagation, the X-axis refers to the sequential stations (A – F) on a trip, the Y-axis refers to the accumulated delay time, and the following Figures 3.10 to 3.12 are the same and case sensitive

step-by-step predictions for the trip level prediction. Meanwhile, as that delayed trips can be influenced by various factors, which are introduced above, the spatial prediction performance of our model is quite acceptable. It demonstrates the model's capability to predict the spread of delays and their impact on other lines on large-scale networks.

3.3.4   DELAY PROPAGATION IN DIFFERENT SCENARIOS

In this part, we utilize our proposed model to predict the delay in different propagation scenarios mentioned above and compare the predictions with real-world operational records. When a primary delay occurs at a particular station, we calculate the means and confidence intervals of secondary predicted delays for the influenced following, cross-line, and connected trips.

Figures 3.9 – 3.12, illustrate the four different kinds of delay propagation scenarios: self-, cross-line, backward, and train-connection delay propagation. In all figures, the X-axis represents the stations, the blue line corresponds to the predicted mean, the blue band refers to the confidence interval, and the red line refers to the actual running records. The dots indicate the predicted/actual dwell time at stations, while the stars indicate the predicted/actual runtime between consecutive stations.

Regarding self-delay propagation, depicted in Figure 3.9, we applied the model at the beginning of the trip and adopt the starting time to obtain subsequent stations

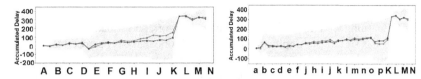

Figure 3.10   Delay cross-line propagation occurs when the train trips, denoted as A.. and a.., running on different lines, eventually converge onto the same sequence of stations (K, L, M, N) after a certain duration of time. This overlay leads to the propagation of delays between the two train lines

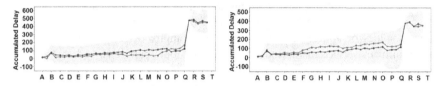

Figure 3.11   Backward delay propagation

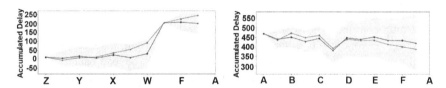

Figure 3.12   Train-connection delay propagation

prediction. The means of the predicted results closely align with the real records. Additionally, when we specify a delay occurring between Station C and Station D (a runtime delay), the input of our model is updated to predict the delay conditions for the following stations. Our predicted delay propagation results match the actual one fairly well, with the difference between the actual and predicted mean at the trip destination being less than 30 seconds.

Regarding cross-line propagation, presented in Figure 3.10, Figure 3.10 (a) reveals that cross-line trains are affected by the primary delay occurring at Station K. Figure 3.10 (b) displays that the predicted delays of cross-line trips are closely aligned with the actual delays.

Regarding backward propagation, as shown in Figure 3.11, Figure 3.11 (a) indicates that following trains are affected by the primary delay occurring at Station Q. Figure 3.11 (b) demonstrates that the predicted delays of the following trip are in close agreement with the actual delays.

Lastly, train-connection propagation, illustrated in Figure 3.12, represents delay propagation related to train connections. Figure 3.12 (b) presents the starting delays caused by train-connection delays shown in Figure 3.12 (a).

3.4 SUMMARY

Using machine learning techniques for infrastructure network performance evaluation in smart cities has significant implications from a network analysis perspective. These techniques provide in-depth insights into the functioning and efficiency of the network infrastructure, enabling proactive management and optimization.

Machine learning algorithms analyze network data to identify patterns, anomalies, and trends. This allows for the detection of bottlenecks, congestion points, or areas of suboptimal performance within the network. By understanding these issues, smart cities can take targeted actions to improve network capacity, throughput, and reliability.

Real-time monitoring using machine learning algorithms ensures that network performance is continuously assessed. Any deviations from normal behaviour, such as sudden traffic spikes or abnormal patterns, can be promptly detected and addressed. This minimizes service disruptions, maintains smooth operations, and enhances the overall user experience.

Predictive maintenance becomes possible through machine learning techniques. By analyzing historical network data, models can anticipate potential failures or performance degradation. This enables proactive interventions, reducing downtime and improving the longevity of network infrastructure components.

Machine learning contributes to optimizing resource allocation within the network. By analyzing network traffic, usage patterns, and user behaviour, models can suggest optimal routing protocols, bandwidth allocation strategies, or load balancing techniques. This ensures efficient utilization of network resources and enhances overall performance.

Intelligent traffic management is another area where machine learning plays a crucial role. By analyzing real-time traffic data from various sources, such as sensors, cameras, and connected vehicles, models can optimize traffic flow, identify congestion patterns, and dynamically adjust traffic signals. This reduces congestion, improves transportation efficiency, and promotes a smoother urban environment.

Machine learning also enables data-driven decision-making for network infrastructure upgrades and planning. By analyzing historical and real-time data, models can provide insights into future network requirements, allowing smart cities to make informed decisions about infrastructure investments, capacity expansions, and network enhancements.

In summary, the use of machine learning techniques in infrastructure network performance evaluation from a network analysis perspective enables proactive management, real-time monitoring, predictive maintenance, optimized resource allocation, intelligent traffic management, and data-driven decision-making. These advancements lead to improved network capacity, reliability, efficiency, and overall performance in smart cities.

4 Network Status Monitoring – Signal Aspect Detection for Railway Networks

4.1 BACKGROUND

Network monitoring stands as a fundamental component in the operational integrity of various industries, transcending beyond the specific context of railway systems. It involves the vigilant surveillance and analysis of numerous parameters within an organization's network infrastructure. This includes monitoring traffic flow, performance metrics, and system health to preemptively identify and rectify potential issues. The objective is to maintain an optimal state of operations, ensuring that all interconnected systems and services function harmoniously and efficiently. By employing a suite of advanced technological tools, network monitoring can provide a granular view of the network's performance, facilitating swift responses to irregularities and safeguarding against disruptions. In essence, network monitoring is pivotal for any sector that relies on robust and reliable network systems, serving as the bedrock for continuous operational excellence.

Train signal detection plays a crucial role in the complex realm of railway operations [168, 62]. These signals serve as the primary communication medium between the vast railway network and train drivers, ensuring the safe and efficient movement of trains. They determine when a train should stop, slow down, or proceed [142]. The accuracy and timeliness of interpreting these signals are vital; even a minor oversight can result in significant disruptions, delays, and potential safety hazards [54].

New South Wales Train Services (Australia) shoulders the responsibility of providing rail services across the Greater Sydney area. With a vision focused on delivering safe, customer-centric, reliable, and clean services, they are instrumental in keeping Sydney in motion. Their extensive network spans over 813 km of track, includes 175 stations across nine lines, and accommodates approximately 1.3 million passenger journeys each weekday [103]. This vast operation necessitates meticulous management and maintenance of tracks, trains, signals, overhead wiring, stations, and other vital facilities.

However, a significant challenge persists. Train speed, essential for upholding scheduled operations and ensuring a positive customer experience, is primarily influenced by the signal conditions observed by train drivers [165]. For example, observing a caution aspect can reduce the speed by 50%. Current data collection

DOI: 10.1201/9781003473893-4

methods, mainly from control systems, record temporal changes in signal aspects. However, they often fall short in providing the detailed and comprehensive data needed for advanced analytics. While these systems document the times when signal aspects change from "stop" to "proceed", they don't capture the nuances of various "proceed" indications [77]. This data limitation impedes the extraction of actionable insights crucial for ongoing operational improvements and strategic planning [117].

Identifying the need for a more sophisticated solution, the New South Wales Train utility partners with the UTS Data Science Institute. Renowned for its innovative and research-intensive ethos, the institute garners a strong reputation for its practice-based learning programs and industry collaborations. With a global perspective, they emphasize collaborative research with the goal of enhancing individual lives and the broader society. The proficiency of institutes in Information and Communications Technology (ICT), advanced analytics, autonomous systems, and AI places them at the vanguard of transportation transformation, striving for increased reliability, safety, and environmental sustainability [104, 105, 190]. Consequently, we embark on a joint initiative with NSW train utilities to harness advanced machine learning techniques and develop the Signal Aspect Transition Detection model. This model aims to equip train utilities with a profound understanding of historical performance, facilitating the achievement of performance metrics and rapid incident recovery.

The primary goal of this chapter is to devise an AI-powered object detection methodology capable of accurately capturing signal aspect states and transitions using video footage from front-facing cameras on the Waratah train sets. The approach is bifurcated. Initially, an object detection model for signals is formulated, consolidating what is previously a multi-step procedure into a unified neural network-driven process. This network undertakes both classification and prediction of bounding boxes for identified objects. Recognizing the distinct challenges tied to track detection, a separate image segmentation method is proposed. This method harnesses both detailed and high-level semantics, aiding in the identification of tracks and the subsequent localization of relevant signals. Through this pioneering approach, the research seeks to transform train signal detection, bolstering the safety, efficiency, and dependability of railway operations.

4.2   PRELIMINARY

Railway traffic signals are pivotal assets. Their accurate detection is essential for both automating locomotive movements and maintaining a comprehensive track asset database. In collaboration with NSW train utilities, our objective is to establish a computer vision (CV)-based model for signal detection within the Sydney railway system. Utilizing video frames from moving trains, we employ advanced computer vision methodologies for precise object detection. This research encompasses four primary parts: data amalgamation, footage examination, AI model formulation, and system alignment. These parts are detailed below:

Data Cleaning and Quality Review: This part emphasizes data pre-processing, encompassing data acquisition, purification, and amalgamation to ensure data veracity. The data under consideration includes (1) Video footage; (2) Fleet and timetable data (TLS-OTR); (3) Control system data from NSW train utilities (ATRICS); and (4) Track-level maps of specific railway lines.

After obtaining these data, the data undergoes a cleansing process to rectify corrupt, redundant, or erroneous entries through methods like flagging and imputation. Given the diverse data sources and formats, a standardization process is implemented post-cleansing. Subsequently, a rigorous review is conducted to ensure data quality, completeness, and consistency, laying the foundation for subsequent analyses and model development.

Traffic Light Detection and Signal Aspect Recognition: Leveraging state-of-the-art computer vision and machine learning techniques, we aim to devise a methodology for precise signal transition identification. Initial efforts focus on understanding the spatial and visual attributes of signal aspects, followed by the extraction of salient visual features from the videos. Insights garnered from this study guide the training of a machine learning classifier tailored for signal aspect recognition within video footage. Emphasis is also placed on harnessing the temporal attributes of video frames to ensure seamless signal tracking and change detection.

Data Fusion for Performance Analysis: Data fusion entails the synthesis of multiple data streams to yield information that is more consistent, accurate, and actionable than any singular data source. Upon finalizing the CV-based detection model, a strategy is devised to correlate signals identified in video footage with data sourced from the ATRICS control systems.

Model Evaluation: The assessment phase involves comparing the constructed model with manually annotated ground truth data, focusing on metrics like accuracy, efficiency, and robustness. The findings from this part guide further refinements to the model.

4.3 OBJECT DETECTION MODEL FOR SIGNAL DETECTION

In signal light detection, we employ an advanced object detection algorithm. This innovative approach amalgamates what is traditionally a multi-step procedure into a singular process. Utilizing a unified neural network, the algorithm concurrently performs object classification and predicts bounding boxes for the identified objects. This integrated methodology offers a significant optimization in detection performance. Notably, it exhibits superior efficiency compared to the conventional approach of deploying two distinct neural networks for object detection and classification. The underlying mechanism capitalizes on repurposing conventional image classifiers, adapting them for the regression task of delineating bounding boxes around detected objects.

In the realm of object detection, our model operates on the principle of image segmentation. Specifically, the image is partitioned into a grid of dimensions $S \times S$, as illustrated in Figure 4.1:

The grid cell encompassing the centre of an object (e.g., the centre of a signal) assumes the responsibility for detecting that specific object. Each cell is designed to predict B bounding boxes, each with a confidence score. By default, this architecture predicts two bounding boxes per cell. The confidence score spans from 0.0 (lowest

Figure 4.1   The sample of image grids

confidence) to 1.0 (highest confidence). In the absence of an object within a cell, the confidence score is 0.0. These scores encapsulate the confidence of the model regarding the presence of an object and the accuracy of the bounding box prediction.

Each bounding box prediction comprises five parameters: x-coordinate, y-coordinate, width w, height h, and confidence. The coordinates (x, y) pinpoint the centre of the bounding box, while the width and height are expressed relative to the overall image dimensions. The confidence score embodies the Intersection Over Union (IOU) between the predicted and the ground truth bounding boxes. IOU quantifies the overlap between these boxes, calculated as the ratio of their intersection area to their union area.

Beyond the predictions of bounding boxes and confidence levels, each cell additionally forecasts the class of the object. This class is represented through a one-hot vector with a length of C, where C signifies the total number of distinct signal classes present within the dataset. Notably, while a cell can predict multiple bounding boxes, it predicts only one class. This inherent limitation implies that the algorithm may falter in accurately classifying multiple objects of distinct classes within a single cell. Consequently, each prediction from a cell has a shape of $C + B \times 5$, where B is the number of predicted bounding boxes. The parameter B is multiplied by 5 because it accounts for these five parameters: x, y, w, h, and confidence, for each bounding box. Given $S \times S$ grid cells per image, the overall prediction of the model is a tensor of shape $S \times S \times (C + B \times 5)$.

Take an output Figure 4.2 of our model as an example, a single bounding box is predicted per cell. The true centre of the signal in the image is marked by a cyan circle labeled "object centre". The grid cell containing this dot, emphasized in dark blue, is responsible for detecting the dog and defining its bounding box. The predicted bounding box consists of four elements: the centre, denoted by a red dot, with coordinates (x, y) and the width and height, symbolized by orange and yellow markers. It is noteworthy the model predicts the centre and dimensions for the bounding

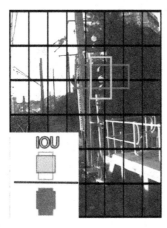

Figure 4.2   The sample of IOU

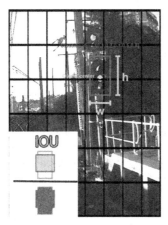

Figure 4.3   Classification and Confidence

box instead of the top-left and bottom-right corners. Classification uses one-hot encoding, and in this example, there are five classes. The model confidently identifies the signal as the fifth class. Figure 4.3 would typically present all bounding boxes and class predictions, leading to the final detection outcome. The overall signal detection process is shown in Figure 4.4.

4.3.1   MODEL ARCHITECTURE

In our model, it consists of three primary components: the backbone, neck, and head, as shown in Figure 4.5. The backbone employs convolutional layers, focusing on the identification and processing of salient image features [75]. Initially trained on datasets like ImageNet [46], the backbone operates at a resolution less refined

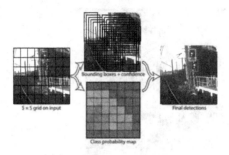

Figure 4.4   Our system models detection as a regression problem

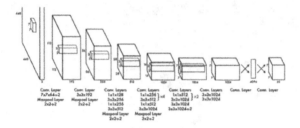

Figure 4.5   Model Architecture

than the eventual detection model, given the intricate details demanded by detection compared to classification. Drawing from the features discerned by the convolutional layers of the backbone, the neck integrates fully connected layers to forecast probabilities and delineate bounding box coordinates. The head, acting as the terminal output layer, offers flexibility, allowing interchangeability with layers of identical input configurations, and facilitating transfer learning. As previously mentioned, the structure for the head is represented as an $S \times S \times (C + B \times 5)$ tensor and is $7 \times 7 \times 30$ in the model with a split size S of 7, 20 classes C, and 2 predicted bounding boxes B. Consequently, these model segments collaborate to extract pivotal visual features, subsequently classifying and encapsulating them.

4.3.2   MODEL TRAINING

As aforementioned, the backbone of the model undergoes an initial training phase using the ImageNet dataset, which is renowned for its 1000-class competition set. Out of the 24 convolution layers present, 20 are subjected to pre-training. This is succeeded by the integration of an average-pooling layer and a fully connected layer. Subsequent enhancements to the model include the addition of four convolution layers and two fully connected layers. Such augmentations empirically demonstrate improvements in model performance. To cater to the intricate requirements of detection, the resolution is amped up from 244×244 pixels to a more detailed 448×448 pixels. The terminal layer of the model, responsible for predicting class probabilities and bounding box coordinates, employs a linear activation function. In contrast, the preceding layers utilize the leaky ReLU activation function. In this research, we undertake the manual labelling of over 1000 typical signal lights, capturing varied statuses like red, yellow, and green, extracted from video screenshots. The model is subjected to a rigorous training regimen spanning 135 epochs, utilizing a batch size of 64. To counteract the potential pitfalls of overfitting, strategies like data augmentation and dropout are employed. Specifically, a dropout rate of 0.5 is implemented between the inaugural and secondary fully connected layers. This strategic placement aimed to diversify the learning patterns of the layers, thereby mitigating co-adaptation.

Loss function of Detection Model The foundational loss function employed is a squared sum. However, this rudimentary approach necessitates refinements. In its unaltered state, the model indiscriminately weighs the localization error, which is the discrepancy between the predicted and actual bounding box coordinates, and the class prediction error. Furthermore, in instances where a grid cell is devoid of an object, its confidence score gravitates towards zero. This can overshadow the gradient contributions from other cells that do house objects. To address these challenges, two coefficients, λ_{coord} and λ_{noobj}, are introduced. These coefficients modulate the loss associated with coordinates and object absences, respectively. By setting λ_{coord} to 5 and λ_{noobj} to 0.5, the model accentuates detection significance while diminishing the weightage of cells without objects. A pivotal modification is the square-root transformation applied to the differences in bounding box dimensions. This ensures that errors, irrespective of bounding box size, are treated uniformly. Without this, the model might exhibit a bias against predicting larger bounding boxes. To elucidate, consider a predicted bounding box width of 10 against an actual width of 8. Using the equation $(w_i - (\hat{w_i}))^2$, the resultant loss is 4. Scaling this to a predicted width of 100 versus an actual 98, the loss remains 4. However, a width discrepancy of 2 in the context of 98 is trivial compared to the same discrepancy in the context of 8. Thus, the disparity between 10 and 8 should be more penalized than that between 100 and 98. This insight leads to the adoption of the equation: $\left(\sqrt{w_i} - \sqrt{\hat{w_l}}\right)^2$. With this equation, the loss values for the aforementioned examples are 0.111 and 0.010, respectively. It is imperative to understand that the absolute loss value is not intrinsically informative; rather, the relative differences between loss values are of essence. The square-root transformation underscores the importance of equitable treatment for bounding boxes, regardless of their size.

Within each grid cell, multiple bounding box predictions are generated. However, only a singular bounding box is designated as the primary detector for the object. This principal bounding box is identified based on its Intersection Over Union (IOU) score, with the highest scorer being selected. A notable consequence of this approach is the emergence of specialization among bounding boxes. Certain bounding boxes become adept at predicting specific object shapes and dimensions, while others hone their skills in different object morphologies. This specialization phenomenon can be attributed to the following dynamics: When a grid cell encounters a large object, and multiple bounding boxes make their predictions, the bounding box that offers the closest match (or the best fit) is reinforced. Consequently, this bounding box becomes

Figure 4.6 Example of semantic segmentation

increasingly proficient at predicting larger objects. Conversely, when a smaller object is presented, the bounding box that previously excelled at predicting larger objects might not provide an optimal fit due to its oversized dimensions. In such scenarios, a different bounding box, which offers a better fit for the smaller object, is reinforced. Over the course of training, these bounding boxes progressively refine their predictions, gravitating towards the object sizes and shapes they are initially more adept at detecting.

4.4 IMAGE SEGMENTATION MODEL FOR TRACK DETECTION

For track detection, traditional object detection methods are unsuitable due to the irregular boundaries of tracks compared to signals. Consequently, we introduced an image segmentation approach that leverages both low-level details and high-level semantics. This approach employs an aggregation layer to enhance the interplay and fusion of these feature representations. Through this model, an image is divided into multiple segments, facilitating the identification of tracks. Image segmentation yields segments that together encompass the entire image or produce a collection of contours derived from the image. Pixels within a segment share similarities in attributes like colour, intensity, or texture. In contrast, neighbouring segments exhibit pronounced differences in these attributes. Semantic segmentation, a pivotal domain in computer vision, aims to allocate semantic labels to individual pixels in an image, such as identifying entities like cars, houses, or persons, as shown in Figure 4.6.

4.4.1 SPATIAL PATH

For semantic segmentation tasks, several methodologies have been proposed [135, 71]. Some strategies prioritize retaining the resolution for input image to encapsulate ample spatial information, often achieved using dilated convolution [34]. Conversely, other techniques focus on encompassing an extensive receptive field, employing mechanisms like pyramid pooling modules, atrous spatial pyramid pooling, or using "large kernels". The emphasis on both spatial information and receptive

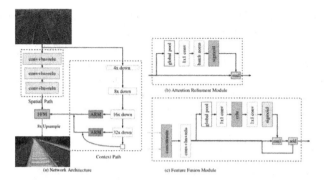

Figure 4.7 An overview of the Bilateral Segmentation Network

field stems from their significance in ensuring precision. Yet, harmonizing these two requirements remains challenging. Particularly in real-time semantic segmentation scenarios, contemporary methods often resort to smaller input images or employ lightweight foundational models to expedite the process. Unfortunately, reducing the input image size results in a significant loss of spatial information inherent in the original image. Similarly, lightweight models, often achieved through channel pruning, compromise the spatial information integrity.

Given the aforementioned challenges, our approach incorporates a Spatial Path designed to maintain the spatial dimensions of the original input image, thereby capturing abundant spatial information. The architecture of the Spatial Path comprises three distinct layers. Each of these layers integrates a convolution operation with a stride set to 2, which is subsequently succeeded by batch normalization and a ReLU activation function. As a result, the Spatial Path yields output feature maps scaled down to 1/8 of the dimensions of the original image. Despite this reduction, the feature maps retain a wealth of spatial information attributed to their considerable spatial dimensions. A comprehensive depiction of this architecture can be observed in Figure 4.7 (c).

4.4.2   CONTEXT PATH

To achieve a balance between a vast receptive field and computational efficiency, we introduce the Context Path. This path leverages a lightweight model, such as Xception [36], coupled with global average pooling to ensure an expansive receptive field. The lightweight model swiftly downsamples the feature map, capturing high-level semantic context. Subsequently, we append a global average pooling at the end of this model, offering the broadest possible receptive field infused with global context. The culmination involves merging the upsampled feature output from global pooling with the features for lightweight model. Within the lightweight model, we employ a U-shaped structure to integrate features from its final two stages, resulting in a modified U-shaped design. The comprehensive architecture of the Context Path is illustrated in Figure 4.7 (c).

Attention refinement module: Within the Context Path, we incorporate a distinct Attention Refinement Module (ARM) to enhance the features at every stage. As depicted in Figure 4.7 (b), the ARM utilizes global average pooling to seize the global context, subsequently computing an attention vector that directs feature acquisition. This mechanism fine-tunes the resultant feature of each stage present in the Context Path. By seamlessly integrating global context information, it eliminates the need for any up-sampling processes, ensuring minimal computational overhead.

4.4.3   NETWORK ARCHITECTURE

Leveraging both the spatial path and context path, we present a comprehensive framework for real-time semantic segmentation, as depicted in Figure 4.7 (a).

For the backbone of the Context Path, we employ the pre-trained Xception model, while the Spatial Path consists of three convolution layers with a designated stride. Subsequently, the output features from these two paths are integrated to produce the final prediction. This design ensures a balance between real-time execution and optimal accuracy. Delving into the computational aspect, the Spatial Path, despite its expansive spatial size, comprises merely three convolution layers, ensuring it remains computationally efficient. In contrast, the Context Path utilizes a lightweight model, facilitating swift down-sampling. Notably, the concurrent computation of these two paths significantly bolsters efficiency. From an accuracy perspective, the Spatial Path is adept at encoding abundant spatial information, whereas the Context Path offers an expansive receptive field. Their combined capabilities complement each other, culminating in enhanced performance.

Feature fusion module: The fusion of features from the Spatial and Context Paths necessitates careful consideration due to the distinct levels of feature representation they offer. The Spatial Path primarily captures intricate details, providing a rich spatial representation, while the Context Path predominantly encodes contextual information. In essence, the Spatial Path offers low-level features, whereas the Context Path provides high-level features. To effectively combine these disparate features, we introduce a specialized Feature Fusion Module.

Given the varying feature levels, our initial step is to concatenate the output features from both paths. To harmonize the feature scales, we then apply batch normalization. Following this, the concatenated feature undergoes pooling to produce a feature vector, from which a weight vector is computed. This weight vector serves to re-weight the features, effectively performing feature selection and combination. The intricacies of this fusion process are illustrated in Figure 4.7 (c). Regarding the loss function, we incorporate an auxiliary loss function to guide the training of our proposed model. While the primary loss function supervises the entire model's output, we introduce two specific auxiliary loss functions to oversee the Context Path's output. All these loss functions employ the Softmax loss, as depicted in Equation 1. To strike a balance between the primary and auxiliary losses, we use the parameter α, as outlined in Equation 2. In our implementation, α is set to 1. This combined loss approach facilitates a more streamlined optimization process for the model.

Loss function of Segmentation Model

In this research, the training of the proposed model is enhanced using an auxiliary loss function. The primary loss function is responsible for supervising the entire model's output. In addition, we introduce two distinct auxiliary loss functions specifically tailored to oversee the Context Path's output. All these loss functions employ the Softmax loss, as depicted in Equation 4.1. To ensure a harmonious balance between the main and auxiliary losses, we incorporate the parameter α. As indicated in Equation 4.2, this parameter adjusts the weightage between the primary and auxiliary losses. For our study, we set the value of α to 1. By employing this combined loss approach, the optimization process becomes more efficient and streamlined for the model.

$$Loss = \frac{1}{N}\sum_i L_i = \frac{1}{N}\sum_i -\log\left(\frac{e^{p_i}}{\sum_j e^{p_j}}\right) \tag{4.1}$$

where p is the output prediction of the network.

$$L(X;W) = L_p(X:W) + \alpha\sum_{i=2}^{K} l_i(X_i;W) \tag{4.2}$$

here l_p represents the primary loss derived from the concatenated output. The feature output from the Xception model's stage i is denoted by X_i. The auxiliary loss corresponding to stage i is represented by l_i. In our study, the value of **K** is set to 3. The joint loss function is symbolized by **L**. It is crucial to note that the auxiliary loss is exclusively utilized during the training phase. For the purpose of training, we employed a publicly available dataset tailored for semantic rail scene comprehension [189]. Subsequently, the model is implemented on the NSW train utilities' dataset.

4.5   TARGET SIGNAL DETECTION MODEL

In real-world scenarios, a complex network of railway tracks intertwines, catering to various routes. Cameras positioned at the train's forefront often capture a myriad of tracks and their associated signal lights simultaneously, as illustrated in Figure 4.8. For seasoned train drivers, with their vast experience, identifying the specific signal light that governs their current train is almost second nature. However, for a computer system, autonomously pinpointing the relevant signal light amidst such a multifaceted backdrop is a formidable challenge. To tackle this issue, we introduce a series of optimization techniques. These methods utilize the data from prior detections of signal lights and tracks, aiming to accurately identify the signal light that oversees the train's operations. Leveraging our proposed strategies, we can effectively ascertain the target signal lights and tracks pertinent to the current train. This refined information then aids in the precise detection of signal aspect transitions.

Figure 4.8 Sample frames that multiple signals and tracks appear in the camera simultaneously

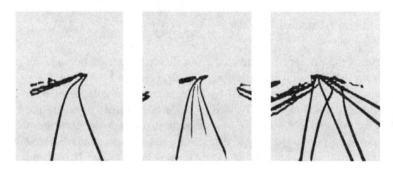

Figure 4.9 Sample of track detection results in different cases: the purple line refers to the detected tracks

4.5.1 CURRENT TRACK LOCATION

To pinpoint the specific signal light that governs the movement of an active train, it is essential to discern the spatial relationship between the signal lights and the trains. This essentially translates to understanding how train drivers ascertain which signals to adhere to. Drawing from the insights shared by experts at NSW train utilities, the governing signal light for trains is invariably situated to the train's left. Consequently, to identify the pertinent signal light for a given train, our primary object is to determine the train's current track. Our hands-on research delineate a sequence of steps to effectively capture the current track's location:

Step 1 – Current Track Location: As illustrated in Figure 4.9 (a), which displays the tracks identified by our proposed image segmentation model, it is evident that only the current track makes contact with the frame's bottom. This is attributed to the positioning of the train camera, which is situated at the train's forefront.

Consequently, we can straightforwardly determine the current track by identifying the one that touches the bottom of the frame.

Step 2 – Tracks do not connect with the bottom: However, in certain exceptional scenarios, our image segmentation model struggles to detect the entire track from the bottom due to issues with brightness. Specifically, when the frame's bottom is dimly lit, track detection becomes challenging, as depicted in Figure 4.9 (b). To mitigate this, if we're unable to identify the current track from the frame's bottom, we initiate a scan of the tracks from the bottom upwards until the current track is identified.

Step 3 – Merging tracks: In real-world scenarios, there are instances where two separate tracks converge into a single one, facilitating the merging of trains from different directions. This results in multiple tracks appearing at the bottom, as illustrated in Figure 4.9 (c). In such situations, pinpointing the exact track on which the train is running becomes challenging. Given that these merging tracks often emerge abruptly, when multiple tracks are detected at the bottom, we compare the positions of these detected tracks with the track from the previous frame. We then identify the track closest to the previous frame's track as the current one. Leveraging this proposed track location technique, our model can swiftly and accurately determine the current track.

4.5.2   TARGET SIGNAL LIGHT LOCATION

As mentioned above, the controlling signal light for the current train is invariably situated to its left. Once we've identified the track the train is operating on, this principle aids us in pinpointing the target signal light from among multiple options. Nonetheless, train networks present a myriad of intricate scenarios. To adeptly and efficiently identify the signal lights in these diverse situations, we've devised a comprehensive set of optimization techniques tailored to address each unique circumstance.

Step 1 – Determine the position of the signal lights relative to the current tracks: The target signal for the current train is consistently positioned to its left, allowing us to concentrate solely on the left-side signal lights and disregard those on the right, thereby simplifying the process. To ascertain the relative positioning of the signal lights, it is imperative to first establish a dividing line based on the current track. In this study, we employ the skeletonization algorithm to determine this dividing line, given that the detected train tracks can be approximated as triangular regions, as shown in Figure 4.10. The skeletonization algorithm is a technique that extracts the central lines or "skeletons" from binary images by progressively thinning the regions. By leveraging the skeletonization algorithm, the dividing line can adeptly discern the prospective direction of the train, regardless of whether it is proceeding straight or making a turn. Consequently, any signal light situated to the left of this dividing line is considered a potential candidate for the target signal light, while all others are disregarded.

Step 2 – Locate target signal light on the left: After determining the detected signal lights on the current track's left side, we can pinpoint the target signal lights based on their relative positions. To enhance the accuracy and speed of this identification,

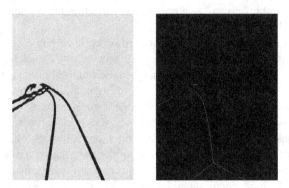

Figure 4.10   Sample of split lines(skeleton) of tracks

the location process is categorized into four distinct scenarios: (1) Single signal light
with no left tracks: Here, the lone signal light is directly identified as the target, as
there are no additional left tracks (i.e., tracks on the left of the current track and on
the frame's left side). This indicates that this signal light directly governs the current
train. (2) Single signal light with left tracks: In this scenario, the relationship between
the signal light and various tracks is ascertained. The skeletonization algorithm is
employed to determine the dividing line of left tracks. If the signal light is positioned
on the upper left of this dividing line, it is deduced that this light controls the left
track and not the current one. However, if the signal light lies between the dividing
lines of the current track and its nearest left track, it is designated as the target signal
light. (3) Multiple signal lights with no left tracks: This situation typically arises
when the train's front camera simultaneously captures both distant and proximate
signal lights. However, only the closer signal light controls the train. The signal light
with a larger apparent size (i.e., a longer diagonal distance) is selected as the target
based on the principle that closer objects appear larger. (4) Multiple signal lights
with left tracks: Analogous to the second scenario, if multiple signals are detected
between the current track and its adjacent left track, the signal light closest to the
current track is identified as the target.

Utilizing the proposed target signal light location methods, the detected signal
lights and tracks can be optimized in complex situations. The identified target signal light and current tracks are then employed for the final signal aspect transition
detection.

4.6   SUMMARY

Large-scale rail systems, such as NSW train utilities, play a pivotal role in
metropolitan areas, ensuring the smooth movement of people across the city. The
primary rail service provider in the Greater Sydney area is committed to offering
safe, customer-centric, reliable, and clean services. One of the critical factors influencing the efficiency of train operations is the speed, which is largely determined

by the signal conditions that train drivers observe on the railway network. Notably, train speeds can decrease by up to 50% upon encountering a caution signal. Such fluctuations in speed adversely affect the scheduled train operations, leading to a compromised customer experience. The data currently sourced from control systems primarily captures the moments when signal aspects transition from stop to proceed. While there is a singular signal aspect for " stop ", multiple aspects indicate " proceed ". This data limitation hinders the extraction of actionable insights that could drive continuous operational and planning enhancements.

Against this backdrop, the primary objective of this chapter is to devise an AI-driven object detection methodology capable of accurately identifying signal aspect states and their transitions. This is achieved by analyzing video footage sourced from front-facing cameras installed on the Waratah train sets. Our approach involves a two-tiered detection model tailored for track detection tasks. The initial phase involves the creation of an object detection model specifically for signal detection. This model amalgamates what is previously a multi-step procedure, utilizing a singular neural network to classify and predict bounding boxes for identified objects simultaneously. Given the irregular boundaries of tracks compared to signals, the same object detection technique isn't applicable for track detection. As a solution, we've introduced an image segmentation method. This method, guided by both low-level details and high-level semantics, employs an aggregation layer to bolster mutual connections and merge both feature representations. Through this, the model can segment an image into multiple parts, enabling the identification of tracks. Conclusively, target signals are pinpointed based on the current location of the track, and the signal status is subsequently reported.

5 Underground Vessel: Water Pipe Failure Prediction

5.1 BACKGROUND

Water pipe failure prediction plays a critical role in maintaining the integrity of water supply systems. This chapter focuses on data-driven methods for water pipe failure prediction, complementing existing physical models. These data-driven methods are particularly valuable in situations where obtaining micro-level data is challenging. The chapter addresses two key questions in prediction: replacement and maintenance. The replacement question pertains to predicting the retirement of pipes, assuming only one final failure needs to be predicted. Maintenance, on the other hand, involves further inspection and repair of risky pipes, allowing them to continue being used. Failures can occur at various locations along the pipe, necessitating repairs in specific areas. The modelling approach for replacement allows for the label to be represented in multiple ways to fit different models and provide varying levels of information. Time-to-event labelling, risky scores represented in the probability space, and grid representation as multiple tasks are discussed. For maintenance prediction, both parametric and non-parametric models are considered, with parametric models offering easier inference but limited flexibility, and non-parametric models capturing more detailed information.

Water companies make sure people have enough clean water for drinking and sanitation by managing a big network of underground pipes. These pipes, which stretch for thousands of kilometres, were mostly built a long time ago. Recently, many of them have started to break down and need fixing. Keeping up with all these repairs is tough and expensive. To deal with this, water companies are focusing more on fixing and replacing old pipes to stop them from failing. They know they need to predict when pipes might break to stay on top of things, as old pipes keep getting worse over time. Leveraging the rising computing power, machine learning has seen rapid growth in recent years. Many water companies are exploring the use of machine learning to predict the chances of pipes breaking and are planning to hire experts to test prediction models for pipe failures. If these models work well in the water distribution network, they could help find and fix faulty pipes early on.

To decide which pipes need attention first, water companies must understand the risk of failure and how likely it is to happen, which helps estimate potential costs. Experts have studied why pipes break for many years, and different models based on factors like pipe thickness [57], material decay due to the environment and manufacturing [151], and hydraulic properties [134] have been developed to predict how long

DOI: 10.1201/9781003473893-5

pipes will last. But checking pipe condition without digging them up is still difficult and expensive. This step, called condition assessment, often involves digging, using special equipment, and disrupting the public. To avoid this, water companies are working with machine learning experts on projects to analyze and predict pipe failures. The main goal of these projects is to test advanced machine learning techniques using real pipe data.

Predicting water pipe failure is crucial for several reasons. Firstly, it helps prevent water loss, mitigating the environmental and economic impacts associated with such losses. Secondly, it ensures the maintenance of water quality, as pipe failures can lead to contamination and health risks. Additionally, predicting failures allows for targeted and efficient maintenance and replacement, reducing infrastructure costs. It also helps avoid service interruptions, minimizing inconvenience and costs for customers. Lastly, predicting failures enhances safety by preventing flooding and other hazards associated with pipe failures, thereby promoting a safer environment.

Predicting water pipe failures serves various purposes at different levels of decision-making. At the decision and planning level, predictions provide valuable information about the scale and magnitude of potential problems. At a more granular level, users can prioritize and schedule repairs or inspections for risky pipes based on the predictions. Furthermore, predictions offer insights into the factors and mechanisms that contribute to pipe failures. In this chapter, our focus is on providing predictions for individual pipes within a supply water network. These predictions rely on data-driven approaches that complement traditional physical models and leverage readily available information such as pipe attributes. Throughout the chapter, we delve into the challenges, complexities, proposed solutions, and machine-learning models relevant to water pipe failure prediction.

5.1.1 PIPE FAILURE PREDICTION AS A MACHINE LEARNING PROBLEM

Machine learning methods are valuable in addressing the aforementioned issue. Generally, there are two kinds of models for predicting water pipe failures: physical models and statistical models. Physical models heavily rely on domain expertise and aim to understand the causes of failures, such as soil corrosion. However, they have limitations, like budget constraints for experiments, when applied to large and complex water networks. On the other hand, statistical models require fewer resources and can uncover hidden statistical patterns caused by various physical factors. Therefore, they can be used for large-scale water networks to guide preventive maintenance. These statistical machine-learning models are trained using historical failure data, pipe characteristics, and environmental factors. The utility of statistical machine learning methods is enhanced if they can be explained using domain expertise. In the following sections, we will explain why domain expertise is essential for each task using the example of predicting water main failures.

The strategy for predicting water pipe failures (WPFP) can be divided into two distinct categories, each posing unique challenges for data scientists. Firstly, there is the replacement prediction, which involves identifying scenarios where entire pipes need to be replaced. In replacement prediction, the focus is on identifying pipes that have reached the end of their lifespan and require complete replacement. The cost of replacing a pipe is high, but it is necessary to ensure the longevity of the network. After replacement, the probability of failure is reduced significantly. It is important to note that each pipe can only fail once, and even if it exceeds the budget, the replacement must be done. Therefore, the cost is not a significant factor in this prediction approach. In machine learning terms, this becomes a binary classification problem, where the prediction for each pipe is either 1 (replace) or 0 (not replace).

The second category is rehabilitation through maintenance. This strategy offers lower costs and greater feasibility. Rehabilitation prediction aims to forecast the frequency and quantity of pipe failures. Maintenance activities are then carried out to inspect these pipes and address any detected issues. The machine learning problem is to predict failure frequency and probability. The Maintenance prediction is focused on the inspection and maintenance of water pipes, with the goal of reducing the frequency of failures in high-risk pipes while staying within budget constraints. Therefore, the problem requires identifying pipes with a high probability of failure and prioritizing maintenance efforts accordingly. To address this problem, the prediction model is designed to identify highly risky pipes within the network. For such a prediction, we consider a pipe network where, for each pipe $i = 1 \cdots N$, we aim to determine the best subset of pipes for maintenance, denoted by $r_i = 1$ if the pipe is selected, and $r_i = 0$ otherwise. However, this prediction problem faces two key challenges:

- The budget constraints limit the number of pipes that can be selected for maintenance, so it is important to identify the pipes that are most likely to fail. In such circumstances, only the prediction accuracy for the top of the list is the focus.
- The expected probability of failure for each pipe is unknown and must be estimated based on historical data, which may be censored or not.

Although the prediction is based on statistics, we use machine learning because the entire process of failures is complex. We need to consider a large number of factors for each pipe, and machine learning can explore and learn the patterns and rules from the data when used as proxy reasoning. The major reason for using machine learning is its ability to learn from the data and provide insights into the underlying patterns that may not be apparent through traditional statistical methods. Hence, data volume is critical to ensure that the learned patterns are consistent and representative of the underlying phenomena.

Machine learning is a fascinating field of study that revolves around the development of algorithms that can learn from data and make predictions or decisions based on that learning. It involves building models that can recognize patterns and relationships in data, which can then be used to perform a specific task. Although there are many statistical works and models used in water pipe failure prediction, the advantages of machine learning models are numerous. One of the most significant benefits is that they avoid the need for complex model design that reflects the true physical world, which is often unavailable or uncertain. Machine learning techniques assume highly flexible models that offer much greater freedom of degree than statistical models. This flexibility means that if the highly flexible model can be learned to fit reality, it will be equal to or even better than a statistical model. If the statistical model is optimal, it will be simulated by a fitted machine-learning model. If the statistical model is sub-optimal, the machine learning model will likely find a better solution to the problem. However, this does not mean machine learning is definitely better than statistics; on the other hand, machine learning can be seen as an extension of statistics. Because it is built based on the statistics. usually, machine learning is also based on the pre-design of a model, and then the algorithms focus on how to design a program for a computer to find the optimal model parameter that can best fit the data with a predefined cost function.

Machine learning models are built to fit the data, even unsupervised models incorporate the designer's experience in their manual design. There is no universal method to fit the data, and either manual design or large-scale models with abundant data are used to achieve the fitting standards. In predictive problems, data is often split into training and validation data, as the unknown part cannot be accessed. Cross-validation is commonly used, where the training data is further split into training and testing data.

The goal of a model is to find a mapping from the data to the target as accurately as possible: $f(x) = y$ structure. For example, $[1\ 2\ 3\ 4] \rightarrow [2\ 4\ 6\ 8]$: $f(x) = 2x$. Despite the presence of noise or additional factors, if the mapping is not perfect, it can still be inferred, such as $[1\ 2\ 3\ 4] \rightarrow [2\ 4\ 6\ 9]$, where we can still infer $f(x) = 2x$. More complex mappings require more complex models. Underfitting occurs when the relationship is not properly captured, and overfitting occurs when the relationship is too well captured for the training data but cannot be generalized to the validation data (generalization problem).

The process of building a machine learning model typically involves training the model on a dataset that has been labelled or annotated with the correct output. The model is then tested on a separate dataset to evaluate its performance and determine if it is accurately predicting the correct output. If the model does not perform well, it can be adjusted and retrained until it achieves the desired level of accuracy. While the underlying mathematics and algorithms of machine learning can be complex, the basic principles and techniques can be learned and applied with practice and experience. In fact, many of the tools and frameworks used in machine learning are freely available and accessible to anyone with an internet connection. With dedication and perseverance, anyone can learn how to use machine learning to solve real-world problems and make data-driven decisions.

5.2   REPLACEMENT PREDICTION

5.2.1   REPLACEMENT PREDICTION AS A MACHINE LEARNING PROBLEM

The water pipe replacement problem requires the prediction of pipe lifespan. This is because, in this strategy, the pipe must be replaced before it enters the high breakage stage. Although breakage and leakage occur from time to time, and even if they are fixed, the pipe's length means that we can expect the break/leak rate to increase significantly after a certain age stage. To simplify the problem, we only need to assume a retirement age for each pipe. For each pipe i, we define $y_i(t)$ to be the failure label at time t. At time t_0, which is present with $y_i(t_0) = -1$, we aim to predict all $y_i(t)$ or $t - t_0$ until we find $y_i(t) = 1$. Otherwise, $y_i(t') = -1$, where $t' < t$, since for any $t' > t$, we still have $y_i(t') = 1$. Historical pipe replacement data is usually used to learn such a problem, with x_i being the vector of descriptors for pipe i. x_i is usually referred to as the pipe attribute or feature, with a possible dynamic descriptor represented by $x_i(t)$.

The most similar problem is survival analysis, which is also known as time-to-event analysis. It is a statistical method developed to analyze data in which the outcome variable of interest is the time until an event, which is pipe replacement time or time of pipe death. The origins of survival analysis can be traced back to the field of actuarial science, which was concerned with studying the mortality rates of life insurance policyholders. In the early times, medical researchers began to use survival analysis to study the time to death of patients with diseases such as cancer and to evaluate the effectiveness of different treatments. Survival analysis is widely used in various fields, including epidemiology, engineering, economics, and social sciences.

The early survival analysis methods were based on the assumption that the probability of an event occurring was constant over time and that the censoring of data (when the event of interest has not yet occurred or cannot be observed) was random. However, more advanced methods have since been developed that allow for non-constant hazards (the probability of an event occurring changing over time) and non-random censoring, we will discuss both scenarios in below sections.

5.2.2   MACHINE LEARNING IN SURVIVAL ANALYSIS

Machine learning is a natural fit for survival analysis, as the trained model can be trained to predict time-to-event or failure using current pipe status as input. There are two ways to consider this. First, time-to-event, as a continuous number, can be predicted as a regression problem. Second, whether the pipe will fail at the next time interval can be viewed as a binary classification problem. The time interval can be chosen to be a month or a year. The below section will discuss time-to-event prediction with deterministic output, probability-based output, and binary classification.

5.2.3   PREDICT DETERMINISTIC TIME-TO-EVENT

Standard regression learning is based on optimizing the loss function such that the predictions are as close as possible to the observed values for all training data. In some cases, such as predicting time-to-event, the problem is deterministic in nature. For such learning problems, as shown in Figure 5.1, observations are available for each pipe across multiple years. For each year, there are two sets of inputs for pipe i: static pipe attributes, denoted by x_i, which do not change with time, such as material, laid year, and pipe length, and dynamic pipe attributes, denoted by $x_i(t)$, which change with time, such as pipe age and historical maintenance records. Each year, a pair of inputs $(x_i, x_i(t))$ and output $y > 0$ is observed at any time t, where y represents

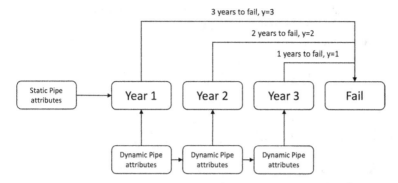

Figure 5.1 The time-to-event prediction framework. The example is for 1 pipe

the time-to-event, such as how many years until the pipe fails. These pairs are used to train a machine-learning model. When a new observation is available for a pipe in a new year, the corresponding inputs $x_i(t)$ can be obtained and updated, and the trained model can be used to predict the time-to-event. The example in Figure 5.1 shows four data pairs, but in a real dataset, there would be a large number of pipes, and the dataset would be correspondingly larger.

Within the framework, there are several additional considerations that need to be addressed, even though the task may initially seem straightforward. One important consideration is the completeness of the input data. Various factors influence pipe failures, but obtaining all of them may not be feasible. In such cases, we often rely on marginal factors instead of potential factors. However, when these factors are incomplete, a naive solution would be to build a separate model for each pipe, assuming that all pipe information is contained within the historical data.

Alternatively, if we can classify pipes based on their similarity, we can assume that pipes with similar latent factors exhibit similar behaviours. This classification process can be based on observed factors. By doing so, the model learned from pipes with similar latent factors does not need to consider those latent factors explicitly. However, without access to the latent data, employing domain knowledge becomes crucial for accurate classification.

Another approach is to estimate the uncertainty of predictions. Uncertainty estimation provides an understanding of the reliability of the data. If the learned model relies on data with critical latent information, the resulting predictions may have a large range of uncertainty. Machine learning offers various algorithms for uncertainty estimation. When the uncertainty range is significant, it may be necessary to decompose the group into smaller subgroups, considering the balance between data volume and reliability.

The "cold start" problem is another important consideration. In machine learning, the cold start problem arises when there is either no data or very limited data available. While traditional approaches are effective for typical data prediction problems, the challenge arises in pipe replacement because there may be no observed positive cases (failure data labels) or only a limited number of positive data labels.

This issue arises because each pipe is replaced only once, so there is no need to make predictions for pipes that have already been retired. However, for non-retired pipes, when we need to find data for similar pipes, the challenge is that if the pipes are new, the similar pipes we find may not have any failures. This is because most of the retired pipes are old, creating a cold-start problem. The field of machine learning has extensively studied cold-start problems.

There are two main approaches to address this problem. The first approach is to group different pipes together so that we can use data that is similar to existing pipes. We can create a pipe dataset that contains a number of replaced pipes and another dataset that includes all existing pipes without any failures. The technique called "collaborative filtering" can be applied to this problem. In this method, pipes can be connected based on their attributes. If pipes are similar to each other, the failure data can be used for similar pipes. While the pipe connection method partially solves the problem by finding failure records for pipes without those records, many pipes, especially new ones, do not have many similar failed pipes.

The second approach is based on finding a balance between exploration and exploitation. Exploration and exploitation are two strategies in decision-making. When we have data about some replaced pipes, we can train a model and use it to predict the time-to-event for other pipes that are similar to the known replaced pipe data. This process is exploitation, as we use known information to maximize our benefits and avoid possible losses. However, this approach may cause us to miss the opportunity to replace pipes that are not similar to any of the pipes in the replacement data. Therefore, decision-makers must consider exploitation and exploration, allocating resources for exploration to expand the data. One exploration approach is to inspect pipes with high uncertainty. The challenge then becomes balancing the resources between exploration and exploitation to minimize the general risk of replacement failure. This problem can be addressed using machine learning techniques like the "multi-armed bandit problem". In the cold-start phase, a significant amount of exploration is needed to learn about the rewards of each option quickly. However, excessive exploration may result in losses because low-reward options may be selected.

In the multi-armed bandit problem, balancing exploration and exploitation is crucial for maximizing returns. Here are some examples of strategies for choosing exploration and exploitation:

- ε-greedy algorithm: This algorithm randomly chooses a small portion of actions for exploration and usually chooses the known optimal actions for exploitation. The parameter ε specifies the exploration probability, typically set to a small value (e.g., 0.1), to ensure that exploitation is chosen as much as possible.
- Upper Confidence Bound (UCB) algorithm: This algorithm selects the action with the highest probability of yielding the maximum return based on known return values and unknown uncertainty. This maximizes returns while minimizing uncertainty.
- Thompson Sampling algorithm: This algorithm uses the Bayesian rule and random sampling to select actions based on current knowledge while balancing exploration and exploitation. The probability of each action is updated based on

previous return values and uncertainty, and a random selection is made based on the current probability distribution.

When there are no failure records at all for a specific category of pipes, it represents a pure cold-start problem. On the other hand, if some failure records are available, it indicates an imbalanced data problem. The transition from a cold-start scenario to imbalanced learning is not an abrupt change but rather a gradual process as the data evolves. In situations where there are no labelled data points, obtaining a clear pattern is impossible. However, when we have a small number of positive labelled data, the ratio of positive instances remains uncertain. In such cases, even if we employ imbalanced learning algorithms, the learning pattern lacks confidence. Therefore, it becomes necessary to consider a combination of cold-start learning approaches. Only when we have a more substantial amount of positive data can we gain greater confidence in the learning process?

5.2.4 PREDICTION AS PROBABILITY

When considering risks, it is common to make decisions based on probabilities. In such cases, probability estimation is used to predict outcomes as a distribution rather than a single deterministic value. In order to utilize regression models as probability distributions instead of deterministic predictions, we can make assumptions regarding the distribution based on the problem description.

Assuming a consistent probability, the Bernoulli distribution is used to model each pipe in the pipe failure problem. The parameter p represents the probability of the event occurring, similar to the chance of getting heads on a fair coin (where $p = 50\%$) or rolling a specific side on a six-sided die (where $p = 1/6$). These probabilities remain constant unless the conditions change. In the case of pipe failure, we assume that at time t, each pipe has a probability p of failing. This assumption allows us to estimate the expected time for an event with probability p to occur. For example, if a pipe has a 20% probability of failing at time t, we can expect, on average, that it will fail after approximately three years.

However, the assumption of a consistent probability has two limitations. Firstly, it does not account for variations in the situation, such as how the probability may change over time. For instance, as a pipe ages, its probability of failure may increase due to wear and tear. Secondly, the Bernoulli distribution itself does not incorporate time as an input, preventing it from providing a precise estimation of the most probable time-to-event. In the previous example, the probability of failure does not indicate the specific year when the failure is most likely to occur. Hence, while the Bernoulli distribution is useful for estimating average time-to-event based on a consistent probability assumption, it does not capture temporal dynamics or changing probabilities. To address these drawbacks, alternative models that consider time-dependent factors and evolving probabilities may be more appropriate for accurate predictions in the pipe failure problem.

We can utilize the Normal distribution to estimate probabilities over time by assuming that the time-to-event regression is deterministic but subject to certain noise.

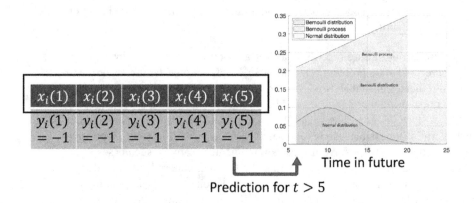

Figure 5.2   The three probability-based predictions

This assumption can be represented as $y = \hat{y} + \varepsilon$, where $\hat{y}$ is the model estimation and $\varepsilon \sim N(0, \sigma)$ follows a Normal distribution with mean zero and standard deviation σ. In this setup, the goal is to estimate $\hat{y}$ and determine the correlation between $\hat{y}$ and y using linear regression. Additionally, the parameter σ captures the variability or uncertainty in the estimation.

By incorporating such an approach, our previous deterministic prediction can be taken as the mean of all possibilities using the Normal distribution. We can then use this mean to estimate the probability of the pipe failing before or after the predicted time, typically represented in a figure. For example, if the figure shows that a pipe has a 50% chance of failing before $\hat{y}$ and a 50% chance of failing after, we can assess the probability of the pipe failing within a given year and consider it as a risk factor in the decision-making process.

The parameter in a probability distribution remains fixed and cannot capture dynamic changes over time. To address this limitation, we can employ a stochastic process to model the dynamic nature of probability. A stochastic process is a mathematical model that describes how a system evolves over time, incorporating randomness and probability. It characterizes the system's state at each time point using random variables or sets of random variables. The evolution of the system is then modelled using probability distributions or stochastic differential equations, which specify the probabilities of different outcomes or the system's behaviour in response to various inputs.

For instance, we can enhance the Bernoulli distribution by introducing a time-dependent parameter $p(t)$, resulting in a Bernoulli process. This allows the probability to vary with time, capturing the dynamic changes in the system. In practice, we can choose a suitable time interval, such as per year, to implement the process. Alternatively, if time is considered continuous, we can consider infinitesimal time intervals.

All three assumptions are depicted in Figure 5.2. On the left side, we observe previous data, and the predicted probabilities based on the Bernoulli distribution remain

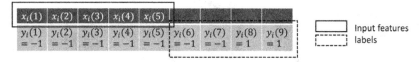

$x_i(1)$	$x_i(2)$	$x_i(3)$	$x_i(4)$	$x_i(5)$				
$y_i(1)$ $= -1$	$y_i(2)$ $= -1$	$y_i(3)$ $= -1$	$y_i(4)$ $= -1$	$y_i(5)$ $= -1$	$y_i(6)$ $= -1$	$y_i(7)$ $= -1$	$y_i(8)$ $= 1$	$y_i(9)$ $= 1$

☐ Input features
⌐ ⌐ labels

Figure 5.3   Multi-task learning scenario

constant over time. However, when using the Normal distribution, we obtain more precise predictions. It is important to note that future conditions can change, such as variations in water usage behaviour (e.g., higher demands). In such cases, where fixed predictions may no longer hold, the Bernoulli process becomes more valuable and applicable.

5.2.5   PREDICT BINARY SURVIVAL BY MULTITASK LEARNING

The case of predicting binary classes is used to predict whether the pipe requires replacement or not. However, such prediction does not take time into consideration, so the usual implementation can only be used to predict the binary label for the next time (e.g., next year), meaning it can only predict whether a failure will occur or not within that specific interval. To fit this into a time-to-replace problem, we can extend the prediction by multiple time intervals, for example, predict the replacement need for multiple years, as depicted in Figure 5.3.

A straightforward approach would be to predict each time interval separately. However, this assumption is not reliable because the predictions between time intervals are dependent on each other. Also there are two constraints that must be considered for the time-to-replace problem: First, the prediction for an unfailed time interval must be before the failure time. Second, the predictions between two time intervals that are close to each other tend to be similar.

To model these constraints, multi-task learning models have been explored. These models aim to jointly learn the predictions for multiple time intervals, taking into account the dependencies and correlations between them. By considering the relationships between adjacent time intervals and incorporating this information into the learning process, multi-task learning models can improve the accuracy and reliability of predictions. For example, multitasking learning can reduce the impact of noise, which cannot be removed from separate learning. The historical replace data can be earlier or after the break, such earlier or late decision can cause the variance of time-to-replace estimation. However, if all time interval needs to be estimated together, including the time intervals the replacement is not needed. The model will average the estimation for all time intervals. So, for the time intervals before the actual replacement, the learned average will be no replacement is needed. For the time intervals after the break, the model will average all cases and consider the time of the break. Such averaging over all time intervals by considering them as multiple tasks to train the model together can remove the notice so the model will be better trained. There are also many other benefits from multitasking learning, including augmented data when one of the tasks is hard to be learned.

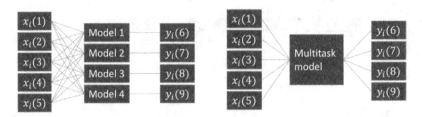

Figure 5.4 The left side represents the traditional model, while the right side illustrates the multitask learning model

In the bellowing multitask learning task, we learn a model for each task, which is associated with the predictions for the corresponding time interval. In other words, a model is trained for all time intervals based on the same input attributes $X = x_i, x_i(t)$ for all pipes indexed by i. The model parameter at the jth time interval is specified by the column $w_{i,j}$ with the coefficient matrix W. The goal is to estimate W by optimizing the following objective function:

$$\min_{W} f(W,X,Y) + \lambda ||W||^2 + \mathcal{L} \tag{5.1}$$

where Y is the label for all pipes defined in subsection 5.2.1. Here all labels must be after attributes, that is, a sample used for training is $x_i(0 \cdots t)$, then we use $y_i(t+1 \cdots t+m)$ with a preset m which is the task number. Here $f(W,X,Y)$, which is shown Equation 5.2, enforces the minimization of the discrepancy between prediction and label. $\lambda ||W||^2$ is the sparse constraint. Here $\mathcal{L}$ defines the constraints in the formulation. it relates to non-recurring setting in which once the survival state of a sample becomes 1 it will not change back to -1. It is termed as the non-increasing constraint, which can be expressed as follows: $y_i(t) \geq \max(\{y_i(k) | k > t\}), \forall i \in \{1, 2, ..., N\}, j, k \in \{1, 2, ..., M\}$. The example shown in Equation 5.2 uses 4 tasks ($y_i(6 \cdots 9)$), with feature in 5 dimensions ($x_i(1 \cdots 5)$). The example uses the data in Figure 5.3.

$$A = g \left(\left(\begin{pmatrix} w_{1,1} & w_{1,2} & w_{1,3} & w_{1,4} & w_{1,5} \\ w_{2,1} & w_{2,2} & w_{2,3} & w_{2,4} & w_{2,5} \\ w_{3,1} & w_{3,2} & w_{3,3} & w_{3,4} & w_{3,5} \\ w_{4,1} & w_{4,2} & w_{4,3} & w_{4,4} & w_{4,5} \end{pmatrix} * \begin{pmatrix} x_i(1) \\ x_i(2) \\ x_i(3) \\ x_i(4) \\ x_i(5) \end{pmatrix} \right) - \begin{pmatrix} y_i(6) \\ y_i(7) \\ y_i(8) \\ y_i(9) \end{pmatrix} \right) \tag{5.2}$$

and

$$f(W,X,Y) = A^2 \tag{5.3}$$

Here g is the nonlinear conversion function otherwise the linear combination is the separate model as the left one in Figure 5.4.

Table 5.1

The Attributes of Water Mains

Pipe ID	Material	Laid year	length
1	1	1962	30
2	1	1960	30
3	2	1976	60
4	1	1980	100
5	3	2003	10
6	3	2001	30
7	1	1916	150

5.3 MAINTENANCE PREDICTION

5.3.1 DATA UNDERSTANDING AND PROCESSING

The maintenance problem is indeed more complex than replacement. Unlike replacement, maintenance assumes that water pipes can be repaired before they need to be replaced, making it a more practical and focused strategy for water utilities. In this context, the problem is defined differently from the previous one. Here, we no longer have the constraint that $y_i(t) \geq y_i(k)$ if $t > k$. Instead, we record $y_i(t) = 1$ to indicate a failure occurring at time t, while the absence of any failure at time k is denoted as $y_i(k) = -1$. Alternatively, we will have a number of timestamps to represent the time of failures. This change in definition allows for a more flexible representation of failure events and non-failure periods, enabling a more comprehensive analysis of the maintenance problem for water pipes.

In most cases, there are two main data sets to be used in the machine learning models: attribute of assets and maintenance records. For instance, a dataset illustrated in Table 5.1 pertains to characteristics of assets (i.e., components within the water main system, typically individual pipes). The additional dataset showcased in Table 5.2 encompasses all asset failure occurrences over recent years (commonly with left-censored data). Domain expertise is crucial when handling such datasets.

5.3.1.1 Categorical Feature

It's crucial for data scientists to grasp the significance of water main attributes. For instance, numerical values may represent categorical attributes without meaningful relationships between consecutive numbers (e.g., material = 2 doesn't imply more material usage than material = 1; they simply denote different material types). Understanding the attributes in failure records is equally vital. For instance, a failure may result from a third party (Failure reason = 'R3') rather than pipe corrosion, so they can't be grouped together for prediction. The shortcoming is obvious for interpolation-based models like the linear regression that will only reflect the change

Table 5.2
The Failure Records of Water Mains

Pipe ID	Failure data	Failure type	Failure reason
1	3/2/2010	Burst	R1
1	11/8/2014	Leak	R2
2	4/2/1998	Burst	R2
2	15/5/2004	Leak	R1
2	30/3/2008	Leak	R3
5	4/4/2011	Burst	R1

of attribute value to an increasing trend, that is, if we have $\hat{y}$ for material = $3 > \hat{y}$ for material = 2, then the model will say $\hat{y}$ for material = $2 > \hat{y}$ for material = 1. The setting creates a problem in that the data correlation is different if we swap the meaning of material = 2 and material = 1.

There are many ways to deal with categorical input. One approach is to treat the input individually. One-hot encoding is a commonly used method. It creates an additional attribute for each category value. For example, representing "material = 3" as $[1, 0, 0]$ and "material = 2" as $[0, 1, 0]$. This encoding results in many columns with mostly 0 values (at least $C - 1$ columns for C distinct values of a categorical input), making the input matrix large and sparse. Moreover, it introduces a constraint that the sum of all encoded columns is 1, which may affect model learning. When dealing with large attribute matrices, methods like PCA can be applied to condense the data into a denser space. In some cases, encoding may be unnecessary; even numerical values can be used for prediction with more flexible models like decision trees. However, flexible models require a large amount of data to prevent overfitting.

Another encoding method involves incorporating the target variable. This method converts categorical features into the label space. If the label is numeric, statistics like mean and median can replace categorical index values. Additionally, multiple statistical measures of the label can represent a single category. For instance, using percentiles such as $25\%, 50\%, 75\%$ as dimensions of input for a category. For point-based data, statistical information such as failure frequency and distribution intervals can be used. However, target-based encoding becomes complex when dealing with multiple categorical features. For instance, if there are 5 categories in each feature and 10 features, 50 model parameters need to be modelled, each with fewer data to maintain robustness.

5.3.1.2 Censored Data

Moreover, there is incomplete data as the observations only span recent years (approximately 5–20 years). This limited timeframe provides uncertain information when dealing with older water mains aged over 100 years. Past occurrences can only

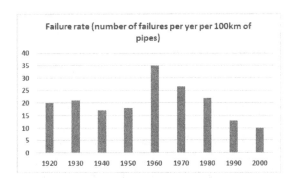

Figure 5.5 The failure rate of pipes varies with the year they were laid. Usually, older pipes are more prone to failure. However, the finding that pipes laid in 1960 have a higher failure rate than those laid in 1920 raises doubts and should be verified by experts in the field

be partially understood and incorporated into models based on expert knowledge. However, this information may be fragmented, leading to omissions or oversights. Additionally, data mining and machine learning specialists have a responsibility to scrutinize the data and pose inquiries, leveraging these queries to extract as much insight as possible from domain experts. For instance, Figure 5.5 illustrates a higher frequency of failures in water mains laid between 1950 and 1980, despite their relatively newer installation compared to those laid between 1920 and 1930. This disparity could stem from missing records, varying material quality, or historical usage patterns. Nonetheless, identifying the underlying cause and consulting domain experts is essential to ensure accurate predictions.

5.3.2 POINT PROCESS TO MODEL MAINTENANCE RECORDS DATA

According to the defined data in subsection 5.3.1, the maintenance records are represented by historical failure data, so it is represented as the event sequence data. The event sequence data (a.k.a. point process) can be modelled by the Poisson process, which is based on a latent parameter about the failure frequency. The Poisson process family has many variations that fit all kinds of situations. Here, our discussion will include the following:

- Homogeneous point process: the failure frequency does not change.
- Non-homogeneous point process (NHPP): the failure frequency is not necessary constant throughout time.

A homogeneous point process is a type of stochastic process that models the random occurrence of points in time, such as each failure history is one point. The process is called "homogeneous" because the probability of a point occurring is constant over time and/or space. The study of homogeneous point processes can be traced back to the early 20th century when it was introduced as a mathematical framework

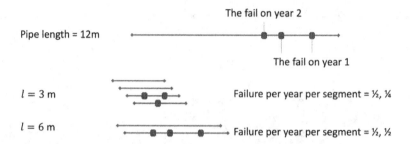

Figure 5.6 The whole pipe length is divided into different smaller segments for different failure rates. When we use shorter segments, the failure rate can be lower

for analyzing phenomena such as radioactive decay, queuing systems, and the distribution of particles in space. One of the key concepts in the theory of homogeneous point processes is the intensity function, usually represented as λ, which describes the rate at which points occur in time or space. For a homogeneous process, the intensity function is constant, and the process is completely described by its intensity. This process is easier to be understood and simple to use, we will focus on discussion of NHPP.

5.3.2.1 Poisson Distribution for Time and Length

The repeated failures of a pipe happen from time to time. The repeating pattern can be predicted to some extent, but uncertainty cannot be removed. Such randomness follows a Poisson process (at least at some moment). That means the failure intensity (average frequency) can vary with time. As introduced in the previous section, such non-homogeneous intensity gives us a challenge of whether the data exists with more uncertainty than the randomness caused by Poisson. All the model predictions are to understand how likely the pipes will fail. This is done by a fundamental assumption that the failure probability follows Poisson distribution, but the parameter could change with time. However, in pipe failure prediction problems, the length is also an important element of failure since it is reasonable that a longer pipe has a higher probability of failure than a shorter pipe.

The Poisson distribution predicts how likely it is to have a certain number of failures in a given time period. However, the length of the pipe can also affect how often failures happen. Here, we present a method to estimate the probability of a pipe failing, taking into account its length, denoted as L. This approach relies on the failure rate, which indicates the number of failures per year per pipe segment. By dividing the pipe into shorter segments during our analysis, we increase the number of segments, thereby reducing the failure rate. The algorithm detailing this process is depicted in algorithm 1.

Algorithm 1: The algorithm to calculate the failure probability and uncertainty for pipes.

Data: Pipe with length L
Result: Failure probability and uncertainty for pipes based on the time and length using Poisson distribution

1 initialization
2 **while** <u>MaxIteration limit</u> **do**
3   Randomly set a length unit $l < 0.1L$
4   **for** <u>all pipe segments with length l</u> **do**
5   We fit the data to Poisson distribution;
6   Calculate the probability of more than 0 failures for all segments for time T;
7   The probability of fail of the pipe $P_L(l)$ is 1- 0 failures for all segments;
8   Average of $P_L(l)$ is the failure probability T;
9   Variance of $P_L(l)$ is the uncertainty;

The procedure outlined in algorithm 1 is applicable when dealing with pipes of varying lengths to assess the likelihood of failures and associated uncertainties. It can serve both for estimating probabilities and for inferring hidden factors. The inference of latent factors becomes necessary due to inevitable data gaps, which are common in practical scenarios. One cluster is typically utilized for probability estimation when employing the data for pipe clustering. However, in cases of missing data, pipes with distinct failure patterns may erroneously fall into the same cluster. In such instances, uncertainty can help identify data gaps and inconsistencies in clustering. Alternatively, the Poisson distribution test can be employed to evaluate the data's suitability for fitting the distribution.

5.3.2.2 NHPP

NHPP stands for Non-Homogeneous Poisson Process. Different from the homogeneous point process, the rate at which the events occur varies over time and is described by a function known as the intensity function. The intensity λ in NHPP is usually considered as $\lambda(t)$ to reflect its variation with time. The major NHPP model inference work is to use the data to find out the parameters of the $\lambda(t)$ as a function. The NHPP model learning includes not only the pattern of historical parameters but also the prediction of the parameter change. We discuss two major types of NHPP models, including estimating $\lambda(t)$ by assuming it is Weibull distribution and Cox distribution.

5.3.2.2.1 Weibull distribution

The Weibull distribution was first introduced by Waloddi Weibull in 1951 and is a widely used probability distribution. The Weibull distribution is a continuous probability distribution that is often used to model the failure time of a system or component. The main purpose of the distribution in point process is that we can use it to estimate the time interval between failures. For example, we can use the probability of failure time interval to estimate the risk of the next failure, or we can estimate the scale of failures like failure numbers in a period of time. It is characterized by two parameters: the shape parameter and the scale parameter. The shape parameter determines the shape of the distribution curve and the scale parameter determines the location of the distribution on the time axis. The Weibull distribution can be used to model different types of failure patterns, including early-life, wear-out, and random failures.

5.3.2.2.2   Cox model

The Weibull distribution and similar distributions have constrained the shape so that they can only represent limited types of failure patterns as a parametric method. The other type of model is the semi-parametric model, which has a more flexible representation. The Cox proportional hazards model, also known as the Cox model, is a widely used semi-parametric model. It also includes the pipe attributes such as x_i. The Cox model was introduced by David Cox in 1972 and is used to analyze the time-to-event data, where the outcome of interest is the time it takes for an event of interest to occur, such as death, failure, or disease onset. The Cox model is a semi-parametric model that estimates the hazard function ($\lambda(t)$), then it can be used to estimate the time to the next event, or it can be used to model event frequency. the model use the equation: $\lambda(t) = h_0(t)e^{\beta \vec{x}_i}$. Here $h_0(t)$ can be any function to describe the change, while the second term is the impact for pipe attribute $\vec{x}_i$

5.3.3   NON-PARAMETRIC MODELS FOR WATER PIPE FAILURE PREDICTION

All the techniques mentioned above rely on our assumed model. Most of them are categorized as parametric models. However, when we lack understanding of the intricate failure process, substantial data enables the use of non-parametric models.

Non-parametric machine learning encompasses methods in machine learning and statistics that refrain from making explicit assumptions about the underlying probability distribution of the data. Instead, these techniques utilize the data itself to infer the problem's structure and the relationship between variables. As a result, non-parametric methods offer greater flexibility, capable of adapting to various data distributions and underlying relationships, especially in cases where the data distribution is poorly understood or where variables exhibit complex, nonlinear relationships.

Non-parametric machine learning techniques possess several advantages over parametric methods. They can effectively handle intricate relationships between variables and are often more resilient to outliers and noise in the data. Moreover, they demonstrate greater flexibility, suitable for addressing a broader spectrum of problems.

Nevertheless, non-parametric methods may incur high computational costs and may necessitate extensive data for optimal performance. Additionally, they may pose challenges in interpretation and may not provide insights into the underlying mechanisms of a problem. Overall, non-parametric machine learning constitutes a crucial set of techniques applicable to diverse problems in machine learning and statistics.

5.3.3.1 Non-Parametric Model for Aging-Pipe Issue

In pipeline analysis, it is often assumed that the failure rate of pipes increases monotonically with age, and this assumption is commonly used in parametric models. However, this assumption may not always hold true. In fact, it confuses the concept of cumulative failure probability with the yearly failure rate. It is true that the cumulative failure probability will continually increase and eventually converge to 100% as the pipe ages. Mathematically, we can represent this as $P(\text{failure} \geq 1) \rightarrow$ 100% for all years with $age < \inf$. Here, inf represents a very large age. It is evident that this representation is not specifically designed to handle repeated failures.

If we consider the failure rate on a year-to-year basis, we observe that it varies but generally follows an increasing trend. This issue becomes more pronounced in the context of predicting pipe failures. In the dataset we utilize, the correlation between age and failure extends across multiple years. For instance, if we have data for the year 2000, the age data pertains to pipes laid in different years. Specifically, the data for pipes with an age of 30 corresponds to pipes laid in 1970, while the data for pipes with an age of 21 corresponds to pipes laid in 1971. Since these are different pipes, when comparing their failure rates, we may observe higher failure rates for pipes laid in 1971 compared to those laid in 1970. Consequently, older pipes may exhibit higher failure rates.

When considering pipe maintenance rather than replacement, it is important to note that the failure rate can vary as pipes enter the failing stage but can still be used. Various factors contribute to this deviation from the age-based assumption, such as differences in surroundings and construction technologies for different pipes. To account for these factors, we use pipe failure frequency data for modelling. However, it is crucial to consider the bathtub failure frequency curve, which also includes installation failures. These failures occur in the early stages, even when the pipes are still new. If we label all failure events as pure failures in our models, we fail to distinguish between installation failures and failures that occur as the pipe ages. To address this, we can employ data processing techniques to remove these early failures. For more detailed modelling, if we also consider the installation failures, we need to examine the relationship between these early failures and failures in later stages. This investigation will reveal whether installation failures have a significant impact on subsequent failures or not.

5.3.3.2 Prediction by Random Forest Model

Random forest is a widely used machine learning algorithm suitable for regression and classification tasks. It is an ensemble method that combines multiple decision trees to make predictions. The name "random forest" originates from the creation of a forest-like structure consisting of decision trees, each trained on a random subset of the available data.

In a random forest, each decision tree is constructed using a subset of the training data and a random subset of the available features. This technique helps mitigate overfitting issues and enhances the algorithm's ability to generalize to unseen data. During training, the algorithm constructs numerous decision trees, with each tree making its own prediction for the output variable. The final prediction is obtained by aggregating the predictions of all individual trees.

One notable characteristic of random forests is their nonparametric nature. Unlike parametric models that involve considering complex physical processes, random forests rely on observations and features (such as pipe attributes and surrounding factors) as inputs. The model's objective is to find an optimized way to utilize a highly flexible function to map the input to the observations. Consequently, the nonparametric nature of the model, with fewer domain knowledge constraints, necessitates a substantial amount of data. With sufficient data, the model can effectively disregard the impact of noisy data, ensuring that the learned patterns are less influenced by irrelevant noise.

Random forest models are readily available in common machine learning packages and are relatively easy to implement when the data can be structured. The key parameters to consider are the number of trees and the depth of each tree, as they control the complexity of the model. Determining these parameters is primarily based on the characteristics of the dataset. It is important to note that when working with limited data or a large number of columns in structured data, the model's complexity should not be overly high. Striking a balance between model complexity and flexibility is crucial in such cases

5.3.3.3 Prediction by Bayesian Non-Parametric Model

Bayesian non-parametric is a field of statistics and machine learning that aims to develop flexible statistical models that can adapt to the complexity of the data without requiring a fixed set of parameters. Unlike traditional statistical methods that assume a specific parametric form for the probability distribution of the data, Bayesian non-parametric models allow the data to determine the complexity of the model. At the same time, it also allows the modeller to set a prop to control the parameter learning. The key idea behind Bayesian non-parametric is to use probability distributions as building blocks for constructing statistical models. Instead of specifying a fixed number of parameters, these models use a flexible and infinite-dimensional space of distributions to model the data. This allows the model to adapt to the complexity of the data and to avoid overfitting or underfitting.

The Bayesian non-parametric method can predict water pipe failures. The model we'll talk about is the hierarchical beta process model. Since there's not much data on failures, we need a Bayesian prior for the model. This protects it from incorrect assumptions about the model's structure and lets it adjust to different failure patterns, making its predictions more precise.

The given model is outlined in [107]. Initially, the model assumes that failures occur randomly, following a Bernoulli distribution with parameter p_k for a specific pipe category k. However, due to limited data, p_k may become unstable. Hence, a Bayesian prior is introduced to prevent p_k from deviating significantly from its true value. To accommodate the changing nature of p_k, the beta process is employed as the prior. A beta process, denoted as $B \sim BP(c, B_0)$, acts as a positive random measure on a space Ω, where c represents the concentration and is a positive value, and B_0 is a fixed measure on Ω. When B_0 is discrete, $B_0 = \sum_k q_k \delta_{\omega_k}$, B features atoms at the same locations, given by $B = \sum_k p_k \delta_{\omega_k}$, with $p_k \sim Beta(cq_k, c(1 - q_k))$ and each $q_k \in [0, 1]$. Subsequently, observation data X is modelled by a Bernoulli process with measure B, represented as $X \sim BeP(B)$. Here, $X = \sum_k z_k \delta_{\omega_k}$, where each z_k is a Bernoulli variable, denoted as $z_k \sim Ber(p_k)$.

Moreover, in cases where a collection of classifications is present, and all data falls under one of these classifications, the hierarchical beta process might be employed to depict the data. Within each classification, the elements and their corresponding utilization are depicted by a beta process. Simultaneously, a shared beta process prior is applied across all classifications. In the context of a water distribution system, let π_{ki} represent the failure probability for a pipe in the k-th group, and the observation time interval (in years) j. The hierarchical structure for Bayesian non-parametric modelling can be expressed as follows:

$$q_k \sim Beta(c_0 q_0, c_0(1 - q_0)), \ where \ k = 1, 2, ..., K,$$
$$\pi_{k,i} \sim Beta(c_k q_k, c_k(1 - q_k)), \ where \ i = 1, ..., n_k, \qquad (5.4)$$
$$z_{k,i,j} \sim Ber(\pi_{k,i})$$

Here q_k and c_k are the mean and concentration parameters for the k-th group, q_0 and c_0 are hyper parameters for the hierarchical beta process, $z_{k,i} = \{z_{k,i,j} | j = 1, ..., m_{k,i}\}$ is the history of pipe failure across $m_{k,i}$ years, $z_{k,i,j} = 1$ means the pipe failed in j-th year, otherwise $z_{k,i,j} = 0$.

For the hierarchical beta process, a set of $\{q_k\}$ are used to describe failure rates of different groups of pipes. For each pipe group, with fixed concentration parameter c_k, our goal is to find $\pi_{k,i}$ for pipe i in group k. This can be estimated from the observation, so we have:

$$p(\pi_{k,i} | z_{k,1:n_k}) = \int p(q_k, \pi_{k,i} | z_{k,1:n_k}) dq_k = \int p(\pi_{k,i} | q_k, z_{k,i}) p(q_k | z_{k,1:n_k}) dq_k \quad (5.5)$$

Each term in Equation (5.5) can be represented by:

$$p(\pi_{k,i} | q_k, z_{k,i}) \sim Beta\left(c_k q_k + \sum_j z_{k,i,j}, \ c_k(1 - q_k) + m_{k,i} - \sum_j z_{k,i,j}\right), \qquad (5.6)$$

and

$$p(q_k|z_{k,1:n_k})(q_k, z_{k,1:n_k}) = p(q_k) \prod_i \left[\int p(\pi_{k,i}|q_k)p(z_{k,i}|\pi_{k,i})d\pi_{k,i} \right]$$

$$\propto q_k^{c_0 q_0 - 1}(1 - q_k)^{c_0(1 - q_0) - 1} \prod_i \frac{\Gamma(c_k q_k + \sum_j z_{k,i,j})\Gamma(c_k(1 - q_k) + m_{k,i} - \sum_j z_{k,i,j})}{\Gamma(c_k q_k)\Gamma(c_k(1 - q_k))}$$

(5.7)

In the model, we observe that the collective failure rate is regulated by hierarchical level parameters c_0 and q_0. These parameters serve to stabilize the learning process, particularly in situations of limited data availability. This aids specialists in grasping the overall performance of a group without delving into every factor affecting an individual pipe.

5.4   SUMMARY

This chapter aims to explore data-driven methods for water pipe failure prediction, complementing traditional physical models. Data-driven methods are particularly valuable for making higher-level decisions when obtaining micro-level data is challenging. The chapter addresses two main prediction questions: replacement and maintenance.

In the case of replacement, the focus is on predicting pipe retirement, assuming only one final failure needs to be predicted. Maintenance, on the other hand, involves further inspection and repair of risky pipes, allowing them to continue being used. Failures, such as bursts, can occur at different locations along the pipe, necessitating repairs in specific areas.

For replacement modelling, even though only one failure is predicted, the label can be represented in various ways to fit different models and provide different levels of information. Time-to-event labelling is discussed, representing the remaining useful life of the pipe as a continuous positive number. Additionally, a risky score can be used to indicate the probability of failure, providing a representation in the probability space. Another approach involves using a grid representation, treating the problem as multiple tasks.

In the context of maintenance prediction, both parametric and non-parametric models are considered. Parametric models offer easier inference with a smaller solution space, but their limited flexibility may prevent them from learning latent information present in the data. Non-parametric models, on the other hand, can capture more detailed information, even unknown to the modellers themselves. However, non-parametric models require additional effort for inference, and it is important to ensure that the volume of data matches the complexity of the model.

Water pipe failure prediction involves more insightful topics to explore. For instance, failures in water pipes can trigger a domino effect, causing disruptions in water flow, pressure, and quality. This, in turn, can burden neighbouring pipes and lead to additional failures. Understanding this cascade of failures and the interconnection between events is crucial. Predicting how failure events can cause other events is an important aspect to consider when analyzing event influence.

Moreover, there is a desire to go beyond static features, such as pipe attributes, and incorporate more detailed data, such as pressure changes or instantaneously captured sensor data. While high-level models may not require large-scale data, the use of sensors can provide dynamic and voluminous data. In such cases, more complex models like deep learning methods can be considered.

6 Long-Term Prediction of Water Supply Networks Condition

6.1 BACKGROUND

The lifespan of infrastructure is typically lengthy, often spanning centuries. Therefore, it is crucial to anticipate potential future risks, such as those within the upcoming decade. Precise long-term prediction equips infrastructure decision-makers with vital data to guide their choices and strategies. Similar to disciplines like finance, governance, and climate studies, infrastructure planners and managers must foresee trends, evaluate risks, and allocate resources efficiently over an extended duration.

The advantages of long-term prediction are diverse. Firstly, in Investment Planning, where infrastructure projects require substantial resource and financial investments, precise long-term predictions assist decision-makers in efficiently allocating resources for constructing new transportation systems, energy grids, or water supply facilities. Secondly, in Population Growth and Urban Planning, long-term predictions are essential for accommodating future population growth and urban expansion. By anticipating changes in population, infrastructure planners can design and implement transportation networks, housing developments, and utility services accordingly. Thirdly, Technological Advancements necessitate the integration of new technologies, such as smart city solutions or renewable energy sources, into infrastructure projects, facilitated by long-term forecasting. Additionally, Environmental Considerations require the incorporation of climate resiliency measures into infrastructure planning and design, guided by long-term predictions of climate change impacts. Resource Management is another area where long-term forecasts assist in managing scarce resources like water and energy sustainably and efficiently. Furthermore, Economic Growth and Development are closely linked to infrastructure development, and accurate long-term predictions aid in planning transportation systems, logistics networks, and utility services to support economic expansion. Lastly, Planning Consistency is ensured through long-term predictions, aligning infrastructure plans with a region's long-term development vision to prevent short-sighted decisions that could lead to inefficiencies or future problems.

In this chapter, we delve into the challenge of long-term prediction. Recognizing its inherent complexity, we explore the viable strategies that can be employed to tackle this task. We shed light on the underlying factors that facilitate predictive capabilities. Subsequently, we delve into the fundamental concepts and frameworks within the domain of machine learning that enable the incorporation of these factors. In essence, we dissect the methodology behind the predictive process.

DOI: 10.1201/9781003473893-6

Furthermore, we delve into the intricate landscape of machine learning models pertinent to this specific challenge. We illustrate this through exemplar models, accompanied by their practical applications, such as their utilization in predicting failures within supply water networks. Concluding our discussion, we contemplate the integration of broader global concerns, such as climate change and population dynamics, into the realm of prediction. These external factors are analyzed for their potential impact on predictive methodologies.

6.1.1   LONG-TERM PREDICTION CLUES

The primary chronological index for predicting future events is time. When considering infrastructure assets, the age of these assets becomes a significant factor. Consequently, we encounter two distinct data alignments: time-aligned data and age-aligned data. Time-aligned data pertains to assets that came into existence simultaneously. As a result, at any given time, these assets share the same or similar age characteristics. For instance, if we denote the age of assets i and j as a_i and a_j, respectively, and the time of the assets at age a as $t_i(a)$ and $t_j(a)$, we establish that when $t_i(a) = t_j(a)$ for the same age a, indicating synchronous emergence. Conversely, age-aligned data refers to instances where $t_i(a_i) = t_j(a_j)$ but with distinct ages a_i and a_j. Throughout our discourse, we often assume that $a_j > a_i$, signifying a logical age progression. The interaction of time and age in infrastructure asset analysis significantly influences our predictive capabilities, accommodating both synchronized and distinct emergence scenarios.

In short-term prediction, the underlying assumption often rests on the idea that the immediate future will resemble recent observations or that existing trends will persist for a certain duration. A critical challenge arises when transitioning to long-term prediction, primarily due to the increased need for information that is often unavailable. Long-term prediction necessitates conjecture regarding the continuity of trends, whether they remain constant indefinitely, undergo gradual evolution, or experience sudden transformations. In this context, age-aligned data emerges as a more informative resource, providing nuanced insights, while time-aligned data tends to offer comparatively less information. The essence of long-term prediction revolves around four key clues, each potentially applicable, as illustrated below:

- The foundation of prediction is rooted in historical data and the application of physical rules to estimate trends. These trends can either be assumed or learned through analysis of historical data. This approach bears the advantage that if the trend exhibits high confidence, then extending the trend using the established rules yields predictions of increased reliability. Furthermore, the versatility of this method allows it to be applied across diverse data types. In the realm of long-term prediction research within the domain of machine learning, a primary focus involves the identification of recurring patterns present over extended periods [106]. Subsequently, these patterns can be leveraged to predict long-term futures. This approach can be categorized under the umbrella of trend prediction, harnessing the power of identified patterns to extend predictions over extended time horizons.

- Second, change point prediction represents a departure from rigid trend assumptions. This method introduces flexibility by allowing predictions to incorporate shifts in trends, often referred to as change points or breakpoints. The challenge here is twofold: predicting not only when a change will occur but also anticipating the nature of the shift that follows. This approach presents a more intricate task that is applicable to both types of data. In the realm of change point considerations, most algorithms tend to prioritize detection rather than prediction. However, there exist specialized change point prediction methods [8] that pivot towards estimating the time until the next change point. Essentially, these methods re-frame the change point prediction challenge as a trend prediction problem. Yet, an underlying challenge remains sparse change points. In scenarios where change points are scarce over extended periods, accurate prediction demands an extensive historical dataset. This requirement stems from the necessity of a prolonged historical record to capture multiple sparse change points effectively. We delve further into the integration of point processes with sparse events to address this intricate facet.

- Third, the adaptive approach takes a distinctive stance by leveraging data far older than that which is intended for prediction. This strategy inherently aligns with age-aligned data scenarios. To illustrate, when predicting the state of asset i at the age of 100 using the information at age 10, we must consider asset j at $a_j = 100$, benefiting from its available observations due to its greater age. This paradigm often finds utility within numerous time series models. The crux of the adaptive method involves utilizing adaptation information gleaned from employing models to predict diverse data sequences encompassing both older and younger assets. Observations from older assets can then guide predictions for their younger counterparts. Although operationally feasible, this process mandates addressing challenges and uncertainties. It necessitates understanding the extent of behavioural similarity among assets and addressing queries like whether younger assets will indeed emulate the patterns of older assets. In the realm of machine learning, this paradigm is encapsulated within adaptation methods. These endeavours frequently tackle a more intricate problem: given two datasets exhibiting domain shifts, how can a larger dataset facilitate learning a model to adapt to the smaller target dataset? This domain is characterized as transfer learning [143]. Transfer learning defines the target model to be acquired from the smaller dataset, alongside the source model/data, which is more extensive yet potentially deviates from the smaller dataset. This paradigm is extensively applied across various AI domains. For instance, pre-trained image models can be fine-tuned using a target dataset to yield a new model adept at accommodating target data.

- Finally, quantifying uncertainty to comprehend the associated risks of utilizing predictions will greatly inform decision-making processes. It is an established fact that all predictions inherently carry uncertainties and risks. Furthermore, these uncertainties in predictions propagate over time, particularly accentuated in the realm of long-term forecasting. The presence of uncertainty can significantly impact various aspects. The concept of uncertainty weaves through various domains, and its application extends far and wide, ensuring informed decision-making across a multitude of scenarios.

6.2 MACHINE LEARNING FRAMEWORKS FOR LONG-TERM PREDICTION

Numerous machine learning algorithms have been devised by adeptly incorporating and aligning with the aforementioned clues. These algorithms exploit the unique characteristics of each clue to augment predictive capabilities across diverse scenarios and data types. They are categorized into frameworks as outlined below:

6.2.1 DIGITISED RULES

The fundamental approach entails an initial comprehension of the mechanism or trend embedded within time series data or sequences of events. Subsequently, this model is employed to incorporate established knowledge, encompassing constraints, physical principles, or prevailing policies. Notably, the model's parameters offer greater flexibility compared to conventional ARMA models when integrated with established insights. This strategic utilization of machine learning methods efficiently resolves parameters even in intricate scenarios, effectively extracting pivotal parameters. Consequently, the model becomes proficient in predicting future statuses in alignment with defined rules.

The advantage of employing machine learning within this framework lies in its aptitude for swiftly approximating solutions to complex optimization problems and substituting intricate model structures. This departs from autoregressive-based predictions, often termed nowcasting. The tailored model excels in furnishing predictions for extended temporal spans due to the robustness of rule-based predictions. Even in the presence of noisy historical data, reliability in forecasting is retained. Furthermore, any modifications in rules yield an updated model, enabling us to anticipate forthcoming events with precision. This attribute empowers the model to assess potential outcomes arising from policy adjustments and settings.

For instance, consider the case of water demand significantly influencing pressure fluctuations, thereby triggering failures within the water supply network, following a discernible pattern in domestic water usage. However, if a city decides to implement an augmented immigration policy, augmenting the allocation of immigrant quotas, the inevitable consequence is an increase in both population and water demand. The ensuing alterations in water demand will inevitably reshape the failure pattern, potentially leading to an upsurge in network failures.

6.2.2 STEP-FORWARDING PREDICTION

Step-forward time series prediction is a technique employed in time series analysis with the goal of forecasting trends across a broader future time horizon.

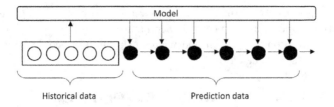

Figure 6.1   The illustration of step-forward prediction

Various implementations exist, one notable example being Amazon's deepAR [156]. In this methodological approach, we incrementally advance through time using available historical data, generating forecasts for forthcoming data points by employing suitable model choices and underlying assumptions. Commencing from an initial historical data point, the technique predicts the subsequent data point using a selected model. This predicted data point is then integrated into the historical dataset, forming a new foundational basis. Utilizing this updated dataset for prediction, the subsequent data point is foretasted, initiating an iterative process that progressively anticipates additional future data points until the desired prediction time range is encompassed. This approach finds pertinence in domains necessitating extended projections of trends and alterations over lengthy temporal spans, such as climatology, economics, and resource allocation. Nevertheless, it is imperative to acknowledge the intricacy and uncertainty inherent in long-term predictions.

The example in Figure 6.1 shows how step-forward prediction is working. The augmentation of step-forward prediction can be achieved through the integration of probability distributions, facilitating the integration of prediction error propagation. These error bands serve to encapsulate either the inherent uncertainty or the underlying risk inherent in the utilization of predictions. The introduction of a Bayesian framework enables the modelling of step-forward prediction by conducting marginalization across intermediary latent layers. These latent layers exhibit variations that are not directly observable, emphasizing their concealed nature. However, these layers can be influenced by prospective policies, modified constraints, or even the inherent uncertainty intrinsic to the model itself. This comprehensive methodology lends itself to a more exhaustive comprehension of potential outcomes and the risk profiles associated with long-term predictions.

6.2.3   GROUPING ASSETS

Another approach to consider within the realm of machine learning involves the distinction between individual asset prediction and grouped asset prediction. Grouping assets has the potential to aggregate data, leading to a reduction in prediction variance. This is mainly because a larger dataset becomes available, which can help mitigate the impact of noisy observations. It's important to note that noise tends to amplify over extended periods, making this variance reduction particularly valuable.

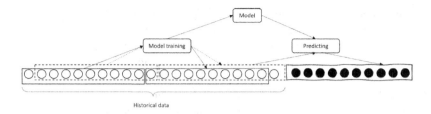

Figure 6.2 The illustration of sequence-to-sequence prediction

However, in the context of long-term predictions, when the influence of certain factors becomes more significant than recent trends used in short-term prediction. Here lies a crucial consideration: when we encounter missing attributes that differentiate one asset from others, the situation becomes complex. If these differentiating features are unobserved, the grouping process might inadvertently combine assets that are distinct in terms of these unobserved factors. This could happen if the observed factors are similar.

Then the challenge arises when an unobserved factor turns out to be a critical variable for predicting future trends. In such cases, grouping assets may introduce bias into predictions, potentially leading to generalized results within the group. This poses a limitation as the actual prediction is the averaged prediction for the group but could significantly vary for each individual asset. Consequently, this is when individual asset-based prediction gains prominence as a more accurate approach.

A suggested approach is to carefully balance the choice between grouping and considering individual assets. When opting for grouping, particularly in situations involving sensitive data, it's essential to assess the alignment between assets being grouped together. Monitoring the consistency among these assets is crucial. If the level of consistency starts to decline, it serves as an indicator that the process of including additional assets within the same group should be halted.

6.2.4 SEQUENCE-TO-SEQUENCE PREDICTION

Sequence-to-Sequence (Seq2Seq) prediction is a (deep) learning technique used for modelling and predicting sequences of data. Usually, it involves two components working together: an encoder and a decoder. Each can be modelled using the deep learning technique: recurrent neural networks (RNNs). The method is suitable for long-term prediction because it can predict a whole sequence instead of one time point and it also focuses on tasks involving sequential data. This model has also been used in translation, text generation, speech recognition, and more. We can imagine the long-term prediction as translating the whole life of an asset to a younger asset, an adaptive manner of prediction. Figure 6.2 illustrates the Seq2Seq learning idea. To get the Seq2Seq model to work, the encoder RNN processes the input sequence step by step, generating a hidden state at each time step. The final hidden state of the encoder captures the information from the entire input sequence and serves as the initial state for the decoder. All this information is encapsulated into the context vector. Then the decoder RNN generates the output sequence step by step, using the context vector as the initial state. At each time step, it produces an output and updates its internal state based on the previous output and the previous hidden state.

As a machine learning model, Seq2Seq models are trained using pairs of input and target sequences. Therefore we need retired assets with entire life for training. During training, the model aims to minimize the difference between its predicted output sequence and the actual target sequence. Therefore the trained model can learn the mapping between input sequences and target sequences. In prediction, given a period of historical observation as a number of years past, we can use the model to predict a sequence of years in the future.

Seq2Seq models have the similar issue when consider the long sequence, that is the long-range dependencies may be "forgotten" in learning since the model tend to find short-term trend. This may have higher learning accuracy, but actually, they are overfitted. To avoid this, the optimisation has been extended and improved over time, with variations like attention mechanisms and transformer architectures that enhance their ability to capture long-range dependencies, which may bring down training accuracy but can avoid overfitting. They are particularly effective for tasks where input and output data are sequences of varying lengths and require understanding context over the entire sequence, making them a suitable choice for long-term prediction research. The method is what we need to input the whole sequence and predict the whole sequence, for example, if we input the history to generate the prediction for a long-horizon future. This can be used in long-term prediction because we can generate a whole sequence, and the length of the sequence can be controlled by us.

6.2.5 CONFORMAL PREDICTION

Conformal prediction is a method that provides probabilistic predictions with a well-calibrated measure of confidence. It's often used to estimate the reliability of individual predictions. Such confidence is also translated as prediction uncertainty. Conformal prediction for long-term prediction is an approach that combines the principles of conformal prediction with the challenges of making predictions over extended time horizons. When applied to long-term prediction, it ensures that predictions are made while accounting for the uncertainty associated with future time points.

Conformal prediction calculates prediction regions (confidence intervals) that are the possible variations of the prediction. These intervals capture the uncertainty associated with each prediction and reflect the inherent variability in long-term forecasting. Such variation can come from many sources. For example, when we have missing observations or records of water pipe material, we may guess about the material and use the uncertain knowledge as model input. Then, what we learned is also uncertain in the long-term future. We may also observe variation of failure rate for all group members, such variation is also the source of uncertainty.

In order to handle long-term prediction, a step-forwarding approach can be used. The approach employs a rolling window. Then the model is trained on a historical window of data and then tested on the next time point. The window is then rolled forward, and the process repeats for each prediction time step. The uncertainty can be calculated using the ground truth in testing and prediction, such as learning the distribution parameter for all the predictions that are as close as to the distribution of ground truth.

The uncertainty is also dynamic prediction, even with some prediction available, as new data becomes available, the model can be updated and the prediction intervals re-calibrated. This adaptation ensures that the model remains accurate over the course of the prediction horizon.

Conformal prediction for long-term prediction provides a way to make informed decisions based on the expected future outcomes while acknowledging the uncertainty associated with those outcomes. It's particularly useful in scenarios where long-term forecasts are critical, such as assets with long-life materials, climate change impact, and resource planning, as it helps decision-makers account for the inherent unpredictability of the future.

6.2.6 MULTIPLE RESOLUTION

Spatiotemporal data aggregated over regions or time windows at various resolutions demonstrate heterogeneous patterns and dynamics in each resolution. Meanwhile, the multi-resolution characteristic provides rich contextual information, which is critical for effective long-sequence forecasting. The importance of such inter-resolution information is more significant in practical cases, where fine-grained data is usually collected via approaches with lower costs but also lower qualities compared to those for coarse-grained data. But this requires the long historical observation data [132].

6.3 LONG-TERM PREDICTION MODELS

6.3.1 POINT PROCESS FOR LONG-TERM PREDICTION

The introduction of point processes in Chapter 5 for survival analysis is pivotal. The model operates under the assumption that the intensity is stationary, or its variation is stationary. Short-term predictions typically favour event-based predictions like time-to-next-event or event count for the next time interval (e.g., 1 year). However, long-term predictions entail forecasting over extended time horizons, resulting in significantly large time intervals. If we aim to predict the number of events over such long intervals, the accumulated number of events becomes substantial. What does this imply? In such cases, the prediction of the number of events follows a Gaussian distribution with the same mean and variance. On the other hand, if we seek to predict the time to next event in long-term forecasting, implying that the time until the next event will be very long, we encounter the challenge of sparse event data.

The properties of stationary are often unavailable in long-term prediction scenarios. In such cases, trend prediction methods can be employed to forecast the future intensity function. Once the trend of the intensity function is predicted, the conventional approach involves predicting the time-to-event, which represents the time until the next event. This method may not necessitate the prediction of individual events.

However, for long-term prediction, multiple events will be encompassed. Utilizing the intensity function, the prediction transforms into the number of events over the long-term future. This is because marginalization is less influenced by long-term futures than single events. Nevertheless, this approach requires the prediction of all infinitesimal values of intensity, which entails integrating the intensity over time:

$$\int_{t_0}^{t_r} \lambda(t)dt, \tag{6.1}$$

given that we are predicting t_r at t_0.

If $\lambda(t)$ is stationary, implying that we can discern some trend from historical data and extrapolate this trend into the future, we can obtain the integral value. However, some trends may not be well-defined, especially when they are complex, as human understanding of underlying physics can be limited. In such cases, deep learning methods can be employed to uncover complex patterns and trends.

It is straightforward to use approximated values for the integral. For instance, we can discretize the problem. Thus, we can express Equation 6.1 in a discrete manner:

$$\sum_{t=t_0,\ldots,t_0+\Delta t,\ldots,t_r} \lambda(t)\Delta t. \tag{6.2}$$

However, this discretization violates the continuous property of point processes. The main risk associated with such discretization is the potential neglect of short but significant variations in the intensity function. For instance, if we consider Δt as 1 year, there could be seasonal variations, such as a higher failure rate in winter and a lower failure rate in summer. Our estimated $\lambda(t)$ can only represent the intensity at time t, which is a single point in time, as shown in Equation 6.2. In the example, if we predict and use $\lambda(t)$ in summer, the higher failure rate in winter will be ignored.

We could increase the resolution, for example, by using monthly λ, but this introduces uncertainty. Each small interval prediction would tend towards zero events if the interval is too small. This becomes riskier when predicting 0 or 1 event when there are actually 2 to 3 events, compared to predicting 10 events when there are actually 12 to 13 events. Thus, larger intervals provide more certainty.

Researchers have explored aggregated information, such as using both coarse and fine resolutions. For example, considering monthly λ and combining them to obtain yearly λ, then making predictions based on this aggregated information. Related research on coarse + finer granularity modelling has been proposed [47]. The approach aims to predict $\lambda(t)$ at two scales in a non-autoregressive manner. However, this method is not self-adaptive if we do not know the appropriate scales for prediction.

6.3.2 SCALE OPTIMISATION

The challenge of implementing these machine learning models is that intervals and scale themselves are also unknown, just like other variables. However, it is necessary to treat them as fixed values when running the model rather than solving for them, as solving would significantly increase the difficulty of finding the optimal solution. We then discuss a Bayesian optimization-based method to find suitable configurations of intervals and scales by iteratively exploring the configurations and model variables.

At its core, Bayesian optimization combines probabilistic modelling and optimization. It utilizes a probabilistic model to forecast the behaviour of the objective function based on the evaluations conducted so far. Initially, assumed configurations are used to evaluate the model, and a probabilistic model is built based on these evaluations. This model is then used to estimate new and more optimal model variables. Consequently, the model incorporates the uncertainty associated with predictions and configurations. The optimization process in Bayesian optimization comprises two main steps:

- Exploitation: The current probabilistic model predicts the likely location of the optimal configuration. This step aims to exploit the current best estimate for the optimal solution.
- Exploration: The algorithm selects the next configuration to evaluate the model in a manner that balances between choosing a point likely to be optimal (exploitation) and exploring uncertain or under-sampled regions of the search space.

The trade-off between exploitation and exploration is managed using an acquisition function, which quantifies the desirability of evaluating a specific configuration based on the current model's predictions and uncertainty.

Bayesian optimization has found successful applications in various fields, including hyper-parameter tuning for machine learning algorithms in our case, optimizing complex simulations, and more. Its ability to efficiently optimize functions with limited evaluations and handle noisy or uncertain observations makes it a valuable tool for finding optimal solutions. In the scale optimization problem, it can provide an optimal scale for machine learning models without exhaustively testing all possibilities.

6.3.3 ADAPTION MODELS

6.3.3.1 Problem Definition

For an asset i, we have its attributes $x_i(a)$, and targeted behaviour (failures) $y_i(a)$ on age a. at age a_0, we wants to predict the long-term behaviour $y_i(a_p)$ here $a_p - t_0 >> 1$. At the same time, we can find at least one asset j, whose observation on a_p, including $x_j(a_p)$ and $y_j(a_p)$ are all available. Therefore our target is to design a model that can use $x_j(a_p)$ and $y_j(a_p)$ to predict $y_i(a_p)$.

The natural sample adaptation issue differs from short-term prediction demands. For comparison, we can delineate a similar procedure with $a_q - t \geq 1$ and $a_q << t_p$. To compare, we can collectively formulate the prediction issue as

$$y_i(a) = h(f_i(w_i, x_i(1 \cdots a_0)), f_j(w_j, x_j(1 \cdots a))). \tag{6.3}$$

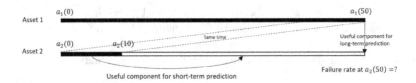

Figure 6.3   The difference between short-term prediction and long-term prediction based on adaption. The short-term prediction relies more on trend, while the long-term prediction relies more on another sequence with long-term observation. We met many such cases in reality, such as predicting new and middle-aged asset failure using old assets

Here we can see there are two major components used in Equation 6.3. First, we used the historical information of i, then we used the historical information of j.

It is noticeable that the age a for j is in the same year with age a_0 for i. Loosely speaking, here f_i and w_i are more important for short-term prediction, while f_j and w_j are more important for long-term prediction. The difference is shown in Figure 6.3. In the figure, we have two assets, asset 1 (j) and asset 2 (i). We would like to predict asset failure for asset 2 when the asset is 50 years old. As of the current time, asset 1 is at the age of 10 ($a_2(10)$), and asset 2 is at the age of 50. We can use the information of $a_1(50)$ to help us predict $a_2(50)$.

Since there is no clear threshold to determine if the forecasted age is a_p or a_q, we will consider a_p to be more indicative of long-term trends and a_q to be more indicative of short-term trends. Therefore, in machine learning, the design of the model will need to find a balance between these two components.

6.3.3.2   Sample Adaption

The model assumption for traditional models, including statistics and machine learning models, does not account for the individual distinctions among data (assets). For instance, when dealing with 100 water pipes, the conventional approach involves representing the data as a list of all assets, with the model distinguishing between assets based on their attributes or behaviours to forecast their future health. This assumes that pipes with the same attributes will exhibit similar behaviours. However, we identify two issues with this assumption.

Firstly, not all attributes may be observed or fully capture the factors influencing future asset health. Hidden factors may have a minor impact in the short term, leading to limited variance observed among assets within the same category. However, over the long term, even small influences can result in significant differences between two assets with similar observed attributes.

Secondly, the degree of similarity between data is unknown. Although we may use feature similarity to pair samples, determining which features are more important remains challenging. Moreover, if we utilize all features to train a model, samples sharing useful features may be perceived as behaving similarly, irrespective of other features.

To address these challenges, we will introduce several models to implement Equation 6.3.

6.3.3.3 Difference Adaption Model

The disparity between two assets can serve as the template. For instance, if one asset consistently experiences failure twice as often as the other, future outcomes can be forecasted based on this correlation. Consequently, a model emerges.

$$y_i(a_p) = u_{y_j}y_j(a_p) + u_0. \tag{6.4}$$

The model uses a linear relationship between i and j for the same age. In addition, we can involve the short-term prediction component as

$$y_i(a_p) = u_{y_i}(a_p - a)(y_i(a) - y_i(a-1)) + u_{y_j}y_j(a_p) + u_0. \tag{6.5}$$

Here we utilize the variance between the most recent observed year and the present year, subsequently adjusting the variance by a factor of $a_p - a$ as the forecast is made after $a_p - a$ years. Nonetheless, such immediate-term tendencies are better suited for short-range predictions. In the implementation, we shall ascertain parameters u_x, u_y, and u_0. The model presented in Equation 6.5, when incorporating white noise, also extends the ARMA model, renowned for its efficacy in time series forecasting. The input is the difference between a and $a - 1$, it is possible to include the difference for longer history. For example, we can generate the first component by

$$u_{y_i}(a_p - a)(y_i(a) - y_i(a-1)) \rightarrow$$
$$\frac{1}{mn}\sum_m\sum_n \frac{u_{y_i}^{m,n}}{m-n}(a_p - a_m)(y_i(a_m) - y_i(a_n)) \tag{6.6}$$

The equation lists all the possible differences that can be calculated from the historical data. actually, when we have a long history, that is, $m - n >> 0$, such long-term differences can inject useful information for long-term prediction.

Likewise, we can extend the second term by incorporating $y_j(a_p)$. This adaptation is necessary when we lack extensive historical data to train the model outlined in Equation 6.4. In Equation 6.4, we require access to $y_i(a_p)$ for model training, which may not always be available. Therefore, assuming we possess data for i up to a_q, where $a_q < a_p$, during training, we operate under the assumption that we are at a, where $a < a_q$. Consequently, we can only train the model as follows:

$$y_i(a_q) = u_{y_j}y_j(a_p) + u_0. \tag{6.7}$$

However, since $y_i(a_q)$ and $y_j(a_p)$ are at different times, we will need to add a temporal difference term, then we have:

$$y_i(a_q) = u_{y_j,a_q-a}(y_j(a_q) - y_j(a)) + y_i(a) + u_0. \tag{6.8}$$

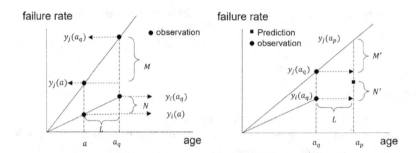

Figure 6.4 The training stage (left) is to learn the parameter that can transform M to N. The ratio is applied in prediction (right) to predict N' using M', considering the translation from L to L'

We can still add the historical data as Equation 6.6 in to train the model. Then, in the forecast, we can use

$$y_i(a_p) = u_{y_j, a_q - a}((y_j(a_p) - y_j(a_q))) + y_i(a_q) + u_0. \tag{6.9}$$

In Figure 6.4, the various phases of training and testing are illustrated. In this context, L is defined as $a_q - a$. When making predictions for i at a_q, we can forecast $a_p = a_q + L$ for asset i. The model can forecast the future for $2n$ years given observations for n years. For longer-term predictions, additional forecasts can be made for subsequent L years, enabling recursive prediction as long as observations for $y_j(a_p)$ are available.

The current setup neglects the incorporation of attributes x_i and x_j, focusing solely on the target within the model. However, if we consider observations, we can enhance Equation 6.4 by incorporating components to leverage the effectiveness of attribute influence. This influence can be dissected into two aspects:

- The evolving trend stemming from the changing attribute.
- The influence from asset j to i, indicating how significant j is in predicting i. If j and i exhibit high similarity, j is considered more influential. Consequently, these two influences can be encapsulated within the weights. The attribute trend can be embedded in u_{y_i}, while the correlation from j can be embedded in u_{y_j}.

A straightforward method is to create lag features. This is by setting

$$u_{y_i} = f(w_i, x_i(a - \Delta a)). \tag{6.10}$$

Here Δa is the lag, for example, we can use attributes in the previous 5 years as the input, given that $\Delta a = 5$.

6.3.4 LONG-TERM RECURRENT NEURAL NETWORK

The input data comprises a collection of sequences $\mathscr{C} = \{S^1, S^2, \ldots\}$. Each sequence $S^i = ((t_1^i, r_1^i), (t_2^i, r_2^i), \ldots)$ consists of pairs (t_j^i, r_j^i), where r_j^i denotes the failure rate of group j at the corresponding time t_j^i, and $t_j^i < t_{j+1}^i$. It's noteworthy that sequences may have varying lengths, allowing groups with shorter lengths to benefit from information shared by longer-length groups. The interpretation of the group and failure rate may vary depending on the specific application. For instance, in the proactive maintenance of water mains, S^i could represent a sequence of observed times for a group of water mains, with r_j^i indicating the frequency of failures for the group at age t_j^i.

In light of this, we aim to develop a model with the following objectives:

- Enabling groups with shorter lengths to leverage information from longer-length groups.
- Predicting multiple failure rates $r_{n+1}^i, r_{n+2}^i, \ldots$ for group i over an extended period, based on a set of sequences with events occurring up to time t_n.

The temporal dynamics of predicting failure events can be effectively captured using traditional survival analysis. An efficient approach to characterize these events is through the hazard function. Within a narrow time window $[t, t + dt)$, the hazard function $\lambda(t)$ quantifies the rate of event occurrences. Defined in relation to the probability density function $f(t)$, the hazard function is formulated as:

$$\lambda(t) = \frac{f(t)}{S(t)} = \frac{f(t)}{1 - F(t)} \tag{6.11}$$

Here, $F(t)$ denotes the cumulative probability of a new event occurring before time t since the last event at time t_n, while $S(t) = \exp\left(-\int_{t_n}^t \lambda(x)dx\right)$ represents the survival function, indicating the absence of new events up to time t since t_n. Estimating the hazard function $\lambda(t)$ facilitates the recovery of the survival function $S(t)$. Consequently, most survival analyses focus on estimating the hazard function.

Different functional forms of the hazard function $\lambda(t)$ are often tailored to capture specific phenomena of interest [3]. Consequently, each parametric form of the hazard function assumes that the underlying distribution of the failure rate follows certain known stochastic processes, such as the Poisson process, Hawkes process, and self-correcting process [51]. However, in practical scenarios, determining the appropriate form to use without sufficient prior knowledge can be challenging. Hence, various specifications for $\lambda(t)$ need to be attempted to fine-tune predictive performance, with the likelihood of encountering errors stemming from model misspecification. To address this limitation, the objective is to develop a general representation for predicting the unknown hazard function.

In the field of machine learning and deep learning, timely information is often represented using RNN (Recurrent Neural Network). RNN is a type of feed-forward neural network with recurrent connections, linking data observed at different time points. This setup allows the outputs of hidden units at one-time point to be used as inputs at the next time point. As a result, the same feed-forward neural network structure is repeated at each time point, with recurrent connections linking the hidden units of neighbouring time points. This setup facilitates the flow of information across time, as hidden units with recurrent connections receive input not only from

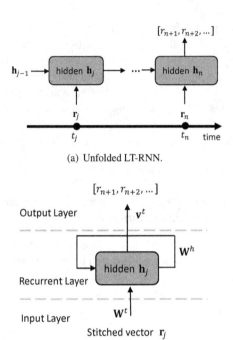

(a) Unfolded LT-RNN.

(b) Structure of LT-RNN.

Figure 6.5   Illustration of LT-RNN [108]

the current data but also from hidden units at the previous time point. This feedback mechanism enables the network to maintain an internal state and preserve the influence of each past data point.

While RNN is usually used for short-term prediction because the hidden states could change after a long time, designing long-term hazard functions for prediction utilising RNN is critical. Since some failure rates cannot be directly observed, it's logical to incorporate prior information from other groups. Hence, shared data, such as the same age observed in different years, can be combined into a unified vector and used as input for RNN. Specifically, depicted in Figure 6.5(a), for the event occurring at the time t_j with the stitched vector of failure rates $\mathbf{r}_j$, the pair $(t_j, \mathbf{r}_j)$ is fed as the input into an RNN unfolded up to the nth event. The embedding $\{\mathbf{h}_{j-1}\}$ represents the memory of the influence from the history of past failure rates. The neural network updates $\{\mathbf{h}_{j-1}\}$ to $\{\mathbf{h}_j\}$ by taking into account the effect of the current event $(t_j, \mathbf{r}_j)$.

Furthermore, 6.5(b) presents the overall structure of the proposed LT-RNN. Given a sequence of failure rates $S = \left((t_j, \mathbf{r}_j)_{j=1}^n \right)$, an RNN is designed to compute a sequence of hidden units $\{\mathbf{h}_j\}$ by iterating the following components.

For the timing input t_j, the associated stitched vector $\mathbf{r}_j$ is projected into a latent space by the weight matrix $\mathbf{W}^t$. We can learn $\mathbf{W}^t$ while we train the network.

The hidden vector is updated after receiving the current input and the memory $\{\mathbf{h}_{j-1}\}$ from the history. In RNN, current hidden units $\{\mathbf{h}_j\}$ can be obtained by using rectification (RELU) activation function

$$\mathbf{h}_j = \max(\mathbf{W}^t \mathbf{r}_j + \mathbf{W}^h \mathbf{h}_{j-1} + \mathbf{b}_h, 0) \tag{6.12}$$

where $\mathbf{W}^h$ is the weight matrix and $\mathbf{b}_h$ is the bias for hidden units.

Based on $\{\mathbf{h}_j\}$, the estimated hazard function can be formulated by

$$\lambda(t) = \exp\left(\mathbf{v}^{t^{\mathrm{T}}} \cdot \mathbf{h}_j + w^t(t - t_j) + b^t\right) \tag{6.13}$$

where $\mathbf{v}^t$ is a m-dimensional column vector, and w^t, b^t are scalars. Therefore, $\lambda(t)$ represents a m-dimensional output corresponding to $[r_{n+1}, r_{n+2}, \ldots r_{n+m-1}]$. Specifically, the first term $\mathbf{v}^{t^{\mathrm{T}}} \cdot \mathbf{h}_j$ represents the accumulative influence from the history. Compared to fixed parametric models, our approach offers a non-parametric function capturing dependencies over historical data. Additionally, the second term highlights the impact of the current timing t_j, while the third term incorporates a baseline failure level for future occurrences. Moreover, the exponential function serves as a nonlinear activation function, ensuring that the failure rate is positive.

6.3.5 CONFORMAL PREDICTION FOR NON-PARAMETRIC MODEL

6.3.5.1 Non-Parametric Conformal Prediction

While numerous studies have been conducted to predict water pipeline failures, several unresolved questions persist regarding the interplay of key factors contributing to pipe failures and their impact on the long-term lifespan of these pipes. This complexity is further compounded by variations in the specific environmental conditions in which the pipes are situated, such as weather conditions, soil composition, ground level, and pressure, as well as how each water utility manages pipe maintenance. Consequently, predicting water main breaks proves to be a formidable challenge due to their infrequent occurrence and the substantial costs associated with inspecting them, resulting in limited availability of historical data.

In the realm of predictive modelling, the concept of an uncertainty interval or confidence interval primarily relies on the probability distribution of predictions. This involves initially assuming and constructing a parametric probabilistic model, from which key parameters are subsequently inferred. The accuracy of this parametric modelling process hinges on the correctness of its underlying assumptions. If these assumptions are incorrect or incomplete, the model may fail to capture the full spectrum of factors at play. Additionally, it's worth noting that models can diverge when updated with new data, necessitating further design efforts and potentially introducing errors.

Alternatively, employing a non-parametric model allows the model to learn the necessary knowledge, particularly with regard to uncertainty in predictions. Non-parametric models require less design effort but capitalize on the complexity of the model itself, leading to greater flexibility. This flexibility enables the model to discern latent and intricate patterns within a high-dimensional input space, particularly when dealing with extensive datasets. In this case study, we introduce a non-parametric model, specifically the random forest algorithm, applied to the framework of conformal prediction for long-term supply water network failure prediction.

6.4   CASE STUDY ON WATER PIPE FAILURE PREDICTION WITH UNCERTAINTY

This research is focused on a comprehensive examination of water pipeline failures in three major cities. These cities collectively boast an extensive water network comprising approximately 500,000 pipelines. Notably, some of these pipelines have a rich history, with origins dating back to as early as 1890. It's worth highlighting that each water main consists of multiple pipes, each featuring various pipe nodes positioned at different ground levels.

The investigation into water pipe failures employs a rigorous analysis involving three primary metrics: failure rate, failure count, and the associated risk factor. These failure rates quantify the number of asset failures per 100 kilometres per year. What's intriguing is that the study reveals a dispersed distribution of elevated failure rates across regions rather than a concentration in specific areas. Additionally, the study delves into the occurrence of pipe breakages within the water main networks.

Across the entire study area, an average of 1500 pipe failures occur annually, resulting in significant disruptions to water supply and a wide range of property and environmental damages. Notably, the research identifies a growing trend in the breakage of critical pipes, with each water utility employing its unique methodology to assess pipe criticality based on associated risks for more than 20 years. The prediction error for the ensemble CHF is assessed using the training/testing split on the data. The model is then trained for a specific set of observation years, such as 2005–2010, and subsequently used to generate predictions for another set of observation years, e.g., 2011–2025 for the long future.

We use an innovative statistical inference technique to quantify prediction uncertainty in supervised learning ensembles [78]. This method leverages quantile regression forests within survival trees. Instead of merely recording the mean values of response variables in each tree leaf, we capture all observed responses within the leaf. This approach allows us to calculate predictions by considering both the mean of response variables and the full conditional distribution of response values for each input. The resulting distribution empowers us to construct prediction intervals for new instances by utilizing appropriate percentiles of the distribution.

These predictions are generated by recording observed responses within leaves, and conditional probability distributions of response variables are computed for given predictor variables for each pipe. These distributions are then used to establish prediction intervals for testing years, with lower and upper bounds of prediction uncertainty calculated based on appropriate percentiles of the distribution.

The distribution outlines various failure patterns, aiding water utilities in assessing the budget required for maintenance investments. By integrating the failure distribution with the associated consequence costs, Value at Risk (VaR) curves can be derived for each year. These curves illustrate the likelihood of consequences of failure exceeding predefined thresholds. Predictions may also consider maintenance budget allocations, indicating that an increased budget could lower the probability of failures. Consequently, users can observe how the distribution changes over time and whether the likelihood of severe consequences surpasses acceptable thresholds in the upcoming decade or any other specified period.

6.5 SUMMARY

Infrastructure development, which often extends over centuries, necessitates a thorough understanding of future risks, particularly in the upcoming decades or longer future. Accurate long-term forecasts play a critical role in providing indispensable insights to decision-makers, empowering them to make well-informed decisions and strategic plans.

Traditionally, forecasting methods heavily leaned on short-term predictions, assuming that future trends would mirror recent observations or existing patterns. However, the challenge of long-term forecasting lies in the requirement for more extensive data, which is frequently unavailable. Consequently, we discussed machine learning techniques to address the intricacies of long-term forecasting.

This chapter explores the intricacies of long-term prediction and presents effective strategies and machine-learning frameworks crafted to address these challenges directly. By analyzing key elements within the infrastructure sector, the document explores fundamental principles and frameworks essential for accurate forecasting. Moreover, it highlights machine learning models applicable to long-term prediction and demonstrates their practical value, such as forecasting failures in water supply networks using real-world instances.

In our discussion of techniques, we emphasized why machine learning models are suitable for long-term prediction by illustrating how these models can effectively organize data. These techniques mitigate data uncertainties and securely assign variable learning tasks to machine learning models, ensuring they capture the correct patterns for future long-term trends. We also explored methods to represent uncertainty to convey the risk and confidence associated with predictions.

Looking ahead, the long-term outlook for infrastructure planning is crucial. However, current predictions tend to be static, focusing solely on infrastructure changes without considering potential shifts in the surrounding environment. These environmental changes, such as climate change, could prompt the adoption of new policies that were previously unforeseen, altering predictions accordingly. We propose incorporating changes in the surrounding environment as input for predictions or periodically reassessing and refining models. In future iterations of the book, we plan to delve deeper into the possibilities presented by automated machine learning models in addressing such dynamic situations.

7 Service Demand Prediction – Passenger Flow

7.1 BACKGROUND

As urbanization accelerates globally, the Intelligent Transportation System (ITS) emerges as a key cyber-physical system in the development of smart cities [102, 45, 73, 131]. ITS, leveraging cutting-edge Internet of Things (IoT) technologies, generates a wealth of data, aiming to utilize this deeply analyzed information to enhance daily transportation. This includes but is not limited to managing traffic congestion, implementing automated road regulations, and orchestrating passenger flow [150, 9, 15]. Within the diverse components of ITS, the railway system stands out as a cornerstone of urban transport networks, attributable to its distinct features such as high dependability, cost efficiency, and environmental sustainability [193, 52].

In contemporary railway systems, a variety of advanced IoT devices are implemented to boost operational efficiency. These include smart card ticketing systems (SCTS), closed-circuit television (CCTV), and train load monitoring systems (TLMS), as illustrated in Figure 7.1 [175, 58, 88]. Particularly, SCTS not only tracks the number of passengers entering train stations, reflecting total footfall, but also offers a user-friendly entry process through Radio Frequency Identification technology [175]. CCTV networks enable train managers to monitor security and crowd dynamics, facilitating swift responses [38]. Meanwhile, TLMS, with its integrated sensors, provides critical train load information to controllers, enhancing their understanding of train capacity [58]. The integration of these IoT devices significantly bolsters the safety and efficiency of railway operations. However, challenges like platform overcrowding and emergency situations still impede the optimal functioning of metropolitan railway systems [97, 35].

Overcrowding typically results from suboptimal train scheduling and unforeseen events, such as special occurrences, train delays, and sudden incidents [181]. These situations not only elevate operational costs but also negatively impact the environment. For example, deploying additional trains to alleviate overcrowding leads to reduced occupancy rates, train congestion, and increased energy consumption. The railway platform, as a critical transit point, plays a vital role in passenger safety and experience [186]. Therefore, accurately assessing real-time crowdedness on platforms is imperative for creating flexible schedules and managing railway incidents [122]. Additionally, with urban expansion and the consequent surge in passenger

DOI: 10.1201/9781003473893-7

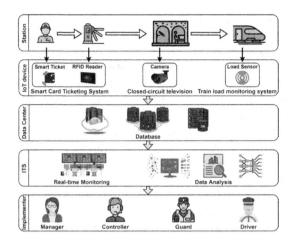

Figure 7.1   An illustration of modern railway systems with integrated IoT devices for passenger flow monitoring

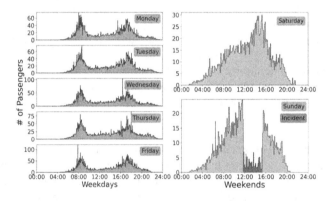

Figure 7.2   An example of daily passenger flow on a platform in the Greater Sydney Area on different days of the week. Weekdays and weekends have clearly different passenger flow patterns. A noticeable deviation from the normal flow pattern (highlighted in red) can be seen on Sunday, which differs from Saturday and is caused by a significant incident near the platform. This unusual observation illustrates how various real-world events can greatly affect passenger flows and underscores the need for our fine-tuning model to effectively handle such situations [103]

demand, coupled with the rapid growth of metropolitan railway networks, these challenges become more complex and pressing.

Extensive research is carried out in recent decades on forecasting passenger flow to enhance railway system operations. This issue is typically treated as a time series forecasting task, as passenger flows often exhibit strong repetitive patterns at identical locations (stations/platforms) and similar times, such as peak commuting hours on weekdays, as depicted in Figure 7.2. Initially, most studies focused on statistical or traditional regression models for future flow predictions [177, 50, 164]. While these methods are computationally fast, they fall short of the standards required for industrial applications in the real world.

The progressive implementation of sophisticated IoT devices and Advanced Train Management Systems (ATMS) in urban rail networks leads to a significant increase in traffic data [58, 96, 17]. Consequently, data-driven approaches, particularly deep learning techniques, gain prominence for their exceptional capabilities in time-series data analysis. Techniques like Recurrent Neural Networks (RNNs) and their variations show promise in predicting passenger flows [116, 118]. Additionally, the attention mechanism, known for its efficiency in pinpointing critical historical data for prediction tasks, is increasingly explored [171]. Its integration into research demonstrates superior prediction accuracy in large metropolitan rail networks [195, 72, 42]. However, most studies focus on forecasting at the station level, using data like inbound passenger numbers (from SCTS) or train boarding records (from TLMS). This approach overlooks the more nuanced needs of railway managers and controllers who are more concerned with platform-level flows. For example, Sydney Central station, with its 25 platforms, requires more specific flow information for effective planning and emergency response. Some researchers attempt to predict station-level flow and then use origin-destination (OD) matrices for platform-level estimates [100, 185]. Yet, estimating passenger interchanges, particularly during emergencies, remains a complex challenge.

While existing studies guide the way in data-driven passenger flow forecasting and demonstrated its potential in railway planning and management, there are significant hurdles in translating these theoretical models into practical, real-world applications:

- Lack of **fine-grained data**: For precise predictions, existing models depend heavily on detailed training data. Yet, in many older railway systems globally, only coarse-grained data is accessible from current IoT devices [13, 16]. This limitation hinders the development of intelligent urban infrastructure. For instance, the railway network in the Greater Sydney Area primarily provides only basic trip boarding records (from TLMS), which include past passenger boarding data. Particularly for smaller stations with infrequent train schedules, these models struggle to accurately track the dynamic flow changes in response to timetable modifications and unforeseen events.
- Lack of **considering delay and interchange**: In intricate railway networks, unexpected events and incidents can drastically affect platform congestion. A single delay can set off a domino effect, leading to further trip delays and altered passenger interchanges – a significant component of platform traffic. To date, no existing models in passenger flow prediction adequately account for both delays and the resultant interchange flows.
- Lack of **real-time predictive ability**: The primary objective of passenger flow forecasting is to assist railway managers and controllers with immediate decision-making. Therefore, the prediction techniques must operate in real-time, without delays. While modern deep learning methods excel in time series forecasting,

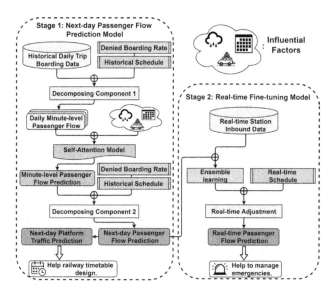

Figure 7.3 The overall framework of the proposed two-stage self-adaptive model [103]

their extensive computational time and the need for substantial data impede their applicability in live operational environments.

In our study, we introduce a novel dual-phase self-adaptive model aimed at overcoming these obstacles to enhance the intelligence of railway systems within ITS. The initial phase involves a unique data decomposition approach that transforms sparse boarding records into a continuous flow estimation. This stage takes into account factors such as the denied boarding rate and the pattern of passenger arrivals. Following this, the restructured data, along with the scheduled timetables and additional external factors, are processed through a self-attention mechanism to predict passenger flow at a minute-level for the following day. In the second phase, our model incorporates a real-time adjustment feature designed to adapt swiftly to emergency situations and short-term changes in passenger numbers. This phase specifically addresses delay propagation and interchange flow. The comprehensive structure of our proposed model is illustrated in Figure 7.3. The key contributions of our work can be summarized as follows:

- In this chapter, we introduce a two-phase self-adaptive model capable of delivering highly accurate, schedule-based daily passenger flow predictions through deep learning, as well as offering real-time adjustments in response to emergency situations and sudden fluctuations.
- We introduce an innovative approach for refining coarse-grained historical data from IoT sources, integrating influential factors and real-time boarding information for detailed daily and real-time forecasts. Our model effectively harnesses

Table 7.1

Summary of Frequent Abbreviations

Abbreviation	Full Name
ITS	Intelligent transportation system
IoT	Internet of Things
SCTS	Smart card ticketing systems
TLMS	Train load monitoring system
CCTV	Closed-circuit television
ATMS	Advanced Train Management System
RFID	Radio Frequency Identification

the data generated by IoT devices, uniquely incorporating a reallocation mechanism to account for delay propagation and passenger interchanges. This aspect is particularly beneficial for high-performance management in extensive railway networks.

- Beyond predicting overall passenger flow, our model extends to provide specific platform traffic forecasts. It considers various elements such as the scheduled timetable, denied boarding rates, interchanges, and real-time emergencies, offering valuable insights for train control and emergency management.

- The efficacy and superiority of our model are demonstrated through comparative analysis with other advanced baseline models. Its real-world application in the railway system of the Greater Sydney Area proves its worth. Our data-driven approach not only assists in precise schedule planning but also supports decision-making during emergencies and unexpected incidents. This contributes significantly to reducing operational expenses and energy consumption in the context of smart city development.

7.1.1   IoT TECHNOLOGIES IN RAILWAY SYSTEM OF SMART CITIES

The rapid advancement and implementation of IoT technology propel smart cities to the forefront of urban development, aiming to integrate physical and information-technology infrastructures to harness the collective intelligence of cities [74]. As a pivotal component of smart cities, Intelligent Transportation Systems (ITS) enhance transportation safety, mobility, and productivity by incorporating cutting-edge IoT technologies. In recent times, a diverse array of IoT devices specifically tailored for transportation systems emerges:

- Smart card ticketing systems: Traditional ticketing methods largely depended on manual processing, which is both labor-intensive and inefficient [28, 79]. The advent of smart cards, employing microchips and RFID technology, significantly mitigates these issues [175]. These cards enable passengers to effortlessly tap in and out at gates and handle payments online, enhancing convenience and reducing bottlenecks [21]. While this system efficiently collects data on station-level passenger flow for the Advanced Train Management Systems (ATMS), it does not provide specific insights into platform-level traffic.

- Closed-circuit television: CCTV allows railway managers to observe real-time passenger conditions [130, 167, 139]. For instance, crowd flows captured by CCTV cameras can be transmitted to control centres, providing direct insights into platform congestion and potential emergencies. Researchers even employ Gaussian processes to forecast pedestrian flows using this data [88, 10]. However, CCTV struggles with accuracy during high congestion and doesn't track the actual number of passengers boarding trains. In this chapter, CCTV data aids in preliminary analyses of platform traffic and distribution. For instance, object detection applied to CCTV footage assists in developing an initial Origin-Destination (OD) matrix. When combined with data from the Train Load Monitoring System (TLMS), which more accurately reflects platform-level passenger flow, a more precise OD matrix is formed. It is important to note that if comprehensive TLMS data is available for all operational train models, the reliance on CCTV data can be reduced.

- Train load monitoring system: Train load is a critical aspect of railway operations, particularly during peak hours in high-traffic areas [58]. Advanced IoT weight sensors gather real-time train load data, which is then relayed to the ATMS, allowing managers to make informed decisions about train scheduling adjustments, such as increasing or decreasing train frequencies [191, 172, 81]. Notably, the train load data can also serve as an indicator of platform-level passenger volumes.

Despite the rapidly increasing volume of data gathered by these IoT sensors, integrating diverse data streams and synthesizing them into a coherent data analysis model remains a formidable challenge. Such a model is essential for train managers and controllers to gain a comprehensive understanding of real-time traffic conditions throughout the network. A critical aspect of these traffic conditions is the passenger flow at the platform level.

7.1.2 PASSENGER FLOW PREDICTION IN ITS

In ITS railway systems, precise forecasting of passenger flow is crucial for everyday operations. The predictability of passenger flow is largely ensured due to the regular patterns in commuters' behaviour. This subject is the focus of researchers for many years, with studies generally falling into two categories: predictions at the station level and at the platform level.

- Station-level passenger flow prediction: This chapter aims at forecasting incoming passenger numbers at stations over specific periods. Utilizing Smart Card Ticketing Systems (SCTS), it becomes feasible to obtain detailed station-level data. This data can then be fed into various time series models, such as Historical Average [177], ARIMA [50], or RNNs [116], to generate reliable predictions. While these station-level forecasts can indicate overall station density, they often over-look the fact that a station comprises multiple platforms, and that passengers are distributed across these platforms.

- Platform-level passenger flow prediction: This study centres on determining the precise number of passengers on a specific platform [194]. Given the stable na-ture of trips between two stations and the advantages of smart card ticketing sys-tems, it is possible to infer the platforms used by passengers based on their en-try and exit data, leading to the creation of an Origin-Destination (OD) Matrix [100, 185]. Current approaches typically involve making station-level forecasts first and then applying the OD matrix to distribute passengers across various plat-forms. Nonetheless, this method often overlooks the dynamics of passenger trans-fers and potential train delays.

7.2 PRELIMINARIES

Forecasting Passenger Flow is a quintessential task in time series analysis, op-erating under the premise that future travel patterns of passengers can be anticipated from their past travel history. This assumption allows us to decode the hidden trends in historical data and examine their time-based dependencies to predict future pas-senger densities for a specific Platform i over the next N time units. This can be represented mathematically as:

$$\widehat{J}_i = \left\{ \widehat{X_i^{t+1}}, \widehat{X_i^{t+2}}, \cdots, \widehat{X_i^{t+N}} \mid H_i, F_i \right\} \tag{7.1}$$

Here, $H_i = X_i^{t-M+1}, X_i^{t-M+2}, \cdots, X_i^t$ symbolizes the last M time units of continuous passenger flow data[1], and F_i denotes a set of additional factors influencing the flow at Platform i. This chapter incorporates various elements that could sway passen-ger behaviour, like severe weather, holidays, school days, and distinctions between weekdays and weekends. Our focus is divided into two temporal scopes: next-day (long-term) and real-time (short-term) predictions. Next-day forecasts aim to pre-dict passenger flow for each minute of the following day (equating to 1440 minutes or time steps per service day), while real-time predictions target the forthcoming 15/20/30 minutes.

Coarse-grained data *vs* **fine-grained data**: "Coarse-grained" data refers to infor-mation that is collected sporadically and without a consistent pattern, in contrast to "fine-grained" data, which is gathered systematically and regularly. In the con-text of this chapter, coarse-grained data specifically pertains to trip boarding data, which tracks the number of passengers boarding at a given platform, as recorded by the Train Load Monitoring System (TLMS). This data is considered coarse-grained because the interval between services[2] varies across different times (such as peak

---

[1] In this study, passenger flow is measured in minute intervals to ensure up-to-date insights on platform conditions.

[2] **Service gap** refers to the interval between the arrivals of two successive trips at a specific platform, indicating the longest potential waiting time for passengers.

and off-peak hours) and locations. Such data doesn't effectively capture the dynamic changes in passenger flow that occur due to timetable adjustments and emergency situations. To address this and achieve precise predictions in complex scenarios, our study delves into the correlation between trip boarding records and passenger entry patterns. We formulate a behaviour-based data decomposition component that reallocates coarse-grained boarding data into a fine-grained, minute-by-minute passenger flow estimation. Further details on this process will be elaborated in the subsequent sections.

Platform traffic indicates the number of passengers on Platform i at a given time point t. It consists of inbound and interchanged passengers, which is influenced by the train timetable on the platform and the denied boarding rate. The platform traffic can reflect the degree of crowdedness on platforms, which has practical significance for train control management and emergency response.

Denied boarding rate is defined as the count of passengers present on Platform i at a specific time t. This figure is a combination of both incoming and transferring passengers. It is affected by factors such as the train schedule for that platform, and the rate of passengers denied boarding. The measurement of platform traffic is a key indicator of how crowded the platform is, providing valuable insights for the effective management of train operations and responding to emergencies.

Passenger flow relative independence refers to the concept that a certain percentage of inbound passengers' behaviours remain unaffected by emergencies or sudden alterations. It is important to note, however, that this assumption does not apply to the flow of transferring passengers.

The concept of Relative Independence in Passenger Flow implies that passengers typically do not react significantly to immediate changes. This insight guides us in creating a two-stage model. In this model, the long-term passenger flow prediction retains considerable accuracy even for short-term forecasting, requiring only minor adjustments. These adjustments are based on the real-time number of accumulated passengers and the flow of interchanging passengers, in accordance with the current train schedule. The comprehensive structure of this model is depicted in Figure 7.3.

7.3 STAGE 1: NEXT-DAY PASSENGER FLOW PREDICTION MODEL

The objective of the daily passenger flow prediction model is to identify and learn from long-term trends in historical passenger data. The next-day predictions generated by this model serve a dual purpose: they act as a foundational layer for real-time adjustments in the second stage and also supply critical data for long-term schedule planning. The primary challenge in this stage lies in effectively harnessing the coarse-grained trip-boarding data from the Train Load Monitoring System for the learning algorithm. To address this, we develop two key components. The first component converts the coarse, discrete boarding records into smoothed, minute-by-minute passenger flow distributions, readying them for input into our prediction model. The second component refines the prediction outputs by incorporating a bimodal distribution and accounting for transferring passengers, thus enhancing the precision of our continuous, fine-grained passenger flow estimates. For the

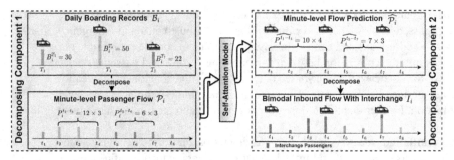

Figure 7.4 The workflow of two decomposing components. DC1 processes data before prediction and DC2 reallocates prediction results based on the scheduled timetable. In DC1, historical daily boarding records $\mathcal{B}_i$ for a given platform i are decomposed into minute-level passenger flow $\mathcal{P}_i$ by recalculating actual arrival passengers and allocating them according to a uniform distribution. In DC2, after obtaining next-day minute-level flow predictions $\widehat{\mathcal{P}_i}$ using the self-attention model, we reallocate prediction results under bi-modal flow estimation and the consideration of interchanged passengers to obtain accurate minute-level inbound flow I_i

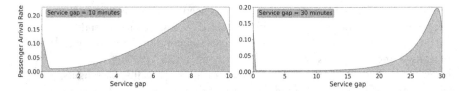

Figure 7.5 Passenger arrival distributions for different service gaps: The x-axis represents time, and the y-axis represents the arrival rate. In both subgraphs, the left peak of the passenger arrival rate corresponds to passengers who missed the previous train, while the right peak represents a dense stream of passengers arriving on the platform near the arrival time of the next train

prediction model itself, we utilize a self-attention mechanism to capture long-term patterns in time series data. Additionally, we estimate the cumulative number of passengers by considering both the predicted flow and the existing train schedule. The complete structure of Stage 1 of our model is illustrated in the left portion of Figure 7.3.

7.3.1   DECOMPOSING COMPONENT FOR MODEL INPUTS (DC$_1$)

Optimizing the use of coarse-grained boarding data from the Train Load Monitoring System (TLMS) for recognizing passenger flow patterns necessitates converting this sporadic data into a continuous format suitable for model inputs. Observations from real-world scenarios indicate that passenger numbers typically peak around the times of train arrivals and departures, creating a bimodal distribution pattern between successive trips, as depicted in Figure 7.5. The shape of this distribution is influenced by factors like the number of passengers, the interval between services, the time of day, and the specific location. These varying distribution shapes can lead to significant data variability, potentially disrupting the learning process for the model. To address this, we craft two distinct data decomposition methods, as illustrated in Figure 7.4: DC_1 aims to generate detailed, minute-level historical passenger flow data for each service gap from the boarding records, while DC_2 creates a bimodal distribution based on the predictions from the model. This approach ensures that the learning process of our prediction model is not adversely affected by data variability while also aligning the outputs from the model with real-world conditions. In this section, we focus on introducing DC_1, and the specifics of DC_2 will be discussed in Section 7.3.4.

Load sensors facilitate the collection of trip boarding data through the Train Load Monitoring System (TLMS), which logs the number of passengers boarding a trip at any given platform, denoted as: $\mathscr{B}_i = \{B_i^{T_1}, B_i^{T_2}, B_i^{T_3}, \cdots\}$.

The term B_i^T is used to signify the quantity of passengers boarding at Platform i at a specific time T. In practical scenarios, it is evident that not every passenger on the platform will manage to board the incoming train, owing to factors like the rate of denied boarding. Consequently, we can establish a mathematical relationship that correlates the cumulative passenger flow during service intervals with the trip boarding data recorded:

$$B_i^{T_k} = (1 - \rho_i^{T_k}) \left\{ I_i^{[T_{k-1}, T_k]} + \rho_i^{T_{k-1}} \left[I_i^{[T_{k-2}, T_{k-1}]} + \rho_i^{T_{k-2}} (I_i^{[T_{k-3}, T_{k-2}]} + \ldots) \right] \right\} \quad (7.2)$$

In this context, $I_i^{[T_1, T_2]}$ denotes the total number of passengers arriving between times T_1 and T_2, which represents the service gap. Meanwhile, ρ_i^T refers to the rate of passengers who are denied boarding at the arrival time of a train, T. Equation 2 employs the inverse chain rule for determining the aggregated number of passengers arriving within a specific service gap, factoring out those who did not board previous trains. For the sake of simplicity and to optimize computational resources, the calculation typically accounts for the passengers missing only the last two trains, as it is commonly observed that most passengers miss no more than two consecutive trips. Following this approach, we obtain:

$$B_i^{T_k} = (1 - \rho_i^{T_k}) \left[I_i^{[T_{k-1}, T_k]} + \rho_i^{T_{k-1}} (I_i^{[T_{k-2}, T_{k-1}]} + \rho_i^{T_{k-2}} I_i^{[T_{k-3}, T_{k-2}]}) \right] \quad (7.3)$$

Given the data on trip boarding and the rates of denied boarding, we can compute the cumulative passenger flow for each service gap using the reverse chain rule. This allows us to extrapolate passenger flow at the minute level from the aggregated data. As mentioned earlier, smoother input data significantly enhances the efficacy of the prediction learning process compared to data with high variability. To achieve this smoothness, we operate under the assumption that passenger flows within any service gap adhere to uniform distributions. Consequently, the calculation for estimating minute-level passenger flow, which will serve as input for the model, can be conducted as follows:

$$P_i^t = I_i^{[T_1, T_2]} / (T_2 - T_1) \quad (7.4)$$

As defined earlier in Section 7.2, P_i^t represents a form of fine-grained data. This estimation of passenger flow at a minute-level offers consistent and even data samples, effectively preserving information that might be lost in the less frequent and more erratic coarse-grained data (such as trip boarding records). Our empirical research indicates that these predetermined fine-grained inputs substantially improve the overall predictive accuracy of the model.

Though utilizing DC_1, we can transfer the coarse-grained trip boarding records on all platforms $\mathscr{B}_i = \{B_i^{T_1}, B_i^{T_2}, B_i^{T_3}, \cdots, B_i^{T_m}\}$ into a series of fine-grained minute-level passenger flow records $\mathscr{P}_i = \{P_i^{t_1}, P_i^{t_2}, P_i^{t_3}, \cdots, P_i^{t_n}\}$, where $n \gg m$.

7.3.2 INFLUENTIAL FACTORS

In addition to historical data on passenger numbers, we identified other key elements influencing passenger flow forecasts. After extensive testing of various potential factors, we selected the three most impactful ones. These factors, along with the minute-level passenger flow data, form the comprehensive input for our next-day predictions from the model: (1) **Weekday/Weekend**: This factor acknowledges the distinct and recurrent daily patterns differing between weekdays and weekends (as exemplified in Figure 7.2). Typical patterns include morning and evening rush hours on weekdays due to work and school commutes, contrasted with a single peak in the afternoon during weekends. (2) **Weather (Rainfall and Temperature)**: Adverse weather conditions, such as heavy rainfall or extreme temperatures, can drastically alter passenger behaviour. For example, passengers may avoid using railways and prefer other transportation modes like taxis during heavy rain. In our study, specific thresholds (e.g., 20 mm of rainfall and temperatures reaching 35°C) are set to denote extreme weather conditions. (3) **School Days/Public Holidays**: The commuting patterns of students significantly contribute to weekday passenger flow. A marked reduction in flow is often seen during school holidays. Public holidays similarly affect passenger flow, mirroring the trend seen during school vacations.

7.3.3 SELF-ATTENTION-BASED PREDICTION COMPONENT

Deep learning methodologies demonstrate remarkable success in tackling time-series forecasting challenges, particularly neural networks, due to their inherent capability to discern underlying patterns in time-series data, often without explicit domain-specific knowledge [111]. In our research, we utilize an encoder-decoder structure combined with a self-attention mechanism for forecasting passenger flow, as illustrated in Figures 7.3 and 7.6. This encoder-decoder framework is specifically tailored for sequential data processing. In essence, the encoder processes the input sequence and transmits this encoded information to the decoder. The decoder then utilizes this encoded data to generate the predicted output. The self-attention component is crucial as it discerns varying degrees of relevance among different pieces of input data, thereby enhancing the accuracy of time-series predictions. This is particularly effective in our context, where passenger behaviour is influenced by multiple factors [171].

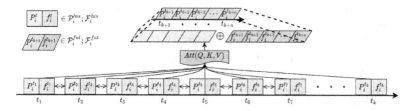

Figure 7.6 An illustration of the proposed self-attention layer

After the data processing in DC_1, we can obtain the fine-grained historical passenger records can $\mathscr{P}_i^{his} = \{P_i^{t1}, P_i^{t2}, P_i^{t3}, \cdots, P_i^{tk}\}$ and influential factors $\mathscr{F}_i = \mathscr{F}_i^{his} + \mathscr{F}_i^{fut} = \{f_i^{t1}, f_i^{t2}, f_i^{t3}, \cdots, f_i^{tk}, \cdots, f_i^{tn}\}^3$, thus we tend to predict the future flow $\mathscr{P}_i^{fut} = \{P_i^{tk+1}, P_i^{tk+2}, P_i^{tk+3}, \cdots, P_i^{tn}\}$.

In the framework of the self-attention mechanism, the core process involves determining correlations using the Query (Q), Key (K), and Value (V) matrices. These matrices are computed as follows:

$$Q = H_l \cdot W^Q; \ K = H_l \cdot W^K; \ V = H_l \cdot W^V \tag{7.5}$$

where H_l represents the input for the l layer of the self-attention module, with the initial input being $H_0 = \mathscr{P}_i^{in} \oplus \mathscr{F}_i^{his}$. The matrix W signifies the weights, which are adjustable throughout the training phase. As an example, considering one particular input flow, the correlation between the historical passenger flow and other influential factors can be ascertained. This is achieved by initially computing the similarity between the Query of the input vector and the Key of other input vectors to determine the weights. Subsequently, a weighted average of the Values, inclusive of the vector itself, is calculated to derive the attention score. This process unfolds as follows:

$$\text{Att}(Q, K, V) = \text{softmax}\left(\frac{Q \cdot K^T}{\sqrt{d_k}}\right) \cdot V \tag{7.6}$$

where $\sqrt{d_k}$ donates to the scaling vector that can be used to reduce the dimension of the attention mechanism. By introducing the future influential factors, the final output of the prediction module is:

$$O = \mathbf{FC}(\text{Att}(Q, K, V) \oplus \mathscr{F}_i^{fut}) \tag{7.7}$$

The term $\mathbf{FC}(\cdot)$ denotes a fully connected layer, which plays a crucial role in amalgamating the predictive outputs from the self-attention layer with upcoming

---

[3]The future weather information can be obtained from weather forecast resources.

influential factors, thereby producing the final forecast. This integration is instrumental in capturing pertinent influential factors, thereby refining the predictive accuracy of the model, as illustrated in Figure 7.6. Additionally, our model incorporates a multi-head self-attention strategy within the encoder-decoder framework, as depicted in Figure 7.3. This approach is particularly effective in sifting through the data to eliminate irrelevant noise and pinpoint crucial information, thereby enhancing the learning efficiency of the model.

7.3.4 DECOMPOSING COMPONENT FOR PASSENGER FLOW REALLOCATION (DC$_2$)

A common trait of data-driven models is their tendency to generate predictions that average out the recurring patterns observed in historical data. In our approach to transform discrete trip records into minute-by-minute passenger flow estimations, we postulate that the flow of passengers during any service gap follows a uniform distribution, as outlined in DC$_1$. Consequently, the outputs of our model tend to smooth the results over short intervals. Moreover, during the prediction phase, the model does not differentiate between interchange passenger flow and inbound passenger flow. As previously discussed in Section 7.3.1, inbound passenger flow typically peaks around train arrivals and departures, leading to a bimodal distribution pattern across successive trips. On the other hand, the peak in interchange passenger flow is largely dependent on the arrival times of transfer trips at the same station. To more accurately gauge the actual passenger numbers during any given service gap, we develop DC$_2$. This component accounts for both the bimodal nature of inbound passenger flow and the interchange passenger flow, as depicted in Figure 7.4.

Bimodal Inbound Flow Estimation

Train schedules on platforms are typically set in a consistent manner, aiding passengers in organizing their daily commutes. In practical scenarios, passengers prefer to arrive at the platform shortly before the scheduled arrival of the train, aiming to minimize wait times (a concept related to Passenger Flow Relative Independence). Consequently, a larger number of inbound passengers tend to gather on the platform at the time of the arrival approaches the next train. However, there are instances where passengers are unable to board due to reasons like insufficient buffer time or early train arrivals. Luethi et al. investigate this behaviour and discover that inbound passenger flows consistently conform to the Johnson S_B distribution within any service gap [124]. The probability distribution of passenger flow is influenced by factors such as the length of the service gap and the passengers' familiarity with the schedule. This relationship can be expressed as follows:

$$f_{sd}(t) = \begin{cases} \dfrac{\alpha_2(b-a)}{(t+b-\delta_{sd}-a)(\delta_{sd}-t)\sqrt{2\pi}}e^{f_1} & \text{if } a < t < \delta_{sd} \\ \dfrac{\alpha_2(b-a)}{(t-\delta_{sd}-a)(b+\delta_{sd}-t)\sqrt{2\pi}}e^{f_2} & \text{if } \delta_{sd} < t < b \\ 0 & \text{otherwise} \end{cases}$$

$$f_1 = -0.5\left\{\alpha_1 + \alpha_2 \ln\left(\frac{t+b-\delta_{sd}-a}{\delta_{sd}-t}\right)\right\}$$

$$f_2 = -0.5\left\{\alpha_1 + \alpha_2 \ln\left(\frac{t-\delta_{sd}-a}{b+\delta_{sd}-t}\right)\right\}$$

(7.8)

where α_1 and α_2 are parameters shaping the distributions, which are derived from the historical data of the specific platform in question; a and b represent the time intervals between two successive trains; and t is a specific time point within these intervals. Furthermore, the degree to which passengers are accustomed to the timetable, which may vary especially in cases of special events such as delays, is factored in by δ_{sd}, a parameter adjusting the distribution based on schedule-dependency and train headways. Therefore, the overall distribution of passenger arrivals can be understood as a combination of two different passenger groups, described as follows:

$$f_a(t, \alpha_1, \alpha_2) = r_{sd} \cdot f_{si} + r_{si} \cdot f_{sd(a,b,\alpha_1,\alpha_2)}$$

(7.9)

where r_{sd} and r_{si} represent the proportions of passengers who are dependent on the schedule and those who are independent of it, respectively. It is important to note that even within the same station, the rates of r_{sd} and r_{si} may vary across different platforms due to the distinct characteristics of the services they offer. For instance, platforms serving business districts typically have a higher proportion of schedule-dependent commuters, whereas those leading to recreational areas may see a lower rate. These rates can be deduced from historical data analysis. Therefore, when we have the cumulative inbound passenger count for a service gap, the Johnson S_B distribution can be applied to accurately estimate a bimodal distribution of passenger flow.

Interchange Passenger Reallocation

In metropolitan cities, complex railway systems often feature several interchange platforms. These platforms are crucial for passengers needing to transfer to reach their destinations where direct trains are unavailable. The flow of interchange passengers forms a significant part of the total passenger movement, and this flow is largely influenced by the timings of arrivals at these interchange platforms. To calculate the probable number of interchange passengers, we utilize interchange rates applicable to different platform pairs. The symbol r_{ij} denotes the rate of passenger transfer from Platform i to Platform j during a specific period. This rate varies depending on the time of day and is determined based on historical data analyses.

As the outputs of the prediction model contain both the inbound passengers and the interchanged passengers, we need to split the predicted flow into two corresponding parts. To be clear, given the predicted flow at Platform i in service gap $[t_m, t_n]$ as

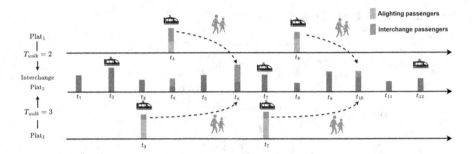

Figure 7.7 An example of interchange passenger flow reallocation. Given a train arriving at Platform Plat$_1$ at time point t_4, the yellow bar refers to passengers who exit the station while the green bar represents interchanged passengers who proceed to the interchange platform Plat$_1$. After a 2-minute walk from Plat$_1$ to Plat$_2$, the interchanged passengers arrive at Plat$_2$ at time point t_6, resulting in an increase in the accumulative number of passengers on Plat$_2$ at t_6. Similarly, when a train arrives at Platform Plat$_3$ at t_3, interchanged passengers spend 3 minutes walking to Plat$_2$ and accumulate at the interchange platform at time point t_6 as well [103]

$\mathscr{P}_i^{fut} = \{P_i^{t_{m+1}}, P_i^{t_{m+2}}, P_i^{t_{m+3}}, \cdots, P_i^{t_n}\}$, the accumulated passenger flow of this service gap is defined as:

$$I_i^{[t_m,t_n]} = \sum_{k=1}^{n-m+1} P_i^{m+k}$$

$$= I_{i(\text{Inbound})}^{[t_m,t_n]} + I_{i(\text{Interchange})}^{[t_m,t_n]} \qquad (7.10)$$

If the interchange rates of all transfer trips to Platform i are $\{r_{1 \cdot i}, r_{2 \cdot i}, r_{3 \cdot i}, \cdots, r_{u \cdot i}\}$, the two different passenger flow can be calculated as,

$$I_{i(\text{Inbound})}^{[t_m,t_n]} = \left(1 - \sum_{j=1}^{u} r_{j \cdot i}\right) \times I_i^{[t_m,t_n]} \qquad (7.11)$$

$$I_{j \cdot i(\text{Interchange})}^{[t_m,t_n]} = r_{j \cdot i} \times I_i^{[t_m,t_n]};$$

$$I_{i(\text{Interchange})}^{[t_m,t_n]} = \sum_{j=1}^{u} I_{j \cdot i(\text{Interchange})}^{[t_m,t_n]} \qquad (7.12)$$

$I_{j \cdot i(\text{Interchange})}^{[t_m,t_n]}$ is adopted in the bimodal inbound flow estimation in Section 7.3.4, while the interchange passenger flow from Platform j to Platform i, $I_{j \cdot i(\text{Interchange})}^{[t_m,t_n]}$, is predicted to arrive Platform i at time point $T_j + T_{\text{walk}}$, where T_j is the planned train arrival time at Platform j and T_{walk} is the walking time from Platform j to Platform i which can be collected from ATMS. Figure 7.7 shows the demonstration of the interchanged passengers.

By combining the bimodal inbound flow estimation with the reallocation of interchange passengers, we arrive at the final predicted minute-level passenger flow, which encompasses both inbound and interchange passenger movements, as depicted in Figure 7.7.

As previously mentioned, understanding the volume of passengers is crucial for effective railway operation management and responding to emergencies. Consequently, the cumulative number of passengers for a particular platform i at a given time T_k can be determined based on the train schedule and the rate of denied boarding using a forward chain rule calculation:

$$C_i^T = I_i^{[T_{k-1}, T_k]} + \rho_i^{T_{k-1}} (I_i^{[T_{k-2}, T_{k-1}]} + \rho_i^{T_{k-2}} I_i^{[T_{k-3}, T_{k-2}]}) \qquad (7.13)$$

Here we select the platform P_i to demonstrate the workflow of the stage 1 model in Algorithm 2.

Algorithm 2: Workflow of Next-day Passenger Flow Prediction Model

---

Input: Historical passenger boarding records $\mathcal{B}_i$ from TLMS.

Output: Next-day passenger flow prediction I_i (minute-level); platform
traffic prediction C_i (minute-level).

1 Historical minute-level (fine-grained) data acquisition: $\mathcal{P}_i^{his} \leftarrow \mathcal{B}_i$ by Eq.
7.2 – 7.4;

2 **if** n # day data is missing **then**

3 $\quad \lfloor$ Fill with historical average passenger flow $\overline{\mathcal{P}_i^{his}}$;

4 Predict next-day passenger flow with attention model:
$\mathcal{P}_i^{fut} \leftarrow \mathcal{P}_i^{his} \oplus \mathcal{F}_i^{his}; \mathcal{F}_i^{fut}$ by Eq. 7.5 – 7.7;

5 Estimate bimodal inbound flow: $\mathcal{P}_i^{fut}$ by Eq. 7.8 – 7.9;

6 Reallocate the interchanged passenger from platform P_j:
$I_i \leftarrow I_{i(\text{Inbound})}; I_{j \cdot i(\text{Interchange})}$ by Eq. 7.10 – 7.12;

7 Obtain next-day platform traffic C_i by Eq. 7.13.

7.4 STAGE 2: REAL-TIME FINE-TUNING MODEL

Predictions of next-day minute-level passenger flow and platform traffic offer valuable foresight for crafting train schedules with a customer-centric approach. However, these predictions may not accurately capture the immediate conditions on platforms during unforeseen emergencies or sudden changes in timetables. Relying on the concept of passenger flow relative independence, we note that inbound passenger flow typically remains unaffected by short-term disruptions. Consequently, next-day forecasts of inbound flow maintain a high degree of relevance and accuracy, serving as a foundational reference in the stage of real-time fine-tuning. Our analysis of railway operation records during emergency situations or temporary schedule alterations reveals that these incidents primarily impact the timing of interchange passenger arrivals and the overall volume of passengers. In response, our second stage of modelling involves adjusting these two aspects to align with real-time occurrences. Additionally, we develop a rapid short-term fine-tuning mechanism. This module swiftly adjusts predictions for an upcoming short-term window (next 15/20/30 minutes) based on the recently concluded short-term periods (previous few trips). This

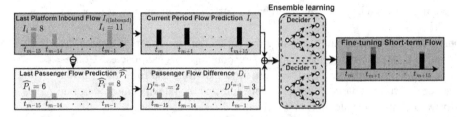

Figure 7.8 The workflow of fast short-term fine-tuning module, fine-tuning short-term flow refers to updating real-time platform flow. Firstly, we calculate the difference D_i between the actual and the predicted passenger flow on Platform i for the recently passed time period. Next, this difference and the current period flow prediction will be input into ensemble learning models to fine-tune and obtain an updated short-term flow prediction [103]

approach is motivated by the observed strong correlation between passenger numbers in successive short-term intervals.

7.4.1 FAST SHORT-TERM FINE-TUNING

In order to respond effectively to short-term fluctuations in passenger flow and bolster our real-time prediction capabilities, we propose a rapid short-term fine-tuning method, outlined in Figure 7.8. Through an analysis of historical operational data, we uncover a strong potential relationship between passenger volumes in adjacent short-term time periods. For instance, higher passenger boarding during the previous trip may lead to lower passenger volumes on the subsequent trip, as observed in historical data for similar time periods. In this stage, we leverage a segment of the next-day prediction results specifically tailored for short-term intervals as input for fine-tuning. Specifically, in the target time period $[t, t+M]$, the short-term predicted passenger flow on Platform i is $\mathscr{P}_i^{[t,t+M]} = \{\widehat{P_i^t}, \widehat{P_i^{t+1}}, \widehat{P_i^{t+2}}, \cdots, \widehat{P_i^{t+M}}\}$ and the predicted passenger flow for "just-passed" time period is $\mathscr{P}_i^{[t-M,t-1]} = \{\widehat{P_i^{t-M}}, \widehat{P_i^{t-M+1}}, \widehat{P_i^{t-M+2}}, \cdots, \widehat{P_i^{t-1}}\}$ extracted from next-day prediction $\mathscr{P}_i^{fut}$.

In Stage 2, we collect real-time inbound station data from the smart card ticketing system to ensure timely accuracy. Nevertheless, as most train stations comprise multiple platforms, accurately tracking passenger numbers on each platform can be challenging. Consequently, we rely on historical boarding records to estimate the distribution of inbound passengers among different platforms using the following approach:

$$\mathbf{p}_i^{[t-M,t-1]} = \mathscr{P}_i^{[t-M,t-1]} \Big/ \sum_{k=1}^{n} \mathscr{P}_k^{[t-M,t-1]} \tag{7.14}$$

where $\mathbf{p}_i^{[t-M,t-1]}$ refers to percentage of inbound passengers to platform i in the time period $[t-M, t-1]$, and n means the number of platforms in the station. Thus,

---

Algorithm 3: Workflow of Real-time Fine-tuning Model

Input: Next-day passenger flow prediction $\widehat{\mathscr{P}_i^{fut}}$; Real-time SCTS operation records $I_{(SCTS)}$.

Output: Short-term Fine-tuning passenger flow C_i (minute-level).

1 Acquire the real-time passenger flow to the platform $I_{i(\text{Inbound})} \leftarrow I_{(SCTS)}$ by Eq. 7.14 – 7.15;

2 Calculate the difference between real-time passenger flow and boarding records prediction: D_i by Eq. 7.16;

3 Fine-tune current short-term flow prediction with RF: $\mathscr{P}_i' \leftarrow \mathscr{P}_i^{fut} \oplus D_i$ by Eq. 7.17;

4 Update the real-time platform traffic prediction: C_i by Eq. 7.18 – 7.19.

---

the estimated real-time passenger numbers on platform i in the "just-passed" time period can be acquired as:

$$I_{i(\text{Inbound})}^{[t-M,t-1]} = I_{(SCTS)}^{[t-M,t-1]} \times \mathbf{p}_i^{[t-M,t-1]} \tag{7.15}$$

where $I_{(SCTS)}^{[t-M,t-1]}$ means the station-level real-time inbound records collected from SCTS. After acquiring the real-time passenger flow to the platform, it is worth noting the passengers who arrive at the platform may not boarding on the train and accumulate on the platform due to the denied boarding rates and missing trains. Therefore, we can obtain the difference between the actual and the predicted passenger flow on the platform of the "just-passed" time period:

$$D_i^{[t-M,t-1]} = I_{i(\text{Inbound})}^{[t-M,t-1]} - \widehat{\mathscr{P}_i^{[t-M,t-1]}} \tag{7.16}$$

$D_i^{[t-M,t-1]}$ and $\widehat{\mathscr{P}_i^{[t,t+M]}}$ are then concatenated and fed into the fine-tuning model for short-term prediction adjustment. Here, we choose an ensemble learning method, which is the Random Forest (RF) model as our fast fine-tuning model due to its high computing efficiency and multi-stream precision which are suitable for online tasks [110],

$$\mathscr{P}_i'^{[t,t+M]} = \mathbf{RF}([D_i^{t-M}, D_i^{t-M+1}, \cdots, D_i^{t-1}] \oplus \widehat{\mathscr{P}_i^{[t,t+M]}}) \tag{7.17}$$

7.4.2 REAL-TIME ADJUSTMENT FOR INTERCHANGE AND PLATFORM TRAFFIC

When emergencies or train schedule changes occur, the interchanged passengers will be influenced which causes differences between the next-day prediction. Thus, we can adjust the interchange and accumulated passenger flow with the same methodology presented in Section 7.3 based on the updated train schedule. For example, if the arrival time of one trip at Platform j will delay M minutes, the interchange

Figure 7.9 The railway network in Greater Sydney Areas. Red points refer to the railway stations

passenger flow from Platforms j to i is recalculated from Equation 7.12 as:

$$I_{j \cdot i (\text{Interchange})}^{[t_m, t_n + M]} = r_{j \cdot i} \times I_i^{[t_m, t_n + M]} \tag{7.18}$$

and the corresponding accumulative passenger flow on Platform j with the rescheduled arrival time of the trip is recalculated from Equation 7.13 as,

$$C_i^T = I_i^{[T_{k-1}, T_k + M]} + \rho_i^{T_{k-1}} I_i^{[T_{k-2}, T_{k-1}]} + \rho_i^{T_{k-2}} I_i^{[T_{k-3}, T_{k-2}]} \tag{7.19}$$

Note that we only consider the near future timetable changes in Stage 2 for short-term prediction, which means only a few future trips are involved in the recalculation process. The changes for the future will be handled when they fall within our target time window. This measurement keeps our real-time model efficient without any loss of accuracy. Similarly, the workflow of the real-time fine-tuning model is shown in Algorithm 3.

7.5 CASE STUDY

Our two-stage self-adaptive model is implemented in a real-world metropolitan railway system, specifically, the Australian NSW network, which operates within the Greater Sydney Area in Australia. This extensive railway network spans over 1,617 kilometers of track, encompasses 175 stations across nine lines, and serves a staggering 377.1 million passengers annually. The intricate nature of this railway system means that the performance of railway operations has a direct and significant impact on the daily lives of the residents in the Greater Sydney Area.

To evaluate the effectiveness of our model, we conduct a series of experiments using operational data collected from the railway network of New South Wales train services, Australia. Our experimental section is organized into two parts, aligning with the design of our model. Firstly, we compare the performance of our Next-Day Passenger Flow Prediction (NDP) model with that of benchmark time-series

Table 7.2
Data Source and Statistics

Data	Source	Data Rate
Trip Boarding Data	TLMS	51,420 Records / Day
Station Inbound Data	SCTS	1,300,000 Records / Day
Weather Conditions	Weather API www.bom.gov.au	Everyday
School day	Official calendar	278 Days / Year
Holiday	Official calendar	12 Days / Year

prediction methods. Secondly, we assess the Real-Time Fine-Tuning (RTF) model on selected platforms with low On-Time Running rates (OTR). It is important to note that OTR represents the percentage of on-time running trips out of all scheduled trips and serves as a critical metric for evaluating the overall operational performance of a railway system. Additionally, we present case studies to illustrate how our real-time fine-tuning stage effectively responds to emergencies and temporary timetable changes, as well as its performance during holidays.

7.5.1 EXPERIMENTAL DATA

In this chapter, we conduct the experiments on a pre-COVID time period spanning 7 months (214 days: May 1, 2019 – November 30, 2019). The railway operation data includes information from 713 platforms located throughout the entire railway network. This data is collected directly from IoT devices used by New South Wales Train Services and includes: (1) Trip boarding data (numeric), which records the number of passengers boarding a train on each platform; (2) Station inbound data (numeric), which refers to the number of passengers entering each station. In addition to essential date attributes such as weekday/weekend status, we also incorporate influential factors such as: (3) Weather conditions data (numeric), including temperature and rainfall measurements for each day (where 0 indicates no rainfall); and (4) School day/Holiday status (attribute), represented using one-hot encoding. The daily average passenger flow for all platforms is approximately 1,650,000 on weekdays and 760,000 on weekends. Table 7.2 presents detailed statistics for our dataset.

Experimental Settings

In this study, 85% of the data (corresponding to the first 6 months) is used for training, while the remaining 15% (the last month) is reserved for testing. The accuracy of passenger flow prediction performance is evaluated using two standard metrics: *Mean Absolute Error* (MAE) and *Root Mean Squared Error* (RMSE). As mentioned earlier, daily passenger behaviours vary between weekdays and weekends. To optimize performance, the previous 5 weekdays are used for future weekday predictions, and the previous 6 weekends are used for future weekend predictions during the experiments.

Table 7.3
Performance of Next-Day Prediction Model and Baselines

Model	Weekdays		Weekends	
	MAE	RMSE	MAE	RMSE
HA	72.22	77.04	68.23	74.34
ARIMA	55.63	58.38	52.87	53.75
SVR	48.34	50.74	44.78	42.87
RF	42.57	45.68	36.88	38.84
FNN	46.42	49.98	40.11	41.97
LSTM	37.58	42.87	31.87	34.24
NDP Model – Without IF	29.78	37.45	20.87	21.12
NDP Model	**28.13**	**35.52**	**18.45**	**20.87**

Baselines

In our evaluation, we compared the performance of our two-stage model with several advanced time-series methods as performance references. These methods include: *Baselines:* (1) **HA** (Historical Average): This baseline calculates predictions based on the historical average of the time series data. (2) **ARIMA** (Auto-Regressive Integrated Moving Average): This model makes predictions by modelling past seasonal information. [136]. (3) **SVR** (Support Vector Regression): It follows the principles of classic Support Vector Machine (SVM) methods for predicting sequential data. [50]. (4) **RF** (Random forest): It utilizes multiple decision trees for regression tasks. [119]. (5) **FNN** (Feed-forward Neural Network): It is a neural network architecture where information flows in one direction. (6) **LSTM** (long-short-term memory): This model is a type of recurrent neural network (RNN) with memory units. [192]. *Proposed Methods:* **NDP model**: Stage 1 – Next-day passenger flow prediction model; **RTF model**: Stage 2 – Real-time fine-tuning model.

7.5.2 PERFORMANCE COMPASSION ON NEXT-DAY PASSENGER FLOW PREDICTION

To evaluate the performance of our next-day passenger flow prediction (NDP) model, we conducted experiments to assess its accuracy based on actual trip boarding records. Since the TLMS records only boarding passenger numbers on the trains, we compared the actual boarding passenger numbers with the aggregated predicted passenger flows, taking into account the denied boarding rate at the train arrival time points. It is important to note that to ensure a fair comparison, we applied our proposed decomposing component to generate fine-grained inputs for all the baseline methods. The results, as shown in Table. 7.3, indicates that our NDP model outperforms other benchmark methods significantly. This improvement is attributed to our

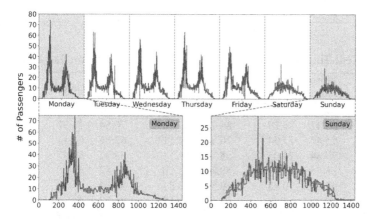

Figure 7.10   The passenger flow prediction and ground truth curve in Platform 24, Sydney Central Station from Nov 11 to Nov 17, 2019 (7 days): the red curve refers to the prediction results while the blue curve refers to the ground truth. The lower sub-figures show the zoom-in view of Monday and Sunday

well-designed passenger flow records transformation process, the incorporation of self-attention to model the unique relationship between historical data and the future, and the consideration of interchanged passengers and influential factors. Furthermore, we analyzed the impact of influential factors by comparing the performance of our model with and without these factors (**With & Without IF**). The results show that incorporating influential factors results in a 3% improvement in MAE.

Figure 7.10 visually demonstrates the next-day prediction compared to the ground truth over a week-long period. The curves show a high degree of fitting, indicating the accuracy of our predictions. Our self-attention model effectively captures the double-peak distribution of weekday passenger flow and the single-peak distribution of weekend passenger flow, as evident in the graph. The zoomed-in view in Figure 7.10 reveals that our model captures not only the overall daily pattern but also the trip-based patterns. This ability is attributed to the relatively fixed daily timetable, with passengers tending to arrive at the same time point for the same trip. Considering the large daily patronage and complex travel situations in the Railway system of New South Wales Train Services, Australia, the performance of our next-day prediction is reasonably acceptable for providing accurate passenger flow predictions for timetable planning, especially when compared to benchmark methods.

7.5.3   PERFORMANCE COMPASSION ON REAL-TIME FINE-TUNING PREDICTION

The real-time fine-tuning experiments aim to assess the effectiveness of our RTF model in real-time train operation scenarios. To provide a meaningful performance comparison, we focus on platforms with major delays, as passenger flow remains relatively stable under on-time operation, making it challenging to distinguish between

Table 7.4

Performance of Real-Time Prediction Model in Different Periods on Bad Days

Model	Morning Peak (7:00 – 10:00)		Evening Peak (17:00 – 20:00)		Off-peak hours	
	MAE	RMSE	MAE	RMSE	MAE	RMSE
HA	88.42	89.29	86.77	87.30	70.54	74.32
ARIMA	75.45	77.94	70.54	74.81	62.84	66.14
SVR	70.84	72.05	65.78	68.14	57.57	59.67
RF	63.15	65.17	58.85	62.10	45.87	48.18
FNN	68.28	70.88	59.82	63.21	50.34	54.19
LSTM	60.08	64.57	53.12	57.19	41.57	44.11
NDP Model	55.74	62.27	46.87	48.75	35.78	39.87
RTF Model	**38.12**	**45.01**	**34.68**	**36.14**	**32.00**	**33.37**

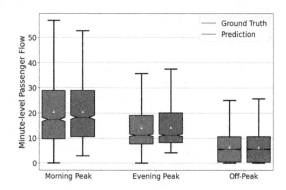

Figure 7.11   Box-plot comparison between Ground Truth and Prediction

next-day predictions and real-time fine-tuning results. In this experiment, we define major delays as instances where there is a gap of more than 5 minutes between the actual arrival time and the scheduled arrival time. We select days with major delays, specifically those in which major delays account for less than 85% of the On-Time Running rate (OTR), indicating "bad days." As a result, we choose 11 eligible days (8 weekdays and 3 weekends) from the testing period in November 2019.

Table. 7.4 presents the prediction performance on bad days for both peak and off-peak hours. We observe that all methods experience a decrease in prediction accuracy due to the influence of train delays and their propagation throughout the network. By applying our real-time fine-tuning, we achieve a significant improvement in accuracy, with more than a 30% improvement during the morning peak and a 26% improvement during the evening peak compared to next-day predictions on bad days. This represents a substantial performance enhancement. The impact on off-peak hours is less pronounced, as lower passenger demand results in fewer scheduled trips and delays during this period. Figure 7.11 visually shows that our prediction results closely

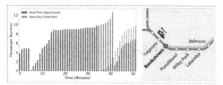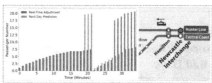

(a) Platform traffic with delayed trips: the planned arrival time of the target train on the platform of Bankstown Station is delayed. The real-time adjustment capability allows for a more accurate reflection of platform traffic, aiding managers in preparing appropriate emergency measures.

(b) Platform traffic with the arrival late of interchanged passengers: the planned arrival time of the target train on the platform of Newcastle Interchange Station is delayed. The real-time adjustment reveals that interchanged passengers arrive on the platform later, allowing the scheduled train to adjust its departure time to accommodate these passengers.

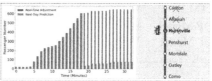

(c) Platform traffic with added trips: the newly added train arrived at the platform of Summer Hill Station. The real-time adjustment reveals that waiting passengers board the added train, leading to a decrease in the number of accumulated passengers on the platform.

(d) Platform traffic with canceled trips: the planned train is cancelled to stop at Hurstville and the following stations. The real-time adjustments demonstrate that arriving passengers accumulate on the platform, providing managers with a clear understanding of the impact.

Figure 7.12 Real-time fine-tuning results based on delays and timetable changes. The blue bars refer to the updated platform traffic by applying the RTF model while the yellow bars represent the next-day prediction by using the NDP model only

align with the ground truth, particularly after minute-level fine-tuning. Additionally, we evaluate short-term prediction performance with different target time windows in Table 7.5. As the target time window increases, the performance degrades, highlighting the influence of the target time window size on real-time passenger flow prediction.

7.5.4 EFFECTIVENESS OF COMPONENTS

To assess the impact of each component in our proposed model, we conducted experiments where we deactivated individual components and analyzed their performance, as depicted in Figure 7.13. From the experiments, we observed that the reallocation of interchanged passengers and real-time adjustments significantly contribute to the performance of our model. These components are crucial in capturing hidden interchange flows and accounting for the influence of emergencies, resulting in more accurate representations of passenger travel behaviours. Additionally, the inclusion of denied boarding rates aids in obtaining precise historical passenger flow

Table 7.5

Performance of Real-Time Prediction Model in Different Target Time Windows on Bad Days

Model	15 Minutes		20 Minutes		30 Minutes	
	MAE	MSE	MAE	MSE	MAE	MSE
HA	75.29	79.87	-	-	-	-
ARIMA	67.30	70.14	67.68	70.45	68.80	71.08
SVR	58.84	62.87	59.05	63.85	59.78	64.13
RF	51.37	55.57	52.27	55.90	52.74	54.01
FNN	55.66	58.02	56.21	58.73	56.65	59.46
LSTM	47.01	50.24	47.22	51.87	47.98	52.93
NDP Model	40.87	43.87	40.90	45.57	41.78	45.12
RTF Model	**34.58**	**37.78**	**34.84**	**37.74**	**35.57**	**38.01**

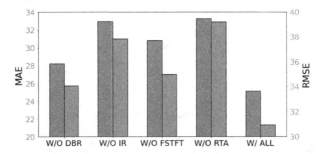

Figure 7.13   Prediction Performance when deactivating components: **DBR** refers to denied boarding rates; **IR** refers to interchanged passengers reallocation; **FSTFT** refers to fast short-term fine-tuning; **RTA** refers to the real-time adjustment; and **ALL** means all components activated

data. Finally, the fast short-term fine-tuning component ensures that predicted results can be promptly updated based on real-world conditions.

7.5.5   FINE-TUNING MODEL ON EMERGENCIES

Real-world railway systems are facing various incidents and emergencies every day, our case study examines four different scenarios to showcase the advantages of our RTF model in responding to real-world incidents and emergencies (Figure 7.12): delayed trips, delayed interchanged passengers, added trips, and cancelled trips. When an emergency occurs, our real-time fine-tuning captures the situation and adjusts the predicted results based on the updated train schedule, providing a dynamic response that next-day predictions cannot achieve. In scenario (a), involving a

Table 7.6

Performance of NDP AND RTF model with Benchmark Methods on Selected Public Holidays

Model	Boxing Day		New Year	
	MAE	RMSE	MAE	RMSE
HA	-	-	-	-
ARIMA	79.23	83.52	75.23	78.95
SVR	68.52	74.12	65.59	67.44
RF	63.24	65.41	61.24	63.06
FNN	64.87	66.41	62.14	60.94
LSTM	54.56	57.96	51.29	54.27
NDP Model	39.64	42.51	34.87	36.11
RTF Model	**31.41**	**32.91**	**28.31**	**29.81**

delayed trip, the updated prediction indicates the accumulation of passengers on the platform until the delayed train arrives. Similarly, in scenario (b) for delayed interchange trips, our model reallocates the influenced interchanged passengers based on the delay time. For scenarios (c) and (d) involving added or cancelled trips, our real-time fine-tuning model effectively updates the real-time passenger numbers on the platform. This case study demonstrates how our real-time fine-tuning can precisely adjust predictions to respond to emergencies or temporary train schedule changes, ensuring accurate passenger flow estimates in dynamic situations.

7.5.6 PUBLIC HOLIDAY SCENARIOS

We evaluate the performance of our model on public holidays, specifically Boxing Day (Saturday, 12-26-2019) and New Year (Wednesday, 01-01-2020), when passenger behaviour significantly differs from other days. On Boxing Day and New Year, the average passenger flow is approximately 750,000 and 550,000, respectively, deviating from the historical passenger flow pattern. Table. 7.6 presents the experimental results, and we can observe that both our NDP and RTF models outperform the baseline methods. This improvement is attributed to our models' ability to capture and learn the features of special days using the attention model. Furthermore, our RTF model effectively fine-tunes and adjusts the prediction results based on the different real-time patterns encountered during public holidays.

7.6 SUMMARY

The development of Intelligent Transport Systems (ITS) serves as a vital indicator of urban intelligence within smart cities, with the objective of providing sustainable and efficient urban services. In the realm of ITS, railway networks play a pivotal role and increasingly incorporate a range of Internet of Things (IoT) devices. These devices are instrumental in monitoring real-time incoming passenger numbers, a critical element in ensuring commuter safety. However, the seamless integration and interpretation of real-time data from diverse IoT sources to facilitate accurate future traffic predictions pose significant challenges. These challenges stem from limitations such as coarse data granularity, unpredictable variations in passenger numbers due to dynamic transfers, and the imperative need for real-time prediction capabilities. These issues considerably impede the progress of ITS in the context of smart city development.

To confront these challenges, our study introduces a dual-phase, self-adjusting model meticulously crafted for the precise and expeditious prediction of commuter traffic within urban rail networks. In the initial phase of our model, we employ an innovative self-attention-based forecasting approach to predict next-day commuter numbers utilizing historical entry data acquired through IoT systems. Our approach, which transforms discrete entry records into continuous patterns, enables accurate predictions at minute-level granularity. In the subsequent phase, we devise a real-time refinement model designed to adapt these predictions in response to immediate emergencies and short-term fluctuations in commuter traffic, as reported by IoT devices. This hybrid approach, integrating an offline deep learning framework with an online adjustment algorithm, facilitates timely responses without compromising precision. This comprehensive system is successfully implemented in the railway network of the Greater Sydney Area in Australia. It demonstrates its capacity to provide accurate forecasts essential for scheduling while offering real-time strategic guidance to operators during urgent situations.

8 Prioritising Risk Assets for Infrastructure Maintenance

8.1 BACKGROUND

Within urban water utilities, the maintenance of water mains has emerged as a critical concern, particularly given the challenges posed by aging infrastructure. Proactive management techniques, specifically proactive maintenance, have gained increasing significance with the advancements in machine learning. In the context of water main maintenance, proactive maintenance heavily relies on the prediction of failure events, such as breaks and leaks, making failure event prediction a crucial element in various applications, including proactive maintenance planning, active investment management, and disease surveillance. Ensuring a consistent supply of high-quality potable water to utility customers becomes paramount, necessitating the prioritisation of addressing disruptions to customer supplies, such as pipe disruptions or compromised water quality. The escalating cost of maintaining aging water mains compounds the challenges faced by urban water utilities, intensifying the urgency to adopt effective asset management strategies.

The issue of water pipe failure prediction has garnered heightened attention due to the aging underground networks for water distribution. In the initial stages, physical models [95, 152] were developed to understand the structural failures of water mains. Subsequently, a plethora of data-driven models emerged, leveraging historical data on pipe failures and incorporating factors such as pipe structural properties, material type, operational pressure, and external biochemical and electrochemical environments. Several statistical methods form the basis of many data-driven models for pipe failure prediction. These include pipe age-dependent models [39], Cox proportional hazard models [144], Weibull and exponential models [128, 66], Kaplan-Meier estimator [37], and Poisson regression [14]. Recent advancements include Bayesian models [83, 112] tailored for specific pipe materials, such as cast iron and ductile iron pipes, offering more nuanced predictions.

As computer science advances, machine learning techniques have further enhanced the understanding of pipe data. Combining evolutionary polynomial regression models with clustering approaches and considering factors like pipe characteristics and weather-related variables, researchers have proposed effective approaches for pipe failure prediction. Machine learning methods, including gradient boosting decision trees [61], have demonstrated superior performance in real-world scenarios, providing valuable insights for proactive asset management. Farmani et al. [55] introduced an innovative approach to predict pipe failures. Their method combines an evolutionary polynomial regression model with a K-means clustering approach, taking into account pertinent data on pipe characteristics and weather-related factors. This integrative approach enriches the predictive capabilities, contributing to a

DOI: 10.1201/9781003473893-8

more comprehensive understanding of the complex dynamics underlying pipe failures. In a separate study, Kumar et al. [94] conducted a thorough evaluation of various machine learning methods using real-world data to forecast pipe failures within a three-year timeframe. Notably, their experimental results highlighted the superior performance of the gradient boosting decision tree model over other machine learning algorithms. This finding underscores the efficacy of employing advanced ensemble learning techniques for accurate and reliable pipe failure predictions. Addressing the need for more dependable long-term predictions, Liang et al. [108] proposed LT-RNN, a novel application of recurrent neural networks (RNN) to the long-term hazard function prediction for failure event forecasting. Through experiments conducted on a water utility dataset, they demonstrated that LT-RNN excels in effectively modelling hidden failure patterns. Notably, it consistently outperforms alternative methods, affirming its robustness and establishing it as a promising tool for advancing the accuracy and reliability of long-term predictions in the context of water infrastructure management.

8.2   WATER PIPE FAILURE PREDICTION

In the sphere of urban water utilities, the foremost concern revolves around the burgeoning costs of maintaining water mains. This chapter presents a collaboration work with a water utility. A concerted effort has been undertaken to harness domain expertise and employ advanced machine learning techniques. The overarching objective is to forge a cost-effective solution for predicting water pipe failures within the expansive water network. However, this endeavour is not without its challenges, including:

- Complexity of multiple information sources: Pipe failures are intricately linked to various characteristics, drawing insights from diverse information sources. The challenge lies in the extraction and aggregation of pertinent information from these multiple sources, presenting a formidable task in ensuring a comprehensive understanding of the factors contributing to pipe failures.
- High-dimensional feature extraction: Extracting features from the amalgamation of data originating from multiple sources can result in a high-dimensional dataset. This complexity necessitates the application of advanced machine learning techniques to effectively navigate and distill meaningful insights, especially as the number of data sources continues to grow.
- Identification of major failure contribution factors: Despite the existing wealth of literature on pipeline failure causes, the crucial task at hand involves discerning the major contribution factors. Unravelling which among the myriad of potential causes holds the most significance for the water utility is paramount. This pursuit requires a meticulous exploration to unveil the primary contributors to pipeline failures, providing essential insights for targeted mitigation strategies.

In tackling these hurdles, we formulate a comprehensive framework designed to unravel the intricacies of the water pipe network. This involves a three-pronged

Table 8.1
Multiple Data sources

Data	Source	Examples
Pipe attributes	Water Utility	length, material, size, laid year
Historical failures	Water Utility	failure date, failure type
Operation	Water Utility	pump pressure, gravity pressure
Soil	CSIRO[1]	water capacity, pH
Topography	ELVIS[2]	elevation

approach: 1) creation of multi-dimensional features using domain knowledge from multi-source data, 2) utilization of ensemble learning to assess and predict the failure likelihood of water main failures, and 3) identification of key features from the developed machine learning model.

8.2.1 FEATURE ENGINEERING WITH DOMAIN KNOWLEDGE

The behaviour of pipe failures is intricately linked to their inherent characteristics, encompassing factors such as materials, sizes, pressures, topography, soil types, and more. A multitude of information is curated from diverse sources to comprehensively understand these dynamics. The water utility has meticulously recorded a substantial volume of historical data, capturing details on pipe attributes and operational parameters. Furthermore, supplementary information on topography and soil has been gathered from publicly available data sources. Table 8.1 provides a comprehensive overview of the data sources utilized in this study.

Effective feature engineering is pivotal in the realm of machine learning, but it comes with inherent challenges and costs. To gain a nuanced understanding of the multi-source data at play, proactive engagement with domain experts from the water utility has been a key initiative. Through insightful interviews, these experts shared considerations regarding factors influencing pipe failures. An illustrative example is the impact of elevation disparities between water mains, which can result in additional water pressure. The determination of practical pressure for each pipe or joint, factoring in considerations such as water flow direction and proximity to the water pump, adds a layer of complexity and is recognized as a significant contributor to pipe failures. In light of the amassed pipe and elevation data, two topographic features have been meticulously extracted: "difference of ground level (DGL)" and "shape type of connection (STC)". These features encapsulate critical aspects identified through collaborative efforts with domain experts, enriching the feature set

---

[1] http://www.clw.csiro.au/aclep/soilandlandscapegrid/

[2] https://elevation.fsdf.org.au/

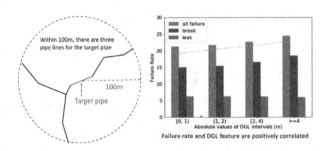

Figure 8.1   The feature *DGL* and its correlation with failure rate [109]

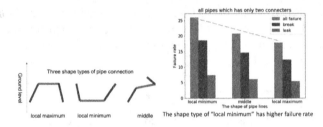

Figure 8.2   The feature *STC* and its correlation with failure rate [109]

and contributing to a more nuanced and comprehensive approach in predicting and understanding water pipe failures.

Illustrated in Figure 8.1, the *DGL* feature represents the average elevation difference between the designated target pipe and those within a 100-meter radius from the centre of this target pipe. Here, the focal pipe for which the feature is crafted is termed the target pipe. Notably, this feature exhibits a discernible positive correlation with the failure rate, emphasizing its significance in capturing key dynamics related to water pipe failures. In addition to the *DGL* feature, another pertinent topographic feature is introduced, namely the *shape type of connection (STC)*. Unlike *DGL*, which solely accounts for elevation differences, *STC* takes into consideration the shape variations in the elevation direction. As depicted in Figure 8.2, there are commonly three distinct shapes of pipe connections. Leveraging pipe layout details and ground-level data, extraction of this feature is straightforward. Notably, *STC* exhibits a robust correlation with the pipe failure rate, underlining its efficacy in capturing significant nuances related to water pipe failures.

8.2.2   ENSEMBLE LEARNING

Ensemble learning, a sophisticated approach in the field of machine learning, has evolved over time, leveraging a rich history and integrating various technical aspects to enhance predictive modelling. The concept of ensemble learning traces its roots to the early 1990s, with the emergence of research on combining multiple models to achieve superior performance compared to individual models. The idea was to exploit the diversity among models, making them collectively more robust and resilient. One of the earliest and most influential ensemble learning techniques is bagging [23]. Bagging, or Bootstrap Aggregating, involves training multiple instances of the same learning algorithm on different bootstrap samples of the training data. By averaging or voting across these models, bagging reduces overfitting and variance, contributing to improved generalization. Subsequently, the boosting algorithm, a key component of ensemble learning, gained prominence. AdaBoost (Adaptive Boosting), proposed by [60], marked a significant advancement. AdaBoost iteratively adapts the weights of misclassified samples, focusing on those instances that were challenging for previous models. This process results in a robust and accurate ensemble model. Gradient boosting, a more recent and widely adopted technique, builds upon the principles of boosting. The introduction of gradient boosting can be attributed to the work of Jerome Friedman in the early 2000s. Notable implementations include XGBoost (Extreme Gradient Boosting), developed by Tianqi Chen in 2016, and LightGBM, created by Microsoft in 2017 [33]. These implementations optimize the boosting process by incorporating techniques such as parallelization and tree-pruning strategies, enhancing both efficiency and performance.

Technically, ensemble learning combines multiple base models, often decision trees, to form a collective model. The diversity among these base models is crucial, as it allows the ensemble to capture a broader range of patterns and nuances within the data. In the case of gradient boosting, the process involves sequentially fitting multiple weak learners, with each iteration focusing on rectifying the errors made by the previous models. The success of ensemble learning lies in its ability to mitigate overfitting, reduce variance, and improve predictive accuracy. It has become a cornerstone in various machine learning competitions and real-world applications, offering a powerful tool for handling complex and high-dimensional data. As the field continues to evolve, ensemble learning remains at the forefront of innovative methodologies, continually pushing the boundaries of what can be achieved in predictive modelling.

In harnessing the wealth of collected multi-source data, this work integrates domain knowledge to construct meaningful features tailored for an advanced machine learning model. However, these crafted features exhibit multiple dimensionalities, posing a challenge for the existing prediction model. Consequently, an upgrade was implemented by employing an advanced ensemble learning technique, specifically XGBoost, to model failure behaviours from these intricate, multi-dimensional features. XGBoost, a decision-tree-based machine learning algorithm, operates within a gradient boosting framework renowned for its flexibility and extendability to accommodate additional features. In the context of gradient boosting for regression, the base learners take the form of regression trees. Each regression tree maps an input data point to one of its leaves, encapsulating a continuous score. The model is then synthesized based on a weighted sum of these base learners. XGBoost minimizes a regularized (L1 and L2) objective function, combining a convex loss function, predicated on the disparity between predicted and target outputs, and a penalty term accounting for model complexity, i.e., the regression tree functions. The training progresses iteratively, introducing new trees that predict the residuals or errors of prior trees, which are subsequently amalgamated with earlier trees to formulate the final prediction. The nomenclature "gradient boosting" stems from its utilization of a gradient descent algorithm to minimize loss during the addition of new models.

The scalability of XGBoost is underpinned by several pivotal algorithmic optimizations:

- A novel tree learning algorithm adeptly manages sparse data.
- A theoretically justified weighted quantile sketch procedure facilitates the handling of instance weights in approximate tree learning.
- Parallel and distributed computing accelerates the learning process, expediting model exploration. The amalgamation of these optimizations equips XGBoost with scalability, efficiency, and adaptability, rendering it a potent tool for modelling complex relationships within diverse datasets.

8.2.3   FEATURE IMPORTANCE

An integral facet of model interpretation, understanding feature importance is pivotal for researchers and practitioners seeking to identify influential variables in predictive modelling. The following methods, each possessing unique strengths and applications across various scenarios, are discussed in detail.

Permutation Importance: Permutation Importance stands out as a versatile method applicable across different models, particularly effective in scenarios involving complex models and high-dimensional data. By randomly permuting feature values and assessing their impact on model performance, this method identifies features that significantly influence predictive accuracy [61].

Random Forest Feature Importance: Well-suited for ensemble models, particularly Random Forests, this method gauges the average decrease in impurity (e.g., Gini impurity) caused by a feature across all decision trees in the ensemble, providing insights into feature relevance [24].

LASSO (L1 Regularization) Coefficient Magnitudes: LASSO Coefficient Magnitudes find utility in linear models, especially when feature selection is paramount. By inducing sparsity in coefficients, the magnitudes of non-zero coefficients indicate feature importance [170].

Recursive Feature Elimination (RFE): Applicable in models supporting feature elimination, such as linear models, RFE is an iterative process that removes the least important features, assessing their impact on model performance until the desired number of features is achieved [70].

SHAP Values (SHapley Additive exPlanations): Suited for explaining the output of any machine learning model, SHAP values, rooted in cooperative game theory, assign a value to each feature, representing its contribution to the difference between the actual model output and the expected output [125].

The selection of a particular method hinges on data characteristics, model type, and the specific goals of the analysis. A judicious combination of these methods often provides a more nuanced understanding of feature importance, enhancing the interpretability and transparency of machine learning models.

A notable advantage of employing gradient boosting in this work is the ease with which importance scores for each attribute can be extracted after constructing the boosted trees. Importance scores offer a quantifiable measure indicating the usefulness or significance of each feature in the creation of the boosted decision trees within the model. Essentially, the more a particular attribute is employed in making crucial decisions within the decision trees, the higher its relative importance becomes. This explicit calculation of importance for each attribute in the dataset facilitates the ranking and comparison of attributes.

In XGBoost, three conventional metrics offer insights into feature importance:

- **Weight**: The count of times a feature is utilized to split the data across all trees. Reflects the frequency with which a feature plays a role in partitioning the data.
- **Cover**: The count of times a feature is employed to split the data across all trees, adjusted by the number of training data points passing through those splits. Quantifies the coverage or reach of a feature's influence, considering the volume of training data affected by the splits.
- **Information Gain (IG)**: The average reduction in training loss achieved by using a feature for splitting. For an individual decision tree, the IG score is computed based on the improvement each attribute split point imparts to the performance measure. This improvement is weighted by the number of observations for which the node is responsible. The performance measure can be the purity, such as the Gini index, used for selecting split points, or a more specialized error function.

Among these metrics, Information Gain emerges as especially harmonized with domain expertise, capitalizing on the principles of entropy to identify the features that wield the most significant influence on predictive accuracy. This nuanced comprehension empowers practitioners to extract profound insights into the fundamental dynamics that shape model predictions.

Based on the feature importance derived from the model, key features can be identified, shedding light on the attributes that significantly contribute to the model's decision-making process. Figure 8.3 visually illustrates the top 5 features for the years 2018 and 2019, providing a succinct representation of their relative importance. It is noteworthy that, beyond pipe attributes, the variance of ground levels emerges as a pivotal feature influencing pipe failures. The inclusion of such diverse factors in the feature importance analysis underscores the comprehensive nature of the ensemble model, which effectively captures the intricate interplay of variables contributing to the prediction of water pipe failures.

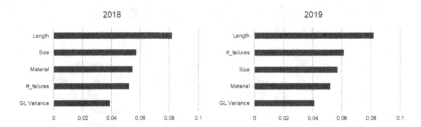

Figure 8.3   Top 5 features for the years of 2018 and 2019. (GL Variance: Variance of ground levels) [109]

8.3   GROUP LEVEL PRIORITISATION

In the realm of water utility management, a shutdown block is a designated section or segment within the water distribution network where temporary shutdowns or isolation can be strategically implemented. These blocks prove indispensable for facilitating maintenance, repairs, or system modifications without causing disruption to the entire water supply network. By isolating specific segments, utilities can efficiently manage and address issues without impacting the broader service area. Shutdown blocks are strategically designated to streamline maintenance activities, repairs, and system upgrades without causing widespread disruptions to the water supply network.

Trunk mains, on the other hand, serve as the primary conduits for water transportation within the distribution network. These large-diameter pipelines play a pivotal role in efficiently conveying substantial volumes of water over longer distances, akin to major arteries connecting various segments of the distribution system. The significance of trunk mains lies in ensuring a consistent and reliable water supply to different regions within the service area. Specifically designed for the efficient transport of large water volumes across significant distances, trunk mains are instrumental in maintaining a dependable water supply to diverse parts of the distribution network.

Recognizing the characteristics and functionalities of shutdown blocks and trunk mains is imperative for effective water utility management. Such understanding empowers utilities to optimize maintenance efforts and guarantee the reliable delivery of water to consumers. Consequently, the ability of a model to provide failure probability and prioritization at the group level—such as the shutdown block and trunk main levels—in addition to the asset level becomes pivotal for enhancing the overall resilience and performance of the water distribution network. In order to obtain failure likelihoods for each shutdown block and trunk main, the following formula is proposed:

$$1 - \prod_{i \in C}(1 - score_i) \tag{8.1}$$

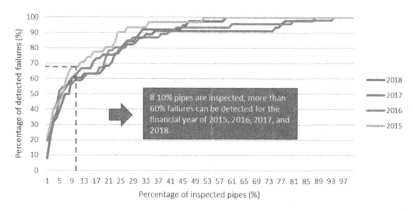

Figure 8.4   Model evaluation based on historical data of different years [109]

where C is a shutdown block or trunk main, and $score_i$ is the failure likelihood of pipe i in the corresponding C. The formula denotes the failure likelihood that at least one pipe fails.

8.4   CASE STUDY FOR WATER ASSETS PRIORITISATION

8.4.1   MODEL VALIDATION

To assess the model's performance, we conducted a comparative analysis by juxtaposing the prediction outcomes against the actual ground truth data. This evaluation involved calculating the percentage of detected failures in relation to the percentage of prioritized pipes, where pipes are arranged in descending order of their likelihood of failure. As illustrated in Figure 8.4, our model achieves a detection rate of over 60% when inspecting the top 10% of pipes. These results affirm the model's capacity to offer significant support in forecasting and strategically planning water main renewals with heightened confidence through the application of predictive analytics.

8.4.2   INTEGRATION OF CONSEQUENCE

In water management, consequence models refer to analytical frameworks or tools used to assess and quantify the potential impacts and outcomes associated with various events, particularly those related to failures or disruptions in the water infrastructure. These models help water utilities and authorities understand the consequences of specific incidents, allowing them to make informed decisions and prioritize actions for mitigation and response. Consequence models are typically applied in scenarios such as pipe failures, system disruptions, or other incidents that could affect the functionality of the water distribution network.

Key aspects and considerations within consequence models in water management may include:

- **Severity Levels**: Assigning severity levels to different types of incidents or failures, such as pipe bursts or contaminations, based on the potential impact on the water supply system and consumers.
- **Infrastructure Impact**: Evaluating the direct impact on water infrastructure, including the extent of damage to pipes, pumps, and treatment facilities, which may affect the overall system operation.
- **Public Health and Safety**: Assessing the potential risks to public health and safety, considering factors like water quality, access to clean water, and the ability to respond to emergencies.
- **Environmental Impact**: Considering the environmental consequences of incidents, including the potential contamination of water sources and the impact on local ecosystems.
- **Economic Implications**: Estimating the economic costs associated with infrastructure repairs, loss of water supply, and potential compensation for affected parties.
- **Operational Disruptions**: Analyzing the extent of operational disruptions, such as service interruptions, water quality degradation, and the time required for system recovery.

Consequence models are crucial tools for risk management and decision-making in water utilities. By understanding the potential outcomes of different scenarios, water managers can proactively implement measures to enhance system resilience, prioritize maintenance and repair activities, and develop effective emergency response plans.

Water utilities have made notable advancements in refining their infrastructure management by incorporating a consequential information model. This model assumes a pivotal role in evaluating the repercussions of individual pipe failures. As an illustration, each pipe can be assigned a level on a scale from 1 to 5, representing the associated consequence impact. This consequence model empowers us to prioritise the efforts effectively, focusing on high consequence pipes that demand immediate attention and proactive maintenance. By incorporating such a comprehensive approach to risk assessment, we can help water utilities optimize resource allocation, minimize potential disruptions, and ensure the longevity and resilience of the water supply network.

Through a seamless integration of the consequence model and pipe failure prediction results, we have successfully prioritized the identification of high-risk pipes based on both their elevated failure probabilities and significant consequences in the event of failure. The integration result can be represented using a risk matrix. An example is shown in Figure 8.5.

The risk matrix serves as a decision-making tool intended for utilization across various facets of the business. Within the water utility domain, this result proves instrumental in enhancing several business functions, including:

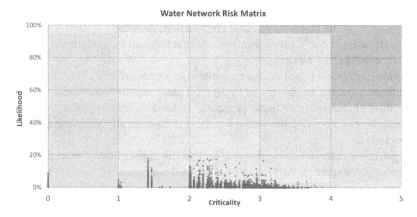

Figure 8.5   Risk matrix populated from the integration of consequence and failure prediction model. Each dot represents a water main asset

- **Informing Operational Areas**: Providing insights to operational areas about sections of the network prone to failures and high risks. This information aids in minimizing disruptions through targeted and planned interventions.
- **Customer Impact Assessment**: Offering guidance to the business on areas where customers are most likely to be affected by water interruptions. This enables proactive measures to mitigate risks and minimize potential impacts on customers.
- **Facilitating Condition Assessment Programs**: Playing a pivotal role in the development of condition assessment programs. The risk model assists in identifying areas that require focused attention, contributing to the strategic planning and execution of comprehensive condition assessment initiatives.

By catering to these functions, the risk matrix empowers the water utility to make informed decisions, enhance operational efficiency, and proactively address potential challenges, thereby contributing to the overall resilience and reliability of the water distribution network.

8.5   SUMMARY

In this chapter, we have explored the multifaceted landscape of water utility management with a focus on risk assessment, infrastructure prioritization, and consequence modelling. The contemporary challenges faced by water utilities, such as aging infrastructure and burgeoning populations, have necessitated a paradigm shift towards data-driven approaches and advanced machine learning models.

The introduction highlighted the increasing concern over the cost of maintaining water mains, prompting the adoption of proactive maintenance techniques, particularly those leveraging machine learning advances. We delved into the evolution of water pipe failure prediction models, ranging from traditional physical models to sophisticated machine learning methods. Notable contributions from the research community, such as Bayesian models, non-parametric approaches, and the integration of recurrent neural networks, were explored.

The subsequent sections focused on the essential components of effective water utility management, namely, shutdown blocks, trunk mains, and the significance of understanding their characteristics. These elements are fundamental in optimizing maintenance efforts, ensuring reliable water supply, and strategically planning infrastructure upgrades.

Feature engineering emerged as a critical aspect in the application of machine learning, with domain experts actively contributing to the creation of meaningful features. We investigated the extraction of topographic features such as the difference of ground level and shape type of connection, showcasing their correlations with pipe failure rates.

The introduction of ensemble learning, specifically XGBoost, brought forth a powerful tool for modelling failure behaviours. The scalability and efficiency of XGBoost, rooted in algorithmic optimizations, make it a formidable choice for handling complex datasets and providing robust predictions.

The discussion on feature importance shed light on various methods, including permutation importance, gain-based importance, and LASSO coefficient magnitudes. These methods play a crucial role in interpreting machine learning models and understanding the contribution of different features.

The concept of consequence models was introduced, emphasizing their role in assessing and quantifying the impacts of water infrastructure failures. The assignment of consequence levels to individual pipes showcases a strategic approach in evaluating the potential outcomes of incidents.

Finally, the integration of risk distribution models was explored as decision-making aids for various facets of the business. These models proved beneficial in informing operational areas, assessing customer impact, and contributing to the development of condition assessment programs.

In conclusion, this chapter underscores the transformative role of data-driven models and advanced machine learning techniques in addressing the challenges in prioritising risk assets. From predicting pipe failures to optimizing infrastructure maintenance and prioritization, the adoption of innovative approaches is paramount. The synergy of domain expertise, feature engineering, ensemble learning, and comprehensive consequence and risk modelling collectively forms a robust framework for enhancing water utility management. This chapter provides a foundation for the subsequent exploration of practical applications and real-world insights within the dynamic landscape of water infrastructure management.

9 Adapting Dynamic Behaviour Evolution in Structural Health Monitoring

9.1 BACKGROUND

With regards to data-driven situation awareness for asset and infrastructure, a significant challenge arises from online applications where data continuously stream in and decisions must be made in real-time to determine whether they are anomalous. In numerous real-world scenarios, the underlying data distributions change over time, meaning that what is considered normal behaviour may evolve over time. Consequently, the current understanding of normal behaviour may not adequately represent future occurrences. This presents a considerable challenge for infrastructure monitoring when dealing with non-stationary data streams. This chapter will explore methods to account for the evolution of normal behaviour in non-stationary data streams.

Taking SHM described in Chapter 2 as an example, data distributions can undergo variations due to changes in environmental and operational conditions that occur periodically, such as fluctuations in ambient temperature and traffic volume [123, 27]. This presents a significant challenge for anomaly detection in the context of non-stationary data streams [53, 49]. Regarding OCSVM, its traditional application assumes a batch formulation where normal data collected within a fixed time period are utilised for one-time training. Such a trained model often yields a high false positive rate for normal test data that possess a different distribution from the training set. Generally, there are two approaches to tackle this issue. One approach involves retraining the OCSVM from scratch when additional normal data become available. However, this approach has two drawbacks. Firstly, it leads to an ever-expanding training set, eventually becoming impractical. Secondly, starting from scratch is computationally inefficient, as some newly arrived samples may have minimal impact on the current decision boundary or surface [161]. Another approach, which is more appealing for addressing this situation, involves incrementally updating the OCSVM model by integrating additional normal data into the existing model. Nowadays incremental or online learning[1] has garnered increasing attention, especially in the realm of big data and learning from data streams. A thorough review of

---

[1]In this chapter, incremental learning and online learning are used interchangeably

DOI: 10.1201/9781003473893-9

online learning algorithms, with a particular emphasis on classification under supervised learning, has been observed in [120].

A fundamental question in OCSVM-based incremental learning for anomaly detection is whether a particular incoming sample should be utilised to update the existing OCSVM model. While several methods have been suggested for anomaly detection in non-stationary data streams [155], their primary focus lies in various data windowing techniques aimed at restricting the number of processed data points. However, they do not explicitly tackle the question of whether a given incoming sample should update the current model based on its estimated category. Existing OCSVM-based incremental learning methods are derived from their counterparts for two-class support vector machine (TCSVM) [29, 48, 98], where a model update occurs solely when a test sample resides within the margin area, signifying highly uncertain classification decisions between the two classes. An incremental SVM learning paradigm with an adiabatic approach was introduced in [29]. A technique referred to as "bookkeeping" was introduced to calculate the new coefficients of the SVM model. This approach was subsequently expanded into a comprehensive framework capable of adjusting the current SVM to variations in regularization and kernel parameters [48]. An expedited version of the bookkeeping method, offering enhanced efficiency, was suggested in [98]. In all these methods, the decision to update the model relies on whether a test sample falls within the margin area between the decision boundaries of the two classes, indicating highly uncertain classification decisions. However, it was determined that these incremental learning methods based on TCSVM cannot be directly applied to the OCSVM scenario [44], as the margin area present in TCSVM does not apply to OCSVM. Instead, the authors in [44] suggested computing an abnormality index for each incoming sample, derived from the decision function of the current model. Model coefficients are updated only when the anomaly index exceeds a predefined threshold. Another online OCSVM was introduced for detecting abnormal events in video sequences in [173]. Likewise, a model update is necessary only if the decision value of an incoming sample, as per the current model, surpasses a predefined threshold. When the training data are transformed into a high-dimensional feature space using a kernel function, there's a possibility that slack variables may not be linearly separable [126]. Given that the margin area in TCSVM corresponds to a collection of error support vectors in OCSVM, the model is updated by including an incoming sample if it exhibits a high degree of similarity with the slack variables [12]. As can be deduced, these online OCSVMs would be effective only when the data distributions remain relatively stable, requiring only minor adjustments to the decision boundary based on the uncertain classification data within the region defined by the decision boundary and error support vectors. A method employing OCSVM for online anomaly detection in wireless sensor networks was introduced in [133], where the primary objective is to decentralize the conventional OCSVM and enable its operation in a distributed manner. However, it does not address the question of whether a particular incoming sample should be utilised to update the current OCSVM model.

Despite the efforts made towards incrementally updating OCSVM for online anomaly detection, we believe that the aforementioned question remains inadequately addressed. It's worth noting that traditional TCSVM-based incremental learning methods were designed to handle training issues with very large datasets, where the underlying data distributions tend to remain relatively stable. In such cases, the decision boundary before and after model updates would exhibit minimal variance. Hence, it's reasonable to update the classifier based solely on the data within the margin area, as they signify class ambiguity. However, it's inappropriate to directly apply this concept to OCSVM-based online learning in non-stationary data streams, where normal behaviour evolves, and the decision boundary requires more adaptation. Clearly, an incoming sample should not be incorporated into the model if it is deemed an anomaly. Instead, an incremental update is warranted only if the new sample reflects normal behaviour and is expected to have significant effects on the current decision boundary upon inclusion in the model. Therefore, the model update criterion should consider the evolution of normal behaviour and not solely rely on the spatial relationship between an incoming sample and error support vectors.

9.2 A CONCEPT DRIFT ADAPTATION PERSPECTIVE

In a broader context, the evolution of normal behaviour in a non-stationary data stream can be viewed as concept drift [63, 121]. On one side, a normal concept might drift towards a novel concept. This novelty could either signify a normal concept that was previously unseen or be triggered by some abnormality. [92]. Regarding SHM, the former corresponds to variations in environmental and operational conditions, while the latter arises from structural damage. Subsequently, the associated drift is termed normal drift and abnormal drift, respectively, hereafter. On the other side, a drift may manifest abruptly, transitioning directly from one state to another, or gradually, with intermediate concepts in between. Within the context of SHM, an abrupt drift could stem from a substantial alteration in environmental or operational conditions or from severe structural damage. Conversely, a gradual drift might be linked to moderate shifts in environmental or operational factors or to minor, progressive structural damage. Given this comprehension, the optimal OCSVM-based incremental learning algorithm should possess the capability to accommodate both gradual and abrupt normal drifts while refraining from updating the model in response to abnormal drifts.

Our objective here is not to provide a comprehensive review of concept drift, as discussed in [121]. It's also important to note that our focus does not lie in detecting concept drift, change, or novelty, as emphasized in [147]. Once a drift, change, or novelty is identified, our primary interest lies in assessing whether the emerging phenomenon is normal or not. Consequently, we delve into reviewing some concept drift adaptation techniques with a particular emphasis on one-class learning. In this context, a method was introduced which employs a one-class classifier ensemble approach to classify batches of samples [196]. Each base classifier assigned weights to samples within a specific chunk. This method employed static one-class classifiers, achieving adaptability by merely incorporating new classifiers into the ensemble.

Building upon this idea, an alternative scheme for computing instance weights was introduced in [114], employing a local kernel-density approach. Our approach diverges from previous works in two key ways: firstly, rather than assigning labels to a batch of samples, which may entail a time delay, a label is promptly determined for each incoming instance without delay; secondly, we employ a single OCSVM to dynamically adapt to the evolving normal concept, rather than utilising multiple models. Assuming that normal behaviour is characterized by gradual changes in data distribution, an exponential weighting window was employed to transition from past to new concepts and adapt accordingly [65]. Nevertheless, normal drifts may not always occur smoothly, and an effective solution should be capable of addressing both abrupt and gradual normal drifts. Inspired by the concept of weighted OCSVM [18], an incremental version was introduced in [93], wherein new instances were integrated by re-weighting support vectors. Two strategies were suggested for assigning weights to incoming samples: firstly, prioritizing the highest weight for the most recent data; secondly, determining weights based on the distance from the hypersphere centre. However, this approach does not explicitly address anomalous data. Moreover, it remains a chunk-based method, thereby restricting its applicability.

Consider $\mathbf{x}_c$ is a new sample provided to a pre-trained OCSVM. For simplicity, let's denote the decision value of this sample based on the current model as g_c. According to 2.2.2, the training data can be divided into three sets: the samples with $\alpha_i \in (0, 1)$ are named margin support vectors which constitute the set $\mathscr{S}$; the samples satisfying $\alpha_i = 1$ are called as error support vectors which form the set $\mathscr{E}$; the remaining data with $\alpha_i = 0$ are referred to as reserve vectors denoted by the set $\mathscr{R}$. Moreover, a distance $d_{c\mathscr{R}}$ between $\mathbf{x}_c$ and reserve vectors in set $\mathscr{R}$ is defined to measure the similarity between them. More specifically, a nearest neighbor distance defined as below is used here:

$$d_{c\mathscr{R}} = \min_{\mathbf{x}_i \in \mathscr{R}} \|\boldsymbol{\phi}(\mathbf{x}_i) - \boldsymbol{\phi}(\mathbf{x}_c)\|. \tag{9.1}$$

The similarity between $\mathbf{x}_c$ and error set $\mathscr{E}$ is measured by $d_{c\mathscr{E}}$ similarly:

$$d_{c\mathscr{E}} = \min_{\mathbf{x}_i \in \mathscr{E}} \|\boldsymbol{\phi}(\mathbf{x}_i) - \boldsymbol{\phi}(\mathbf{x}_c)\|. \tag{9.2}$$

In addition to these metrics, we contend that the distances from reserve vectors and error support vectors to the decision boundary are also crucial properties of the OCSVM model. Here, we utilise the average distance for this assessment, and the distances $d_{\mathscr{R}}$ (or $d_{\mathscr{E}}$) from reserve vectors (or error support vectors) to the decision boundary are defined as follows:

$$d_{\mathscr{R}} = mean_{\mathbf{x}_i \in \mathscr{R}} |g(\mathbf{x}_i)|, \tag{9.3}$$

$$d_{\mathscr{E}} = mean_{\mathbf{x}_i \in \mathscr{E}} |g(\mathbf{x}_i)|. \tag{9.4}$$

Using these definitions, an examination of the relative relationships between an incoming sample and the three sets of vectors is performed, encompassing nearly all conceivable scenarios regarding concept drift. This analysis offers valuable insights into whether $\mathbf{x}_c$ should be integrated into the current OCSVM model.

Let's start by considering a scenario where $g_c > 0$, indicating that the new instance is classified as normal data according to the current model. Initially, it appears that a model update is unnecessary in this case, as the KKT conditions will remain satisfied with $\alpha_c = 0$ when g_c is positive. This holds true when the normal concept is not drifting. However, if the sample belongs to another normal concept that is gradually emerging, the OCSVM should adapt to this gradual drift; otherwise, the current model will eventually fail to recognize the new normal concept in the long run. With this understanding in mind, we further compare $d_{c\mathscr{R}}$ and $d_{c\mathscr{E}}$ to aid in the analysis. If $d_{c\mathscr{R}} < d_{c\mathscr{E}}$, it indicates that the instance bears a strong resemblance to the reserve vectors. In such a case, it's highly likely that the previous normal concept still holds, and thus no update is needed. Conversely, if $d_{c\mathscr{R}} > d_{c\mathscr{E}}$, it suggests less similarity between the sample and the reserve set, potentially implying a gradual drift, whether normal or abnormal, is underway. Our knowledge in SHM suggests that minor and developing structural damage typically leads to a gradual decrease in the decision value for OCSVM. In other words, an abnormal gradual drift could potentially be anticipated by observing a trend of the decision value approaching the decision boundary from the positive side. Motivated by this insight, we introduce the condition $|g_c| > d_{\mathscr{R}}$ as an additional criterion for deciding whether a model update is warranted.

In the scenario where g_c holds a negative value, if $d_{c\mathscr{R}} > d_{c\mathscr{E}}$ is fulfilled simultaneously, it suggests that the incoming sample still bears a strong resemblance to error support vectors, indicating a high likelihood that the sample is an anomaly. Conversely, when $d_{c\mathscr{R}} < d_{c\mathscr{E}}$, if the instance represents another anomaly concept that was not previously encountered, it would not be of interest to us either. However, a certain degree of similarity between $\mathbf{x}c$ and $\mathscr{R}$ expressed by $dc\mathscr{R} < d_{c\mathscr{E}}$, combined with the negative decision value, prompts us to consider the possibility of an abrupt normal drift. Under this assumption, the current OCSVM may lose its ability to accurately classify instances originating from the new normal concept. Rather than being situated far from the current decision boundary, those normal data are expected to be close to the boundary, suggesting uncertain classification decisions. Thus, we adopt $|g_c| < d_{\mathscr{E}}$ as an additional criterion.

In summary, the criteria proposed for updating the model given an incoming sample $\mathbf{x}_c$ are as follows:

- $g_c > 0$, $d_{c\mathscr{R}} > d_{c\mathscr{E}}$, along with $|g_c| > d_{\mathscr{R}}$: gradual normal drift and update the model;
- $g_c < 0$, $d_{c\mathscr{R}} < d_{c\mathscr{E}}$, along with $|g_c| < d_{\mathscr{E}}$: abrupt normal drift and update the model;
- otherwise: not update the model.

9.3   CASE STUDIES

In this section, we apply the concept drift adaptation approach to SHM to assess its effectiveness. We compare two existing OCSVM-based online learning algorithms [173, 12] with the proposed approach. Since an ideal incremental learning model should not only reduce false positives but also detect true positives (i.e., structural damages in SHM), we evaluate the performance of the proposed approach on both healthy and damaged data. We conduct extensive experiments using data collected from three bridge structures, including the Sydney Harbour Bridge in Australia [12], a concrete cantilever beam [87], and the Infante D. Henrique Bridge in Portugal [127, 40]. Each of the subsequent subsections presenting the experimental study related to each bridge structure includes an introduction to the dataset collected from the corresponding structure and the feature extraction process, followed by experimental results and discussions.

9.3.1 THE SYDNEY HARBOUR BRIDGE

9.3.1.1 Data Set and Feature Extraction

The data collected from the Sydney Harbour Bridge [169] (see Figure 2.7) were involved in our first cast study here. When a motor vehicle traverses an instrumented joint (also known as an event trigger), the resulting vibrations are recorded by triaxial (x, y, and z) accelerometers affixed to that joint for a duration of 2 seconds at a sampling rate of 250 Hz. Subsequently, the Fast Fourier Transform (FFT) is applied to this normalized acceleration time response to extract features in the frequency domain. Due to the symmetric nature of FFT, only half of the features in the frequency domain are retained, resulting in a 250-dimensional feature vector for each of the x, y, and z readings. In this investigation, features from all three readings of the central accelerometer are concatenated to create the final feature vector, characterizing this sample event.

In total, eleven joints from various locations on the Sydney Harbour Bridge were examined in this study. Of these, ten were in a healthy condition throughout the observation period from January 2016 to September 2017. There are 20000∼35000 samples for each selected joint as shown in Figure 9.1, which indicates the number of samples for each joint per month is around 952∼1667. More specifically, the mean and standard deviation for the number of samples for each joint across 21 months are plotted in Figure 9.2.

Another joint exhibited an identified crack for a duration of three months in 2012, during which 6886 samples were collected. Furthermore, 15387 samples representing the normal condition of this joint were gathered over consecutive fourteen months from October 2015 to November 2016. The monthly distribution of samples for this joint during the healthy period is illustrated in Figure 9.3.

9.3.1.2 Results and Discussions

We initiate the experiments by demonstrating the concept drift problem in SHM. Data collected from three nodes—Node A, B, and C—attached to three joints in good condition are considered in this experiment. For each node, the sample events collected in January 2016 are utilised to train an OCSVM model, which is subsequently applied to classify the samples collected from February 2016 to September 2017. The

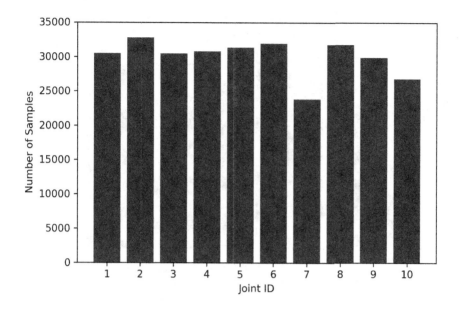

Figure 9.1 Number of samples for each of ten selected healthy joints

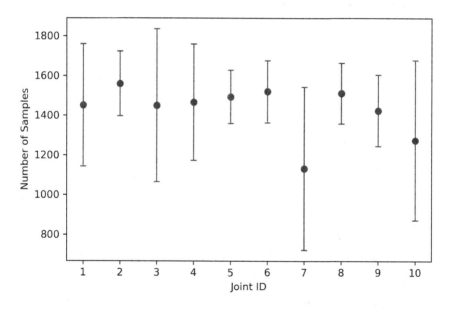

Figure 9.2 Mean and standard deviation for the number of samples for each of ten selected healthy joints across 21 months

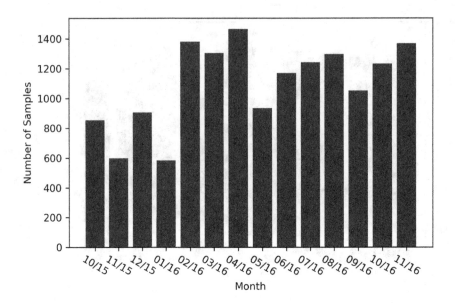

Figure 9.3 Monthly number of samples for a damaged joint when it was in a healthy condition from October 2015 to November 2016

accuracies calculated on a monthly basis are depicted in Figure 9.4. It is evident that the OCSVM model for Node A exhibits relatively stable classification performance throughout the twenty-month observation period. The consistent effectiveness of the OCSVM model indicates the absence of explicit concept drift for Node A during this period. However, for Node B, aside from some fluctuations, the gradual decreasing trend in accuracies suggests a weakening of the discriminative power of the OCSVM model. This phenomenon could be interpreted as a gradual normal drift resulting from moderate environmental and operational changes. Node C experienced sudden changes in classification accuracies twice in 2017: once from February to March and again from May to June. Both instances could be attributed to abrupt normal drift caused by significant changes in environmental and operational conditions. Without incremental learning, both gradual and abrupt normal drifts could lead to an increased false alarm rate in the long run, where more normal/healthy samples might be misclassified as structural damage. Our proposed approach is expected to adapt the OCSVM model to normal drift, thereby reducing the false alarm rate. This will be demonstrated in the next experiment.

Specifically, all ten healthy joints were included in this experiment. For each joint, the sample events collected in January 2016 were utilised to train an initial OCSVM model. Subsequently, for each sample collected from February 2016 to September 2017, a decision was made regarding whether it constituted an anomaly based on the current OCSVM model. Additionally, if the sample satisfied the proposed

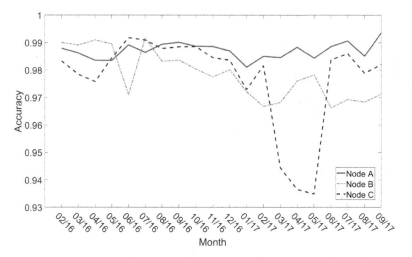

Figure 9.4 An illustration of the concept drift problem in SHM [169]

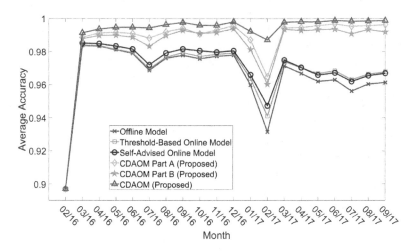

Figure 9.5 Average accuracies for ten healthy joints per month based on different models [169]

criteria for model update, the model would be updated to classify subsequent samples. Monthly accuracies were calculated, and the average accuracies for the ten joints were adopted for performance evaluation. It is important to note that although the classification performance was reported on a monthly basis, the incremental learning was conducted sample by sample sequentially. The average accuracies for the ten joints per month based on the proposed concept drift adaptation online model (CDAOM) are depicted in Figure 9.5. Furthermore, the effectiveness of the proposed

Table 9.1

Average Accuracies and Average Number of Updates for Ten Healthy Joints over the 20-month Period Based on Different Models (AA: Average Accuracy; ANU: Average Number of Updates)

Model	AA	ANU
Offline Model	0.9655	-
Threshold-Based Online Model	0.9683	2.19
Self-Advised Online Model	0.9695	1.42
CDAOM Part A (Proposed)	0.9867	3.51
CDAOM Part B (Proposed)	0.9843	9.12
CDAOM (Proposed)	0.9908	10.28

two criteria for model update was evaluated separately. Specifically, the criteria that $g_c > 0$, $d_{c\mathcal{R}} > d_{c\mathcal{E}}$, and $|g_c| > d_{\mathcal{R}}$ are referred to as CDAOM Part A; while $g_c < 0$, $d_{c\mathcal{R}} < d_{c\mathcal{E}}$, along with $|g_c| < d_{\mathcal{E}}$, are referred to as CDAOM Part B in the subsequent discussion. For comparison purposes, the results based on one offline OCSVM and two online models are also presented in Figure 9.5. The offline model was trained using the data collected in January 2016. Regarding the two online benchmarks, one is the threshold-based online model [173], and the other is the self-advised online model [12]. The accuracies shown in Figure 9.5 are further averaged over the twenty-month period, and the results are provided in Table 9.1.

As anticipated, all online models exhibit an improvement in average accuracy compared to the offline model. Moreover, the individual components of the proposed CDAOM consistently outperform the three baseline models. This validates our assumptions regarding abrupt and gradual normal drift. Overall, CDAOM Part A demonstrates slightly superior performance compared to CDAOM Part B. Combining them in the integrated model further enhances classification accuracy (i.e., true negative rate in this case). The high true negative rates achieved by the proposed CDAOM indicate low false positive rates. This underscores the adaptability of the proposed online OCSVM to environmental and operational changes encoded in the features. Additionally, we computed the frequency of model updates conducted for each joint per month, and the average numbers for the ten joints based on different online models are depicted in Figure 9.6. These figures were further averaged over the twenty-month period, and the results are reported in Table 9.1. It is evident that more updates were performed in the proposed model compared to the two online baselines, aligning more closely with real-world situations involving abrupt and gradual normal drift. Therefore, the proposed approach effectively accommodates changes in environmental and operational conditions.

Furthermore, an experiment was performed using data related to the damaged joint. The sample events collected in October 2015 were utilised to train an initial OCSVM model. Similar to the previous experiment, samples collected from

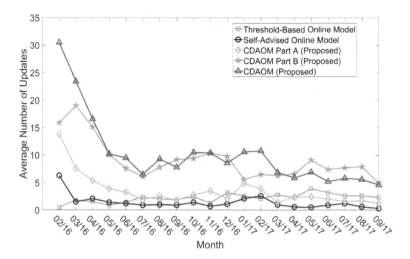

Figure 9.6   Average times of model updates for ten healthy joints per month based on different online models [169]

Table 9.2

Average Accuracies (AA) and F1-Scores for a Damaged Joint Based on Different Models

Model	AA	F1-Score
Offline Model	0.9398	0.9374
Threshold-Based Online Model	0.9489	0.9473
Self-Advised Online Model	0.9821	0.9841
CDAOM (Proposed)	0.9872	0.9892

November 2015 to November 2016 and during the damage period were used for model testing and incremental learning. Monthly accuracies were calculated and are illustrated in Figure 9.7. Once again, the proposed CDAOM was compared with one offline model and two online models. As observed, the proposed CDAOM consistently and significantly reduces the false positive rate when the joint is in a healthy condition. Moreover, achieving 100% classification accuracy for the damage data (the rightmost point in Figure 9.7) indicates a false negative rate of 0, implying that our online model was not mistakenly updated by the damage data. The accuracies shown in Figure 9.7 are further averaged over the observation period, and the results are presented in Table 9.2. Additionally, the F1-score was calculated and included in Table 9.2. Overall, the proposed CDAOM achieved the highest average accuracy and F1-score compared to the other baselines.

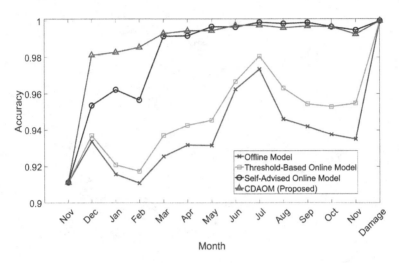

Figure 9.7 Classification accuracies for a damaged joint based on different models [169]

9.3.2 A REINFORCED CONCRETE BEAM

9.3.2.1 Data Set and Feature Extraction

The data collected from a steel reinforced concrete cantilever beam (Figure 2.11) were used in this case study. Similarly, FFT was adopted to extract features in the frequency domain and final features coming from all the three readings have a dimension of 2250. Notice only the accelerometer in the middle position was considered in this study. When the joint was in healthy condition, 200 sample events were collected. Then a crack with a fixed width of 50mm was gradually introduced into the structure with four levels of severity, where the lengths of the crack are 75mm, 150mm, 225mm, and 270mm, respectively. In the condition of each level of damage, 191, 193, 183, and 196 events were collected accordingly.

9.3.2.2 Results and Discussions

One hundred and fifty samples collected in healthy condition were randomly selected to train an initial OCSVM model. The rest 50 samples collected in healthy condition and all the events collected in four levels of damaged conditions were used for model testing and incremental learning in the following order: data of healthy case, data of damaged cases (from less severe to more severe). Classification accuracies and F1-scores were calculated for performance evaluation. The experiment was run five times and the average accuracies and F1-scores are reported in Table 9.3. Similar as before, the proposed CDAOM was compared with one offline model and two online models.

Table 9.3

Average Accuracies (AA) and F1-Scores for a Steel Reinforced Concrete Cantilever Beam Based on Different Models

Model	AA	F1-Score
Offline Model	0.9086	0.9702
Threshold-Based Online Model	0.6941	0.8095
Self-Advised Online Model	0.8514	0.8878
CDAOM (Proposed)	0.9086	0.9702

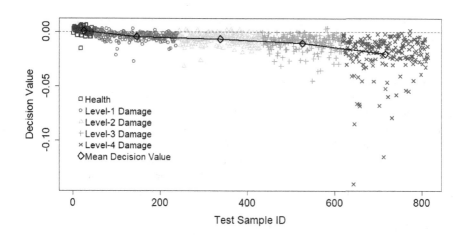

Figure 9.8   The decision values for all the test samples based on the proposed CDAOM

Due to the limited number of samples collected in healthy condition and no normal concept drift, the proposed CDAOM did not update the model and yields the same classification accuracy as the offline model when testing the healthy data. For each sample collected in damaged conditions, it was identified to not follow the defined abrupt or gradual normal drift and hence abandoned for model update. Thus, the proposed online model achieves the same accuracy and F1-score as the offline model as shown in Table 9.3. On the contrary, two online baselines incorporated some samples collected in damaged conditions into OCSVM leading to decreased performance.

Actually, all the test samples can be divided into five groups: one healthy and four damaged. The decision values for all the test samples based on the proposed CDAOM are plotted in Figure 9.8, where the samples coming from each of the five

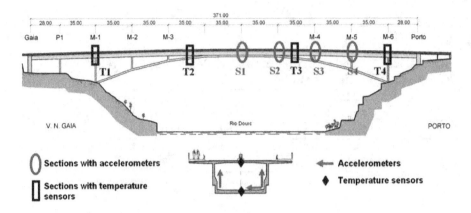

Figure 9.9 A schematic illustration about the locations of the accelerometers and temperature sensors installed on the Infante D. Henrique Bridge [127]

categories are represented by the points of the same colour and type. As can be seen, CDAOM can successfully classify the samples characterizing the healthy and damaged conditions of the structure. Even if the level-1 damage in this study is a quite small crack, it can be distinguished from healthy condition by the proposed online model. Furthermore, the mean values of the decision values for each group of samples were calculated and connected using a solid line as shown in Figure 9.8. The decreasing trend of the mean decision values implies that the proposed CDAOM has potential to detect and assess the evolution of damage in the structure.

9.3.3 THE INFANTE D. HENRIQUE BRIDGE

9.3.3.1 Data Set and Feature Extraction

In this case study, the efficacy of the proposed CDAOM for OCSVM-based incremental learning was evaluated using data collected from the Infante D. Henrique Bridge. The bridge was equipped with 12 force-balance highly sensitive accelerometers. These accelerometers provided acceleration measurements every 30 minutes, which were then subjected to operational modal analysis to ascertain the bridge's modal parameters, including its natural frequencies [115]. For this study, the 12 natural frequencies obtained were utilised as features to characterize the bridge's conditions. Additionally, temperature, believed to influence the bridge's natural frequencies, was recorded every 30 minutes. The positions of the instrumented accelerometers and temperature sensors are depicted in Figure 9.9. Specifically, two years of continuous monitoring data, spanning from September 2007 to September 2009, comprising a total of 35,040 samples, were analyzed in this study. It is noteworthy that no damage occurred to the bridge during this two-year observation period.

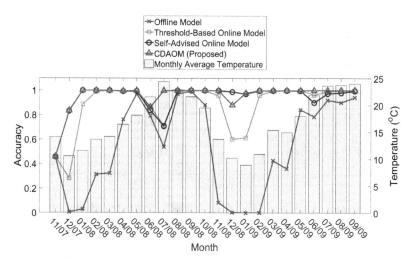

Figure 9.10 Monthly accuracies for the data collected from the Infante D. Henrique Bridge based on different models [169]

9.3.3.2 Results and Discussions

An initial OCSVM model was developed using samples collected in September and October 2007. Subsequently, samples gathered from November 2007 to September 2009 were utilised for model testing and incremental learning. Monthly accuracies were computed for performance assessment. Similarly, the proposed CDAOM was compared with the offline model, threshold-based online model, and self-advised online model. The resulting accuracies, along with the monthly average temperature, are depicted in Figure 9.10.

Noticeably, the average temperatures for September and October 2007 were 22.58°C and 19.06°C, respectively. The influence of temperature on natural frequencies can be inferred from the fluctuation of the classification accuracy based on the offline model. When the temperature was similar to that recorded during the training period, such as from September to October 2008, the offline model achieved high accuracy. Conversely, the performance of the offline model deteriorated drastically during months (e.g., from December 2007 to January 2008 and from December 2008 to February 2009) when the corresponding temperatures were significantly different from those during the training period.

These effects can be alleviated to some extent by the threshold-based online model and self-advised online model. Regarding the proposed CDAOM, its accuracy was initially low but gradually increased to nearly 100% as new samples were incorporated into the model. Despite the sensitivity of the features (i.e., natural frequencies) to environmental changes (i.e., temperature) in this study, the proposed approach can effectively adapt to these changes. The accuracies reported in Figure 9.10 are further averaged over the 23-month period, and the results are presented in Table 9.4.

Table 9.4

Average Accuracies for the Data Collected from the Infante D. Henrique Bridge Based on Different Models

Model	Average Accuracy
Offline Model	0.5357
Threshold-Based Online Model	0.8814
Self-Advised Online Model	0.9405
CDAOM (Proposed)	0.9568

The low average accuracy (53.57%) of the offline model indicates the adverse effects of environmental changes on the discriminative power of the original OCSVM. The proposed CDAOM, however, can adapt to the normal drifts caused by these changes and hence achieves the best performance with an average accuracy of 95.68%.

9.4 SUMMARY

This chapter introduces a novel approach for online anomaly detection in non-stationary data streams, focusing on concept drift adaptation. Incremental learning using OCSVM is selectively performed when a normal drift is detected. Leveraging margin support vectors, error support vectors, and reserve vectors in OCSVM, the relative relationships between an incoming sample and these vectors serve as indicators for predicting a normal drift. To validate the effectiveness of the proposed approach, extensive experiments were conducted in the field of SHM using data from three bridge structures. The experimental results demonstrate that the proposed CDAOM not only reduces the false alarm rate but also effectively detects real structural damage. Compared with other incremental learning methods, the proposed algorithm exhibits superior adaptability to changes in environmental and operational conditions, yielding the best performance. Future work may explore leveraging confidence information returned by the classifier for sample classification to further enhance the robustness of the online model.

10 Smart Sensing and Preventative Maintenance

10.1 BACKGROUND

Ensuring the consistent delivery of safe and reliable potable water to utility customers is paramount, with any disruptions to supply – whether due to pipe failures or compromised water quality – taking precedence. Urban water utilities grapple with the escalating challenge of maintaining aging water mains, a concern that has emerged as a top priority [138]. Developing robust and targeted smart sensing tools, including both mobile and fixed real-time sensors, holds immense promise for utilities. These tools can monitor high-risk areas, validate existing data, and improve the accuracy of leak and break predictions, all while leveraging easily accessible and reliable data sources.

Drawing inspiration from the successful application of breakthrough acoustic and pressure transient sensors in various industries [184, 84], there exists a ripe opportunity to adapt these advancements for the water sector. The deployment of such sensors in critical sections of underground networks, offering real-time input, presents a tangible pathway forward. For instance, Australian water utilities have recently embraced acoustic sensors for leak detection, aiming to mitigate and promptly identify water main leaks and failures [182, 174]. Continuously sensing leaks in real-time provides a wealth of learning data, capturing diverse modalities and enabling proactive identification of leaks and breaks before they escalate.

Leveraging machine learning and multi-modal data analytics tailored to each utility's study areas, optimal site locations for real-time sensing can be determined, maximizing the value of collected data. Validated predictive models, fueled by real-time and mobile sensing data, play a pivotal role in categorizing and prioritizing pipes. These insights seamlessly integrate with evolving condition assessment techniques, facilitating the targeted replacement of pipes as they reach their actual "end of life". This integration heralds a transformative shift towards preemptive asset management, empowering water utilities to effectively safeguard their critical infrastructure.

This chapter presents an ongoing research collaboration with an Australian water utility, focusing on prioritizing zone areas and pipes to mitigate pipe breaks and leaks through the implementation of smart sensing techniques.

- The identification of high-risk zones and pipes has prompted the optimization of sensor deployment strategies. Innovative methods for generating risk maps and adjusting Minimum Night Flow (MNF) have been developed and applied to create prioritization lists at both the zone and pipe levels. Detailed analysis reveals the effectiveness of integrating pipe failure prediction models with MNF analysis, providing a reliable approach to zone prioritization.

DOI: 10.1201/9781003473893-10

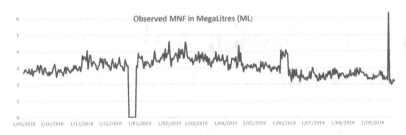

Figure 10.1   An example of observed MNF [109]

- Machine learning techniques have been employed for the development of leak alarm models. Various machine learning models have been tailored and customized to address the specific challenges of leak detection.
- Validation efforts are currently in progress to evaluate the performance of deployed sensors and prioritize pipes accordingly. Alarms triggered by sensors are rigorously compared against prediction results to ensure their accuracy. These validation results underscore the effectiveness of the proposed data-driven approach to leak detection using smart sensors.

10.2   ZONES PRIORITISATION FOR SENSORS DEPLOYMENT

In this section, we present the work focused on prioritizing zones through the utilization of Minimum Night Flow (MNF) analysis coupled with rank aggregation techniques.

The Minimum Night Flow (MNF) within a pressure zone is the measure of water flow observed during nighttime hours. Nighttime is chosen for this assessment because water consumption typically reaches its lowest point during this period. However, certain customers, such as industrial and commercial units, may still utilize water at standard or slightly elevated rates during the night. As a result, it's essential to consistently record a steady flow (or a flow with minor fluctuations) each day. Significant deviations in the recorded MNF over consecutive days from historical data could indicate potential issues, such as leaks or accidentally open valves facilitating water transfer between neighboring pressure zones. Moreover, MNF data plays a crucial role in pinpointing pressure zones for Active Leak Detection (ALD), offering a rapid means of estimating unreported leaks within these zones. An illustrative example of MNF monitoring is provided in Figure 10.1.

To prioritize the deployment of sensors in specific zones or areas, it's essential to identify and prioritize those with higher risks. Utilizing MNF provides a basis for ranking these zones. Additionally, we can assess zones based on predictions of pipe failures as illustrated in Chapter 8. This involves aggregating the risk scores of pressure zones by summing the likelihoods of failure for all pipes within each zone. By combining failure prediction data and MNF values at the zone level, we can achieve more robust outcomes.

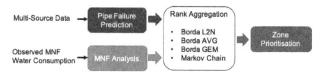

Figure 10.2   Rank aggregation for zones prioritisation [109]

The prioritization process involves ranking pressure zones based on their aggregated risk scores, with zones having the highest probability of risk assigned the top ranks. Each zone is allocated a rank corresponding to its risk probability, with the zone posing the highest risk assigned rank 1, the next highest rank 2, and so forth. Similarly, pressure zones are ranked based on their MNF values, again in descending order.

These two sets of rankings for pressure zones are then combined using various rank aggregation methods such as Borda-Count (L2 norm, Geometric Mean, etc.) [154] and Markov-Chain based techniques [113]. The rank aggregation process is depicted in Figure 10.2. Two main ranking approaches are explored: Borda-Count methods and Markov-Chain based techniques. Each method offers distinct advantages and is suitable for different scenarios.

Borda-Count is a widely used technique for aggregating rankings from multiple sources into a single ranking. It assigns scores to each item based on its position in individual rankings and then aggregates these scores to determine the overall ranking. We discuss three variations of Borda-Count:

- **Basic Borda-Count** In the basic Borda-Count method, scores are assigned based on the rank of each item in individual rankings. The scores are then summed across all rankings, and items are ranked based on their total scores. This method is straightforward and intuitive, making it suitable for cases where multiple independent rankings are available.
- **L2 Norm Borda-Count** The L2 Norm Borda-Count variation adds a square root to the basic formula, emphasizing larger differences between ranks. This method is useful when the magnitude of the differences between ranks is important and can help in capturing more nuanced distinctions between pressure zones.
- **Geometric Mean Borda-Count** In the Geometric Mean Borda-Count, instead of summing the scores across all rankings, the geometric mean is calculated. This method gives more weight to consensus among rankings while mitigating the influence of extreme values. It is beneficial when you want to prioritize zones based on a collective agreement among different rankings.

Markov-Chain based techniques model the transition probabilities between different states based on historical data. By analyzing these probabilities, these techniques predict the most likely future states. The Markov Chain method is particularly useful when there is a sequential relationship between the items being ranked, such as pressure zones, and when historical data is available to model the transitions between

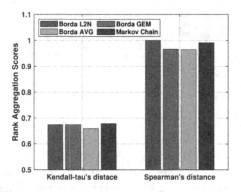

Figure 10.3   Rank aggregation scores with different ranking schemes [109]

states. It inherently considers sequential dependencies and is effective for predicting changes in risk probabilities over time.

The resultant aggregated rankings are illustrated in Figure 10.3. The rank aggregation indicate that, overall, Kendall-tau distance performs better as a metric compared to Spearman's distance for our specific task. Furthermore, employing the Borda-Count scheme with average rank aggregation yields the most effective aggregation outcome across both distance metrics. These aggregated results provide a prioritized list of zones, offering valuable guidance to the water utility in determining where to deploy sensors, with emphasis on the top-ranked zones.

When selecting a ranking methodology for zone prioritization, several factors should be considered:

- **Data Availability:** If multiple independent rankings are readily available, Borda-Count methods may be suitable. However, if there is sequential data and a need to model transitions over time, Markov-Chain based techniques might be preferred.
- **Nature of Rankings:** Consider whether the rankings are ordinal and independent or if there is a sequential relationship between the items being ranked. Borda-Count methods are appropriate for independent rankings, while Markov-Chain based techniques are better suited for sequential data.
- **Weighting Preferences:** Depending on the emphasis on consensus among rankings or the magnitude of differences between ranks, different variations of Borda-Count methods can be chosen. Markov-Chain based techniques inherently consider sequential dependencies but may require additional tuning to incorporate specific weighting preferences.

10.3   SMART SENSING FOR WATER NETWORKS

The advent of Internet of Things (IoT) technology has revolutionized the monitoring of water networks [146, 91], offering more advanced methods than ever before. With IoT, areas can be monitored in real-time using sensors for extended periods, spanning from days to several months. By analyzing the data collected from these sensors, it becomes possible to identify potential failures occurring within underground pipes. Subsequently, necessary actions, such as excavating the pipes for further inspection, can be taken. Notably, a notable example of a successful IoT application in water networks is [163]. This system entails the installation of permanently deployed accelerometer-type acoustic sensors and hydrophone acoustic loggers throughout a central business district. Over a period of 19 months, this system proactively detected 35 main breaks, representing approximately 55 percent of the total number of breaks. This outcome underscores the feasibility of detecting a significant portion of pipe cracks and undertaking timely repairs before catastrophic failure occurs.

10.3.1 SENSOR DEPLOYMENT AND DATA LOGGING

We have developed a water pipe failure prediction tool aimed at identifying high-risk pipes for sensor deployment. This tool utilizes a machine learning model constructed from a combination of historical failure records, pipe characteristics, environmental factors surrounding the pipes, and domain-specific features such as water flow direction and distance to pumping stations. By providing probabilistic predictions of failures, the tool assists in prioritizing the deployment of acoustic sensors on high-risk pipes, enabling real-time monitoring to detect both existing and potential future leaks. Notably, our analysis reveals that approximately 80% of predicted failure locations identified by the prediction tool are located within 200 meters of actual failure sites, significantly enhancing the effectiveness of leak detection with acoustic sensors [109].

Once the high-risk water mains are pinpointed using the pipe prediction tool, a combination of acoustic and pressure sensors is strategically deployed on these structures [178]. The Australian water utility has implemented a system involving the installation of permanent acoustic sensors, as well as lift-and-shift (semi-permanent) sensors, across prioritized pressure zones. Acoustic recordings are scheduled between 2 am and 4 am daily, exploiting the minimal environmental noise from water usage and traffic during these hours, thus facilitating consistent comparisons of recordings across multiple days. To address the challenge of high false alarm rates associated with traditional noise thresholding algorithms or correlation-based leak alarm systems between adjacent sensors, the utility is exploring the integration of machine learning techniques. These approaches hold promise in mitigating false alarms, thereby enhancing the reliability and effectiveness of leak detection systems.

10.3.2 MACHINE LEARNING AND SMART SENSING TECHNIQUES FOR LEAK DETECTION

In this section, we delve into the integration of machine learning techniques and smart sensing technologies for effective leak detection in water distribution systems. These combined approaches offer advanced methodologies for identifying and mitigating leaks, leveraging data from acoustic and pressure sensors deployed in prioritized pressure zones.

Anomaly detection algorithms, such as Isolation Forest, One-Class SVM, or Autoencoders, are employed to identify deviations from normal patterns in sensor data, thus indicating the presence of leaks. These techniques are enhanced by the incorporation of smart sensing technologies, which provide high-resolution data streams for accurate anomaly detection.

Supervised learning techniques, including Decision Trees, Random Forests, Support Vector Machines (SVM), or Gradient Boosting Machines (GBM), utilize labeled datasets to classify sensor readings as indicative of either normal operation or leak events. Smart sensing technologies augment supervised learning by offering real-time data streams for training models and adapting to evolving leak patterns.

Unsupervised learning methods like k-means clustering or Gaussian Mixture Models (GMM) group sensor data into clusters, allowing for the identification of anomalous clusters corresponding to leaks. Smart sensing techniques provide continuous data streams, enabling unsupervised learning algorithms to dynamically adapt to changes in the distribution of sensor data.

Time-series analysis techniques, such as Seasonal Decomposition of Time Series (STL), AutoRegressive Integrated Moving Average (ARIMA), or Long Short-Term Memory (LSTM) networks, capture temporal patterns in sensor data and detect deviations indicative of leaks. Smart sensing technologies offer high-frequency data streams, allowing for fine-grained analysis of temporal trends and patterns associated with leak events.

Ensemble methods like Bagging, Boosting, or Stacking combine predictions from multiple base learners to improve overall performance in leak detection tasks. When coupled with smart sensing techniques, ensemble methods leverage diverse data sources and sensor modalities, enhancing the robustness and reliability of leak detection systems.

Deep learning architectures, including Convolutional Neural Networks (CNNs), Recurrent Neural Networks (RNNs), or Transformers, extract complex features from sensor data and learn intricate patterns indicative of leaks. Smart sensing technologies provide rich, multi-dimensional data streams, enabling deep learning models to capture subtle nuances and variations associated with leak events.

Transfer learning techniques leverage pre-trained models and large-scale datasets to improve performance in leak detection tasks, especially in scenarios with limited labeled data. Smart sensing technologies facilitate transfer learning by providing diverse data sources for model adaptation and fine-tuning.

Semi-supervised learning approaches combine labeled and unlabeled data to train models, making them suitable for scenarios where labeled data is scarce but unlabeled data is abundant. Smart sensing technologies offer continuous data streams, enabling semi-supervised learning algorithms to leverage both labeled and unlabeled data for improved leak detection performance.

By integrating machine learning techniques with smart sensing technologies, water utilities can deploy advanced leak detection systems capable of effectively identifying and mitigating leaks, thereby reducing water loss and improving system efficiency.

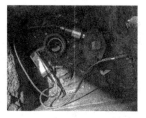

Figure 10.4 An example of deployed sensor [109]

Figure 10.5 An example of automatic leak detection function [109]

10.4 CASE STUDY FOR WATER LOSS SAVING

Sensors have been installed across prioritised pipes and zones. This section presents the validation outcomes of the pipe prioritisation process in relation to the leaks detected.

10.4.1 ACOUSTIC MONITORING FOR LEAK DETECTION

Numerous sensing technologies are available for detecting leaks. Among them, static acoustic sensors serve as a permanent or semi-permanent leak detection solution. These sensors are mounted directly onto the surface of pipelines to monitor real-time information about pipeline integrity [178]. In this study, various sensor types have been tested across different zones, as illustrated in Figure 10.4, which depicts one such deployed sensor. Each type of static acoustic sensor possesses unique data recording capabilities. For optimal performance, these sensors are configured to record ambient noise during the low-usage hours of 2 am to 4 am. This timing minimises environmental noise from traffic and water usage, thereby enhancing the reliability of the data. With reduced background noise, it is possible to consistently compare recorded data over multiple days to detect any changes, indicating potential leaks. Leak alerts are generated from the analysis of acoustic sensor data and are forwarded to water utility crews for further examination. These alerts are automatically triggered by proprietary interpretation systems using a threshold-based method. Typically, these systems employ basic noise level thresholds which, although effective, often result in a significant number of false positive alerts. An example of this automatic leak detection function is illustrated in Figure 10.5, where blue bars signify a detected leak. By leveraging acoustic monitoring, we can assess and enhance our machine-learning models designed for predicting leaks and pipe breaks.

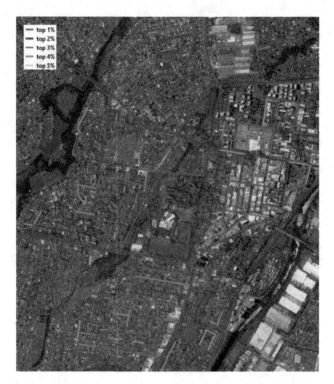

Figure 10.6   An example of the top ranked prioritised pipes (Zone C)

10.4.2   PIPES PRIORITISATION

The machine learning model was trained using the historical pipe failure records up to the end of 2019, which included various types of failures such as leaks, breaks, and main-to-meter issues. After training, this model was utilised to predict and prioritise pipes at risk within Zones A, B, and C of the utility's water network. The pipes are categorised according to their predicted risk of future failures. This prioritisation is depicted in Figure 10.6, highlighting the highest-risk pipes in Zone C. To validate the model, an analysis was conducted by comparing the locations of these prioritised pipes against the actual leak detection, which will be elaborated in the next subsection.

10.4.3   VALIDATION RESULTS

In the first half of 2020, acoustic sensors detected a total of 20 leaks, with 19 of these being confirmed as true positives. Analysis of the locations of these confirmed leaks revealed that 15 overlapped with the pipes identified as high-risk, yielding a matching rate of 75%. This high correspondence rate underscores the effectiveness of our data-driven approach in predicting leaks. Detailed validation statistics are provided in Table 10.1.

Table 10.1
The Validation Results

Zone	#sensors	#detected leaks	#confirmed leaks	#overlaps
A	40	17	17	13
B	25	1	1	1
C	23	2	1	1

Figure 10.7 Validation maps for Zone A, B, and C (from left to right) [109]

Note that Zone A is situated in a metropolitan area, whereas Zones B and C are in rural areas. Consequently, the pipe network in Zone A features higher coverage density compared to Zones B and C. Additionally, more sensors are deployed in Zone A than in Zones B and C, resulting in better coverage of the pipe network in Zone A. This extensive sensor deployment in Zone A likely contributes to its higher number of detected leaks. In contrast, the relatively lower sensor coverage in Zones B and C accounts for fewer detected leaks in these areas.

The validation results for all zones are illustrated in Figure 10.7. In the figure, prioritized pipes are shown in light blue, deployed sensors are marked with red dots, and sensors indicating true positive alarms are denoted by red dots with yellow crosses. The validation involves counting overlaps to determine if true positive alarms coincide with the prioritized pipes in each zone.

10.5 SUMMARY

As aging water mains continue to pose challenges with susceptibility to leaks and breaks, their maintenance has emerged as a critical concern for water utilities worldwide. Fortunately, significant strides have been made in leak detection through the utilization of sensing and analytic technologies. In this chapter, we have presented a data-driven approach for leak detection leveraging smart sensors. The approach encompasses several key procedures, including water pipe failure prediction, Minimum Night Flow (MNF) analysis, and zone prioritization, all of which are integral to effective leak detection. By consolidating historical failure records and MNF, a comprehensive framework for identifying high-risk areas within water distribution networks has been developed. Furthermore, we have validated our leak detection approach using acoustic monitoring data. The validation results are encouraging, demonstrating a matching rate of 75% by overlapping confirmed leaks with our prioritized pipes. This underscores the efficacy of our approach in accurately identifying potential leak locations and prioritizing intervention efforts.

Despite the advancements made in leak detection, there are several avenues for future research and development in this field:

- **Enhanced Data Integration:** Explore methods for integrating additional data sources, such as spatial and temporal factors, socioeconomic data, and sensor fusion techniques, to improve the accuracy and reliability of leak detection models.
- **Advanced Machine Learning Techniques:** Investigate the application of advanced machine learning algorithms, including deep learning architectures and ensemble methods, to further enhance the predictive capabilities of leak detection systems.
- **Real-Time Monitoring:** Develop real-time monitoring capabilities that enable immediate detection and response to emerging leak events, leveraging IoT technologies and cloud-based analytics platforms.
- **Integration of Predictive Maintenance:** Integrate predictive maintenance strategies with leak detection systems to proactively identify and address potential issues before they escalate into costly failures, thereby optimizing asset management practices.
- **Collaborative Research Initiatives:** Foster collaboration between academia, industry, and government agencies to share data, expertise, and resources in advancing the state-of-the-art in leak detection technology and practices.

By pursuing these future directions, we can further enhance the effectiveness and efficiency of leak detection efforts, ultimately contributing to the sustainable management of water resources and the resilience of water distribution infrastructure.

References

1. Fabian Pedregosa, Gaël Varoquaux, Alexandre Gramfort, et al. Scikit-learn: Machine learning in Python. Journal of Machine Learning Research, 12: 2825–2830, 2011.
2. Qiang Yang, Yang Liu, Tianjian Chen, and Yongxin Tong. Federated machine learning: Concept and applications. ACM Transactions on Intelligent Systems and Technology (TIST), 10(2): 1–19, 2019.
3. Odd Aalen, Ornulf Borgan, and Hakon Gjessing. Survival and event history analysis: a process point of view. Springer Science & Business Media, 2008.
4. Evrim Acar, Canan Aykut-Bingol, Haluk Bingol, Rasmus Bro, and Bülent Yener. Multiway analysis of epilepsy tensors. Bioinformatics, 23(13):i10–i18, 2007.
5. Evrim Acar and Bülent Yener. Unsupervised multiway data analysis: A literature survey. IEEE Transactions on Knowledge and Data Engineering, 21(1):6–20, 2009.
6. Dimitris Achlioptas. Database-friendly random projections. In Proceedings of the twentieth ACM SIGMOD-SIGACT-SIGART symposium on Principles of database systems, pages 274–281, 2001.
7. Takao Adachi and Bruce R Ellingwood. Comparative assessment of civil infrastructure network performance under probabilistic and scenario earthquakes. Journal of Infrastructure Systems, 16(1):1–10, 2010.
8. Diego Agudelo-España, Sebastian Gomez-Gonzalez, Stefan Bauer, Bernhard Schölkopf, and Jan Peters. Bayesian online prediction of change points. In Conference on Uncertainty in Artificial Intelligence, pages 320–329. PMLR, 2020.
9. Yoongho Ahn, Tomoya Kowada, Hiroshi Tsukaguchi, and Upali Vandebona. Estimation of passenger flow for planning and management of railway stations. Transportation Research Procedia, 25:315–330, 2017.
10. Hamad Alawad, Min An, and Sakdirat Kaewunruen. Utilizing an adaptive neuro-fuzzy inference system (anfis) for overcrowding level risk assessment in railway stations. Applied Sciences, 10(15):5156, 2020.
11. Nizar Faisal Alkayem, Maosen Cao, Yufeng Zhang, Mahmoud Bayat, and Zhongqing Su. Structural damage detection using finite element model updating with evolutionary algorithms: a survey. Neural Computing and Applications, 30(2):389–411, Jul 2018.
12. Ali Anaissi, Nguyen Lu Dang Khoa, Thierry Rakotoarivelo, Mehrisadat Makki Alamdari, and Yang Wang. Adaptive online one-class support vector machines with applications in structural health monitoring. ACM Transactions on Intelligent Systems and Technology, 9(6):64:1–64:20, November 2018.
13. Mats Anderson, Martin H Murray, Luis Ferreira, and Neal J Lake. Collection and use of railway track performance and maintenance data. In Conference on Railway Engineering, 2004.
14. A. Asnaashari, E. A. McBean, I. Shahrour, and B. Gharabaghi. Prediction of watermain failure frequencies using multiple and Poisson regression. Water Supply, 9(1):9–19, 03 2009.
15. Ayesha Atta, Sagheer Abbas, M Adnan Khan, Gulzar Ahmed, and Umer Farooq. An adaptive approach: Smart traffic congestion control system. Journal of King Saud University-Computer and Information Sciences, 32(9):1012–1019, 2020.

16. JP Bendfeldt, U Mohr, and L Muller. Railsys, a system to plan future railway needs. WIT Transactions on The Built Environment, 50, 2000.

17. Bjarne Bergquist and Peter Söderholm. Data analysis for condition-based railway infrastructure maintenance. Quality and Reliability Engineering International, 31(5):773–781, 2015.

18. Manuele Bicego and Mario A. T. Figueiredo. Soft clustering using weighted one-class support vector machines. Pattern Recognition, 42(1):27–32, January 2009.

19. Ella Bingham and Heikki Mannila. Random projection in dimensionality reduction: applications to image and text data. In Proceedings of the seventh ACM SIGKDD international conference on Knowledge discovery and data mining, pages 245–250, 2001.

20. Christopher M Bishop. Neural networks for pattern recognition. Oxford university press, 1995.

21. Philip T Blythe. Improving public transport ticketing through smart cards. In Proceedings of the Institution of Civil Engineers-Municipal Engineer, volume 157, pages 47–54. Thomas Telford Ltd, 2004.

22. Azzedine Boukerche. Performance evaluation of routing protocols for ad hoc wireless networks. Mobile networks and applications, 9:333–342, 2004.

23. L Breiman. Bagging predictors machine learning 24 (2), 123-140 (1996) 10.1023. A: 1018054314350, 1996.

24. Leo Breiman and RA Cutler. Random forests machine learning [j]. journal of clinical microbiology, 2:199–228, 2001.

25. Rasmus Bro and Henk AL Kiers. A new efficient method for determining the number of components in parafac models. Journal of Chemometrics: A Journal of the Chemometrics Society, 17(5):274–286, 2003.

26. Malachy Carey and Andrzej Kwieciński. Stochastic approximation to the effects of headways on knock-on delays of trains. Transportation Research Part B: Methodological, 28(4):251–267, 1994.

27. F. Necati Catbas, Melih Susoy, and Dan M. Frangopol. Structural health monitoring and reliability estimation: Long span truss bridge application with environmental monitoring data. Engineering Structures, 30(9):2347–2359, September 2008.

28. Brian Caulfield and MO Mahony. Passenger requirements of a public transport ticketing system. In Proceedings of the 8th International IEEE Conference on Intelligent Transportation Systems Vienna, pages 32–37. Vienna, Austria, 2005.

29. Gert Cauwenberghs and Tomaso Poggio. Incremental and decremental support vector machine learning. In Proceedings of the International Conference on Neural Information Processing Systems, pages 388–394, 2000.

30. TH Chan, YQ Ni, and JM Ko. Neural network novelty filtering for anomaly detection of tsing ma bridge cables. Structural health monitoring, pages 430–439, 2000.

31. Varun Chandola, Arindam Banerjee, and Vipin Kumar. Anomaly detection: A survey. ACM Computing Surveys, 41(3):15:1–15:58, July 2009.

32. Bintong Chen and Patrick T Harker. Two moments estimation of the delay on single-track rail lines with scheduled traffic. Transportation Science, 24(4):261–275, 1990.

33. Tianqi Chen and Carlos Guestrin. Xgboost: A scalable tree boosting system. In Proceedings of the 22nd acm sigkdd international conference on knowledge discovery and data mining, pages 785–794, 2016.

34. Bowen Cheng, Alex Schwing, and Alexander Kirillov. Per-pixel classification is not all you need for semantic segmentation. Advances in Neural Information Processing Systems, 34:17864–17875, 2021.

35. Philip S Chodrow, Zeyad Al-Awwad, Shan Jiang, and Marta C González. Demand and congestion in multiplex transportation networks. PloS one, 11(9):e0161738, 2016.

36. Francois Chollet. Xception: Deep learning with depthwise separable convolutions. In Proceedings of the IEEE conference on computer vision and pattern recognition, pages 1251–1258, 2017.

37. Symeon E. Christodoulou. Water network assessment and reliability analysis by use of survival analysis. Water Resources Management, 25(4):1229–1238, Mar 2011.

38. Narumol Chumuang, Mahasak Ketcham, and Thaweesak Yingthawornsuk. Cctv based surveillance system for railway station security. In 2018 International Conference on Digital Arts, Media and Technology (ICDAMT), pages 7–12. IEEE, 2018.

39. Karim Claudio, Vincent Couallier, and Yves Le Gat. Integration of time-dependent covariates in recurrent events modelling : application to failures on drinking water networks. Journal de la société francaise de statistique, 155(3):62–77, 2014.

40. Gabriele Comanducci, Filipe Magalhães, Filippo Ubertini, and Álvaro Cunha. On vibration-based damage detection by multivariate statistical techniques: Application to a long-span arch bridge. Structural Health Monitoring, 15(5):505–524, September 2016.

41. Corinna Cortes and Vladimir Vapnik. Support-vector networks. Machine Learning, 20:273–297, 1995.

42. Yanling Cui, Beihong Jin, Fusang Zhang, and Xingwu Sun. A deep spatio-temporal attention-based neural network for passenger flow prediction. In Proceedings of the 16th EAI International Conference on Mobile and Ubiquitous Systems: Computing, Networking and Services, pages 20–30, 2019.

43. Adnan Darwiche. Modeling and reasoning with Bayesian networks. Cambridge university press, 2009.

44. Manuel Davy, Frédéric Desobry, Arthur Gretton, and Christian Doncarli. An online support vector machine for abnormal events detection. Signal Processing, 86(8):2009–2025, August 2006.

45. Mark Deakin. From intelligent to smart cities. In Smart Cities, pages 27–44. Routledge, 2013.

46. Jia Deng, Wei Dong, Richard Socher, Li-Jia Li, Kai Li, and Li Fei-Fei. Imagenet: A large-scale hierarchical image database. In 2009 IEEE conference on computer vision and pattern recognition, pages 248–255. IEEE, 2009.

47. Prathamesh Deshpande, Kamlesh Marathe, Abir De, and Sunita Sarawagi. Long horizon forecasting with temporal point processes. In Proceedings of the 14th ACM international conference on web search and data mining, pages 571–579, 2021.

48. Christopher P. Diehl and Gert Cauwenberghs. SVM incremental learning, adaptation and optimization. In Proceedings of the International Joint Conference on Neural Networks, volume 4, pages 2685–2690, July 2003.

49. Gregory Ditzler, Manuel Roveri, Cesare Alippi, and Robi Polikar. Learning in nonstationary environments: A survey. IEEE Computational Intelligence Magazine, 10(4):12–25, November 2015.

50. Harris Drucker, Chris JC Burges, Linda Kaufman, Alex Smola, Vladimir Vapnik, et al. Support vector regression machines. Advances in Neural Information Processing Systems, 9:155–161, 1997.

51. Nan Du, Hanjun Dai, Rakshit Trivedi, Utkarsh Upadhyay, Manuel Gomez-Rodriguez, and Le Song. Recurrent marked temporal point processes: Embedding event history to vector. In Proceedings of the 22nd ACM SIGKDD International Conference on Knowledge Discovery and Data Mining, pages 1555–1564. ACM, 2016.

52. Gabriel Dupuy. Network geometry and the urban railway system: the potential benefits to geographers of harnessing inputs from "naive" outsiders. Journal of Transport Geography, 33:85–94, 2013.

53. Ryan Elwell and Robi Polikar. Incremental learning of concept drift in nonstationary environments. IEEE Transactions on Neural Networks, 22(10):1517–1531, October 2011.

54. Alessandro Fantechi, Francesco Flammini, and Stefania Gnesi. Formal methods for railway control systems. International Journal on Software Tools for Technology Transfer, 16:643–646, 2014.

55. Raziyeh Farmani, Konstantinos Kakoudakis, Kourosh Behzadian, and David Butler. Pipe failure prediction in water distribution systems considering static and dynamic factors. Procedia Engineering, 186:117–126, 2017.

56. Charles R Farrar and Keith Worden. An introduction to structural health monitoring. Philosophical Transactions of the Royal Society A: Mathematical, Physical and Engineering Sciences, 365(1851):303–315, 2007.

57. Philip Ferguson, Mark Heathcote, Greg Moore, and Dave Russell. Condition assessment of water mains using remote field technology. WATER-MELBOURNE THEN ARTARMON-, 23:6–8, 1996.

58. Francesco Flammini, Andrea Gaglione, Francesco Ottello, Alfio Pappalardo, Concerta Pragliola, and Annarita Tedesco. Towards wireless sensor networks for railway infrastructure monitoring. In Electrical Systems for Aircraft, Railway and Ship Propulsion, pages 1–6. IEEE, 2010.

59. Livio Florio and Lorenzo Mussone. An analytical model for the simultaneous calculation of capacity of lines, junctions and station tracks. WIT Transactions on The Built Environment, 37, 1998.

60. Yoav Freund, Robert Schapire, and Naoki Abe. A short introduction to boosting. Journal-Japanese Society For Artificial Intelligence, 14(771-780):1612, 1999.

61. Jerome H Friedman. Greedy function approximation: a gradient boosting machine. Annals of statistics, pages 1189–1232, 2001.

62. Yamato Fukuta, Gen Kogure, Takashi Kunifuji, Hiroyuki Sugahara, Reiji Ishima, and Masayuki Matsumoto. Novel railway signal control system based on the internet technology and its distributed control architecture. In Eighth International Symposium on Autonomous Decentralized Systems (ISADS'07), pages 77–82. IEEE, 2007.

63. João Gama, Indrė Žliobaitė, Albert Bifet, Mykola Pechenizkiy, and Abdelhamid Bouchachia. A survey on concept drift adaptation. ACM Computing Surveys, 46(4):44:1–44:37, March 2014.

64. Ramashish Gaurav and Biplav Srivastava. Estimating train delays in a large rail network using a zero shot markov model. In 2018 21st International Conference on Intelligent Transportation Systems (ITSC), pages 1221–1226. IEEE, 2018.

65. Vanessa Gómez-Verdejo, Jerónimo Arenas-García, Miguel Lázaro-Gredilla, and Ángel Navia-Vázquez. Adaptive one-class support vector machine. IEEE Transactions on Signal Processing, 59(6):2975–2981, June 2011.

66. Mofid Gorji-Bandpy and Majid Shateri. Analysis of pipe breaks in urban water distribution network. GMSARN International Journal, 2:117–124, 01 2008.

67. Rob MP Goverde. A delay propagation algorithm for large-scale railway traffic networks. Transportation Research Part C: Emerging Technologies, 18(3):269–287, 2010.

68. Rob MP Goverde and Ingo A Hansen. Delay propagation and process management at railway stations. In 5th World Conference on Railway Research (WCRR 2001), Köln, November 25-29, 2001. WCRR, 2001.

69. Stephen Graham. Constructing premium network spaces: reflections on infrastructure networks and contemporary urban development. International journal of urban and regional research, 24(1):183–200, 2000.

70. Isabelle Guyon, Jason Weston, Stephen Barnhill, and Vladimir Vapnik. Gene selection for cancer classification using support vector machines. Machine Learning, 46:389–422, 2002.

71. Shijie Hao, Yuan Zhou, and Yanrong Guo. A brief survey on semantic segmentation with deep learning. Neurocomputing, 406:302–321, 2020.

72. Siyu Hao, Der-Horng Lee, and De Zhao. Sequence to sequence learning with attention mechanism for short-term passenger flow prediction in large-scale metro system. Transportation Research Part C: Emerging Technologies, 107:287–300, 2019.

73. Colin Harrison and Ian Abbott Donnelly. A theory of smart cities. In Proceedings of the 55th Annual Meeting of the ISSS-2011, Hull, UK, 2011.

74. Colin Harrison, Barbara Eckman, Rick Hamilton, Perry Hartswick, Jayant Kalagnanam, Jurij Paraszczak, and Peter Williams. Foundations for smarter cities. IBM Journal of Research and Development, 54(4):1–16, 2010.

75. Kaiming He, Georgia Gkioxari, Piotr Dollár, and Ross Girshick. Mask r-cnn. In Proceedings of the IEEE international conference on computer vision, pages 2961–2969, 2017.

76. Jacob SW Heglund, Panukorn Taleongpong, Simon Hu, and Huy T Tran. Railway delay prediction with spatial-temporal graph convolutional networks. In 2020 IEEE 23rd International Conference on Intelligent Transportation Systems (ITSC), pages 1–6. IEEE, 2020.

77. Yoshiyuki Hirano, Takashi Kato, Takashi Kunifuji, Tetsunori Hattori, and Tamotsu Kato. Development of railway signaling system based on network technology. In 2005 IEEE International Conference on Systems, Man and Cybernetics, volume 2, pages 1353–1358. IEEE, 2005.

78. Hemant Ishwaran, Udaya B Kogalur, Eugene H Blackstone, and Michael S Lauer. Random survival forests. 2008.

79. Gražvydas Jakubauskas. Improvement of urban passenger transport ticketing systems by deploying intelligent transport systems. Transport, 21(4):252–259, 2006.

80. Chaozhe Jiang, Ping Huang, Javad Lessan, Liping Fu, and Chao Wen. Forecasting primary delay recovery of high-speed railway using multiple linear regression, supporting vector machine, artificial neural network, and random forest regression. Canadian Journal of Civil Engineering, 46(5):353–363, 2019.

81. Long Jin, Weili Deng, Yuchen Su, Zhong Xu, Huan Meng, Bin Wang, Hepeng Zhang, Binbin Zhang, Lei Zhang, Xinbiao Xiao, et al. Self-powered wireless smart sensor based on maglev porous nanogenerator for train monitoring system. Nano Energy, 38:185–192, 2017.

82. Predrag Jovanović, Pavle Kecman, Nebojša Bojović, and Dragomir Mandić. Optimal allocation of buffer times to increase train schedule robustness. European Journal of Operational Research, 256(1):44–54, 2017.

83. Golam Kabir, Solomon Tesfamariam, and Rehan Sadiq. Predicting water main failures using bayesian model averaging and survival modelling approach. Reliability Engineering and System Safety, 142:498–514, 2015.

84. Pugalenthi Karkulali, Himanshu Mishra, Abhisek Ukil, and Justin Dauwels. Leak detection in gas distribution pipelines using acoustic impact monitoring. In IECON 2016-42nd Annual Conference of the IEEE Industrial Electronics Society, pages 412–416. IEEE, 2016.

85. Eamonn Keogh, Kaushik Chakrabarti, Michael Pazzani, and Sharad Mehrotra. Dimensionality reduction for fast similarity search in large time series databases. Knowledge and Information Systems, 3:263–286, 2001.

86. Nguyen LD Khoa, Bang Zhang, Yang Wang, Fang Chen, and Samir Mustapha. Robust dimensionality reduction and damage detection approaches in structural health monitoring. Structural Health Monitoring, 13(4):406–417, 2014.

87. Nguyen Lu Dang Khoa, Bang Zhang, Yang Wang, Wei Liu, Fang Chen, Samir Mustapha, and Peter Runcie. On damage identification in civil structures using tensor analysis. In Proceedings of the Pacific-Asia Conference on Knowledge Discovery and Data Mining, pages 459–471, 2015.

88. Stefan H Kiss, Kavindie Katuwandeniya, Alen Alempijevic, and Teresa Vidal-Calleja. Constrained gaussian processes with integrated kernels for long-horizon prediction of dense pedestrian crowd flows. IEEE Robotics and Automation Letters, 2022.

89. Tamara G. Kolda and Brett W. Bader. Tensor decompositions and applications. SIAM Review, 51(3):455–500, 2009.

90. Tamara G Kolda and Jimeng Sun. Scalable tensor decompositions for multi-aspect data mining. In 2008 Eighth IEEE international conference on data mining, pages 363–372. IEEE, 2008.

91. Dan Koo, Kalyan Piratla, and C John Matthews. Towards sustainable water supply: schematic development of big data collection using internet of things (IoT). Procedia engineering, 118:489–497, 2015.

92. Bartosz Krawczyk, Leandro L. Minku, João Gama, Jerzy Stefanowski, and Michał Woźniak. Ensemble learning for data stream analysis: A survey. Information Fusion, 37:132–156, September 2017.

93. Bartosz Krawczyk and Michał Woźniak. One-class classifiers with incremental learning and forgetting for data streams with concept drift. Soft Computing, 19(12):3387–3400, December 2015.

94. Avishek Kumar, Syed Ali Asad Rizvi, Benjamin Brooks, R Ali Vanderveld, Kevin H Wilson, Chad Kenney, Sam Edelstein, Adria Finch, Andrew Maxwell, Joe Zuckerbraun, et al. Using machine learning to assess the risk of and prevent water main breaks. In Proceedings of the 24th ACM SIGKDD International Conference on Knowledge Discovery & Data Mining, pages 472–480, 2018.

95. Senro Kuraoka, Balvant Rajani, and Caizhao Zhan. Pipe-soil interaction analysis of field tests of buried pvc pipe. Journal of Infrastructure Systems, 2(4):162–170, 1996.

96. CC Lai, Jacob CP Kam, David CC Leung, Tony KY Lee, Aiken YM Tam, Siu Lau Ho, Hwa-Yaw Tam, and Michael SY Liu. Development of a fiber-optic sensing system for train vibration and train weight measurements in Hong Kong. Journal of Sensors, 2012, 2012.

97. William HK Lam, CY Cheung, and YF Poon. A study of train dwelling time at the hong kong mass transit railway system. Journal of advanced Transportation, 32(3):285–295, 1998.

98. Pavel Laskov, Christian Gehl, Stefan Krüger, and Klaus-Robert Müller. Incremental support vector learning: Analysis, implementation and applications. Journal of Machine Learning Research, 7:1909–1936, December 2006.

99. Jong Jae Lee, Jong Won Lee, Jin Hak Yi, Chung Bang Yun, and Hie Young Jung. Neural networks-based damage detection for bridges considering errors in baseline finite element models. Journal of Sound and Vibration, 280(3-5):555–578, 2005.

100. Biao Leng, Jiabei Zeng, Zhang Xiong, Weifeng Lv, and Yueliang Wan. Probability tree based passenger flow prediction and its application to the Beijing subway system. Frontiers of Computer Science, 7(2):195–203, 2013.

101. Javad Lessan, Liping Fu, and Chao Wen. A hybrid Bayesian network model for predicting delays in train operations. Computers & Industrial Engineering, 127:1214–1222, 2019.

102. Boyu Li, Ting Guo, Ruimin Li, Yang Wang, Amir H Gandomi, and Fang Chen. A two-stage self-adaptive model for passenger flow prediction on schedule-based railway system. In Pacific-Asia Conference on Knowledge Discovery and Data Mining, pages 147–160. Springer, 2022.

103. Boyu Li, Ting Guo, Ruimin Li, Yang Wang, Amir H Gandomi, and Fang Chen. Self-adaptive predictive passenger flow modelling for large-scale railway systems. IEEE Internet of Things Journal, 2023.

104. Boyu Li, Ting Guo, Ruimin Li, Yang Wang, Yuming Ou, and Fang Chen. Delay propagation in large railway networks with data-driven Bayesian modeling. Transportation Research Record, 2675(11):472–485, 2021.

105. Boyu Li, Ting Guo, Yang Wang, and Fang Chen. The future of transportation: How to improve railway operation performance via advanced AI techniques. Humanity Driven AI: Productivity, Well-being, Sustainability and Partnership, pages 85–110, 2022.

106. Shiyang Li, Xiaoyong Jin, Yao Xuan, Xiyou Zhou, Wenhu Chen, Yu-Xiang Wang, and Xifeng Yan. Enhancing the locality and breaking the memory bottleneck of transformer on time series forecasting. Advances in neural information processing systems, 32, 2019.

107. Zhidong Li, Bang Zhang, Yang Wang, Fang Chen, Ronnie Taib, Vicky Whiffin, and Yi Wang. Water pipe condition assessment: a hierarchical beta process approach for sparse incident data. Machine learning, 95:11–26, 2014.

108. Bin Liang, Zhidong Li, Yang Wang, and Fang Chen. Long-term rnn: Predicting hazard function for proactive maintenance of water mains. In Proceedings of the 27th ACM international conference on information and knowledge management, pages 1687–1690, 2018.

109. Bin Liang, Sunny Verma, Jie Xu, Shuming Liang, Zhidong Li, Yang Wang, and Fang Chen. A data driven approach for leak detection with smart sensors. In 2020 16th International Conference on Control, Automation, Robotics and Vision (ICARCV), pages 1311–1316. IEEE, 2020.

110. Andy Liaw, Matthew Wiener, et al. Classification and regression by randomforest. R News, 2(3):18–22, 2002.

111. Bryan Lim and Stefan Zohren. Time-series forecasting with deep learning: a survey. Philosophical Transactions of the Royal Society A, 379(2194):20200209, 2021.

112. Peng Lin, Bang Zhang, Yi Wang, Zhidong Li, Bin Li, Yang Wang, and Fang Chen. Data driven water pipe failure prediction: A Bayesian nonparametric approach. In

Proceedings of the 24th ACM International Conference on Information and Knowledge Management, CIKM '15, page 193–202, New York, NY, USA, 2015. Association for Computing Machinery.

113. Shili Lin. Rank aggregation methods. Wiley Interdisciplinary Reviews: Computational Statistics, 2(5):555–570, 2010.

114. Bo Liu, Yanshan Xiao, Philip S. Yu, Longbing Cao, Yun Zhang, and Zhifeng Hao. Uncertain one-class learning and concept summarization learning on uncertain data streams. IEEE Transactions on Knowledge and Data Engineering, 26(2):468–484, February 2014.

115. Chengyin Liu and John T. DeWolf. Effect of temperature on modal variability of a curved concrete bridge under ambient loads. Journal of Structural Engineering, 133(12):1742–1751, December 2007.

116. Lijuan Liu and Rung-Ching Chen. A novel passenger flow prediction model using deep learning methods. Transportation Research Part C: Emerging Technologies, 84:74–91, 2017.

117. Wentao Liu, Zhangyu Wang, Bin Zhou, Songyue Yang, and Ziren Gong. Real-time signal light detection based on yolov5 for railway. In IOP Conference Series: Earth and Environmental Science, volume 769, page 042069. IOP Publishing, 2021.

118. Yang Liu, Zhiyuan Liu, and Ruo Jia. Deeppf: A deep learning based architecture for metro passenger flow prediction. Transportation Research Part C: Emerging Technologies, 101:18–34, 2019.

119. Yunxiang Liu and Hao Wu. Prediction of road traffic congestion based on random forest. In 2017 10th International Symposium on Computational Intelligence and Design (ISCID), volume 2, pages 361–364. IEEE, 2017.

120. Viktor Losing, Barbara Hammer, and Heiko Wersing. Incremental on-line learning: A review and comparison of state of the art algorithms. Neurocomputing, 275:1261–1274, January 2018.

121. Jie Lu, Anjin Liu, Fan Dong, Feng Gu, João Gama, and Guangquan Zhang. Learning under concept drift: A review. IEEE Transactions on Knowledge and Data Engineering, pages 1–1, 2018.

122. Kai Lu and Baoming Han. Congestion risk evaluation and precaution of passenger flow in metro stations. The Open Civil Engineering Journal, 10(1), 2016.

123. Yinghui Lu and Jennifer E. Michaels. A methodology for structural health monitoring with diffuse ultrasonic waves in the presence of temperature variations. Ultrasonics, 43(9):717–731, October 2005.

124. Marco Luethi, Ulrich Weidmann, and Andrew Nash. Passenger arrival rates at public transport stations. In TRB 86th Annual Meeting Compendium of Papers, pages 07–0635. Transportation Research Board, 2007.

125. Scott M Lundberg and Su-In Lee. A unified approach to interpreting model predictions. Advances in neural information processing systems, 30, 2017.

126. Yashar Maali and Adel Al-Jumaily. Self-advising support vector machine. Knowledge-Based Systems, 52:214–222, November 2013.

127. Filipe Magalhães, Álvaro Cunha, and Elsa Caetano. Vibration based structural health monitoring of an arch bridge: From automated OMA to damage detection. Mechanical Systems and Signal Processing, 28(SI):212–228, April 2012.

128. Alain Mailhot, Geneviève Pelletier, Jean-Francois Noël, and Jean-Pierre Villeneuve. Modeling the evolution of the structural state of water pipe networks with brief

recorded pipe break histories: Methodology and application. Water Resources Research, 36(10):3053–3062, 2000.

129. Luke JW Martin. Predictive reasoning and machine learning for the enhancement of reliability in railway systems. In International Conference on Reliability, Safety, and Security of Railway Systems, pages 178–188. Springer, 2016.

130. Michael McCahill and Clive Norris. CCTV in London. Report deliverable of UrbanEye project, 2002.

131. Rodolfo I Meneguette, R De Grande, and AA Loureiro. Intelligent transport system in smart cities. Cham: Springer International Publishing, 2018.

132. Chuizheng Meng, Hao Niu, Guillaume Habault, Roberto Legaspi, Shinya Wada, Chihiro Ono, and Yan Liu. Physics-informed long-sequence forecasting from multi-resolution spatiotemporal data. In IJCAI, pages 2189–2195, 2022.

133. Xuedan Miao, Ying Liu, Haiquan Zhao, and Chunguang Li. Distributed online one-class support vector machine for anomaly detection over networks. IEEE Transactions on Cybernetics, 49(4):1475–1488, April 2019.

134. Dalius Misiūnas. Failure monitoring and asset condition assessment in water supply systems. Vilniaus Gedimino technikos universitetas, 2008.

135. Yujian Mo, Yan Wu, Xinneng Yang, Feilin Liu, and Yujun Liao. Review the state-of-the-art technologies of semantic segmentation based on deep learning. Neurocomputing, 493:626–646, 2022.

136. H Zare Moayedi and MA Masnadi-Shirazi. ARIMA model for network traffic prediction and anomaly detection. In 2008 International Symposium on Information Technology, volume 4, pages 1–6. IEEE, 2008.

137. Luis E Mujica, Josep Vehí, Magda Ruiz, Michel Verleysen, Wieslaw Staszewski, and Keith Worden. Multivariate statistics process control for dimensionality reduction in structural assessment. Mechanical Systems and Signal Processing, 22(1):155–171, 2008.

138. Bureau of Infrastructure and Transport Research Economics. Australian infrastructure statistics-yearbook 2014 and key Australian infrastructure statistics booklet, Dec 2019.

139. Sehchan Oh, Sunghuk Park, and Changmu Lee. Vision based platform monitoring system for railway station safety. In 2007 7th International Conference on ITS Telecommunications, pages 1–5. IEEE, 2007.

140. Luca Oneto, Emanuele Fumeo, Giorgio Clerico, Renzo Canepa, Federico Papa, Carlo Dambra, Nadia Mazzino, and Davide Anguita. Dynamic delay predictions for large-scale railway networks: Deep and shallow extreme learning machines tuned via threshold-out. IEEE Transactions on Systems, Man, and Cybernetics: Systems, 47(10):2754–2767, 2017.

141. Luca Oneto, Emanuele Fumeo, Giorgio Clerico, Renzo Canepa, Federico Papa, Carlo Dambra, Nadia Mazzino, and Davide Anguita. Train delay prediction systems: a big data analytics perspective. Big data research, 11:54–64, 2018.

142. Jörn Pachl. Railway signalling principles. Braunschweig, June, 2020.

143. Sinno Jialin Pan and Qiang Yang. A survey on transfer learning. IEEE Transactions on knowledge and data engineering, 22(10):1345–1359, 2009.

144. Suwan Park, Hwandon Jun, Newland Agbenowosi, Bong Jae Kim, and Kiyoung Lim. The proportional hazards modeling of water main failure data incorporating the time-dependent effects of covariates. Water Resources Management, 25(1):1–19, Jan 2011.

145. Krzysztof Pawlikowski, H-DJ Jeong, and J-SR Lee. On credibility of simulation studies of telecommunication networks. IEEE Communications Magazine, 40(1):132–139, 2002.

146. Thinagaran Perumal, Md Nasir Sulaiman, and Chui Yew Leong. Internet of things (Iot) enabled water monitoring system. In 2015 IEEE 4th Global Conference on Consumer Electronics (GCCE), pages 86–87. IEEE, 2015.

147. Marco A.F. Pimentel, David A. Clifton, Lei Clifton, and Lionel Tarassenko. A review of novelty detection. Signal Processing, 99:215–249, June 2014.

148. Miguel A Prada, Janne Toivola, Jyrki Kullaa, and Jaakko Hollmén. Three-way analysis of structural health monitoring data. Neurocomputing, 80:119–128, 2012.

149. Andrii Prokhorchenko, Artem Panchenko, Larysa Parkhomenko, G Nesterenko, Mykhailo Muzykin, G Prokhorchenko, and Alina Kolisnyk. Forecasting the estimated time of arrival for a cargo dispatch delivered by a freight train along a railway section. Eastern-European Journal of Enterprise Technologies, 3(3):30–38, 2019.

150. Luo Qi. Research on intelligent transportation system technologies and applications. In 2008 Workshop on Power Electronics and Intelligent Transportation System, pages 529–531. IEEE, 2008.

151. Balvant Rajani and Yehuda Kleiner. Comprehensive review of structural deterioration of water mains: physically based models. Urban Water, 3(3):151–164, 2001.

152. Balvant Rajani and Yehuda Kleiner. Comprehensive review of structural deterioration of water mains: physically based models. Urban Water, 3(3):151–164, 2001. Ground Water in the Environment.

153. Anders Rytter. Vibrational Based Inspection of Civil Engineering Structures. PhD thesis, Denmark, 1993. Ph.D.-Thesis defended publicly at the University of Aalborg, April 20, 1993 PDF for print: 206 pp.

154. Donald G Saari. Selecting a voting method: the case for the borda count. Constitutional Political Economy, 34(3):357–366, 2023.

155. Mahsa Salehi and Lida Rashidi. A survey on anomaly detection in evolving data: [with application to forest fire risk prediction]. ACM SIGKDD Explorations Newsletter, 20(1):13–23, June 2018.

156. David Salinas, Valentin Flunkert, Jan Gasthaus, and Tim Januschowski. Deepar: Probabilistic forecasting with autoregressive recurrent networks. International Journal of Forecasting, 36(3):1181–1191, 2020.

157. Bernhard Schölkopf, John C. Platt, John C. Shawe-Taylor, Alex J. Smola, and Robert C. Williamson. Estimating the support of a high-dimensional distribution. Neural Computation, 13(7):1443–1471, July 2001.

158. Bernhard Schölkopf and Alexander J. Smola. Learning with Kernels: Support Vector Machines, Regularization, Optimization, and Beyond. MIT Press, Cambridge, MA, USA, 2001.

159. Pieter M Schrijnen. Infrastructure networks and red–green patterns in city regions. Landscape and Urban Planning, 48(3-4):191–204, 2000.

160. George AF Seber and Alan J Lee. Linear regression analysis, volume 329. John Wiley & Sons, 2012.

161. Alistair Shilton, Marimuthu Palaniswami, Daniel Ralph, and Ah Chung Tsoi. Incremental training of support vector machines. IEEE Transactions on Neural Networks, 16(1):114–131, January 2005.

162. Hoon Sohn, Jerry A Czarnecki, and Charles R Farrar. Structural health monitoring using statistical process control. Journal of Structural Engineering, 126(11):1356–1363, 2000.

163. ML Stephens, Jinzhe Gong, Angela Marchi, et al. Field testing of Adelaide CBD smart network acoustic technologies. In WDSA/CCWI Joint Conference Proceedings, volume 1, 2018.

164. Hongyu Sun, Henry X Liu, Heng Xiao, and Bin Ran. Short term traffic forecasting using the local linear regression model. 2002.

165. Tetsuo Takashige. Signalling systems for safe railway transport. Japan Railway & Transport Review, 21:44–50, 1999.

166. David M.J. Tax and Robert P.W. Duin. Support vector data description. Machine Learning, 54(1):45–66, January 2004.

167. Christine Teague, Lelia Green, and David Leith. Watching me, watching you: The use of cctv to support safer work places for public transport transit officers. 2010.

168. Gregor Theeg and Sergej Vlasenko. Railway signalling & interlocking. In International Compendium, volume 448. Eurail-press Publ Hamburg, 2009.

169. Hongda Tian, Nguyen Lu Dang Khoa, Ali Anaissi, Yang Wang, and Fang Chen. Concept drift adaption for online anomaly detection in structural health monitoring. In Proceedings of the 28th ACM International Conference on Information and Knowledge Management, pages 2813–2821, 2019.

170. Robert Tibshirani. Regression shrinkage and selection via the lasso. Journal of the Royal Statistical Society Series B: Statistical Methodology, 58(1):267–288, 1996.

171. Ashish Vaswani, Noam Shazeer, Niki Parmar, Jakob Uszkoreit, Llion Jones, Aidan N Gomez, Łukasz Kaiser, and Illia Polosukhin. Attention is all you need. In Advances in neural information processing systems, pages 5998–6008, 2017.

172. Hao Wang, Qingxin Zhu, Jian Li, Jianxiao Mao, Suoting Hu, and Xinxin Zhao. Identification of moving train loads on railway bridge based on strain monitoring. Smart Structures and Systems, 23(3):263–278, 2019.

173. Tian Wang, Jie Chen, Yi Zhou, and Hichem Snoussi. Online least squares one-class support vector machines-based abnormal visual event detection. Sensors, 13(12):17130–17155, December 2013.

174. SA Water. Continued sensor success for SA water's smart network.

175. Morten Welde. Are smart card ticketing systems profitable? Evidence from the city of trondheim. Journal of Public Transportation, 15(1):8, 2012.

176. Chao Wen, Ping Huang, Zhongcan Li, Javad Lessan, Liping Fu, Chaozhe Jiang, and Xinyue Xu. Train dispatching management with data-driven approaches: a comprehensive review and appraisal. IEEE Access, 7:114547–114571, 2019.

177. Billy M Williams, Priya K Durvasula, and Donald E Brown. Urban freeway traffic flow prediction: application of seasonal autoregressive integrated moving average and exponential smoothing models. Transportation Research Record, 1644(1):132–141, 1998.

178. L Wong, R Deo, S Rathnayaka, B Shannon, CS Zhang, J Kodikara, WK Chiu, and H Widyastuti. Leak detection and quantification of leak size along water pipe using optical fibre sensors package. Electron. J. Struct. Eng, 18:47–53, 2018.

179. Keith Worden and Graeme Manson. The application of machine learning to structural health monitoring. Philosophical Transactions of the Royal Society A: Mathematical, Physical and Engineering Sciences, 365(1851):515–537, 2007.

180. Keith Worden, Graeme Manson, and Nick RJ Fieller. Damage detection using outlier analysis. Journal of Sound and Vibration, 229(3):647–667, 2000.

181. Linda B Wright. The analysis of UK railway accidents and incidents: a comparison of their causal patterns. PhD thesis, University of Strathclyde, 2002.

182. Staff Writer. Acoustic sensing project to help sydney water prevent pipe breakage, Jan 2020.

183. Jianqing Wu, Luping Zhou, Chen Cai, Fang Dong, Jun Shen, and Geng Sun. Towards a general prediction system for the primary delay in urban railways. In 2019 IEEE Intelligent Transportation Systems Conference (ITSC), pages 3482–3487. IEEE, 2019.

184. Rui Xiao, Qunfang Hu, and Jie Li. Leak detection of gas pipelines using acoustic signals based on wavelet transform and support vector machine. Measurement, 146:479–489, 2019.

185. Dan Yang, Kairun Chen, Mengning Yang, and Xiaochao Zhao. Urban rail transit passenger flow forecast based on lstm with enhanced long-term features. IET Intelligent Transport Systems, 13(10):1475–1482, 2019.

186. Fuya Yuan, Huijun Sun, Liujiang Kang, and Jianjun Wu. Passenger flow control strategies for urban rail transit networks. Applied Mathematical Modelling, 82:168–188, 2020.

187. C Zang, M Imregun Friswell, and M Imregun. Structural damage detection using independent component analysis. Structural Health Monitoring, 3(1):69–83, 2004.

188. C Zang and M Imregun. Structural damage detection using artificial neural networks and measured frf data reduced via principal component projection. Journal of Sound and Vibration, 242(5):813–827, 2001.

189. Oliver Zendel, Markus Murschitz, Marcel Zeilinger, Daniel Steininger, Sara Abbasi, and Csaba Beleznai. Railsem19: A dataset for semantic rail scene understanding. In Proceedings of the IEEE/CVF Conference on Computer Vision and Pattern Recognition Workshops, pages 0–0, 2019.

190. Bang Zhang, Ting Guo, Lelin Zhang, Peng Lin, Yang Wang, Jianlong Zhou, and Fang Chen. Water pipe failure prediction: A machine learning approach enhanced by domain knowledge. Human and Machine Learning: Visible, Explainable, Trustworthy and Transparent, pages 363–383, 2018.

191. Yuliang Zhao, Xiaodong Yu, Meng Chen, Ming Zhang, Ye Chen, Xuanyu Niu, Xiaopeng Sha, Zhikun Zhan, and Wen Jung Li. Continuous monitoring of train parameters using iot sensor and edge computing. IEEE Sensors Journal, 21(14):15458–15468, 2020.

192. Zheng Zhao, Weihai Chen, Xingming Wu, Peter CY Chen, and Jingmeng Liu. Lstm network: a deep learning approach for short-term traffic forecast. IET Intelligent Transport Systems, 11(2):68–75, 2017.

193. Chen Zhong, Michael Batty, Ed Manley, Jiaqiu Wang, Zijia Wang, Feng Chen, and Gerhard Schmitt. Variability in regularity: Mining temporal mobility patterns in london, singapore and beijing using smart-card data. PloS one, 11(2):e0149222, 2016.

194. HJ Zhou, Y Liu, YW Feng, and GR Zheng. Passenger flow prediction and control at peak hour for transfer stations of urban mass transit. Advances in Transportation Studies, 1, 2017.

195. Xian Zhou, Yanyan Shen, Yanmin Zhu, and Linpeng Huang. Predicting multi-step citywide passenger demands using attention-based neural networks. In Proceedings of the Eleventh ACM International Conference on Web Search and Data Mining, pages 736–744, 2018.

196. Xingquan Zhu, Wei Ding, Philip S. Yu, and Chengqi Zhang. One-class learning and concept summarization for data streams. Knowledge and Information Systems, 28(3):523–553, September 2011.

Index

Note: Locators in *italics* represent figures and **bold** indicate tables in the text.

Printed in the United States
by Baker & Taylor Publisher Services